We DO Have Future Choices

Strategies for fundamentally changing the 21st century

Dedication

To those who provided me with financial and moral support when I was struggling with oesophageal cancer. I hope that this work will provide a creative return on your human investment.

We DO Have Future Choices

Strategies for fundamentally changing the 21st century

Robert Theobald

Southern Cross
University Press

Southern Cross University Press
PO Box 157
Lismore NSW 2480
Australia
E-mail: scupress@scu.edu.au

National Library of Australia
Cataloguing-in-Publication data

Theobald, Robert, 1929-
We DO have future choices : strategies for fundamentally changing the 21st century

Includes index

ISBN   1 875855 41 6

1. Nature conservation. 2. Environmental protection. 3. Nature – Effect of human beings on. 4. Technology and civilization. I. Title

333.72

Edited and indexed by Barbara Bowden

Typeset by Michelle Sharpe

Contents

Foreword

In my childhood, I went to a boarding school where we sang hymns every morning, and twice on Sunday. We opened our mouths wide and chorused our supreme confidence in holding dominion over the earth and all its creatures. We were God's head prefects, vastly superior to all other forms of life. In the western tradition, our science lessons gave us faith in a world which was ordered, predictable and neatly divisible into its component part – a Newtonian view which had altered little since the seventeenth century.

One of the most profound shifts in my lifetime has therefore been our reluctant acceptance that we are not masters of our fate. Life isn't mechanistic but organic. Our very existence depends upon achieving harmony with the earth and with every living thing – something Aboriginal peoples have always known. Their relationship to the land, which was once dismissed as primitive, is now recognised as a source of spiritual nourishment and strength.

Another radical challenge to our way of thinking came in the late sixties and seventies when a science of process rather than state was born – a turning away from reductionism towards looking for the whole.

Scientists began examining how and why even the smallest of changes in any given system can produce unexpected and at times dramatically magnified results. These theories of chaos were popularised by a New York science writer, James Gleick, in his 1988 book *Chaos,* which described how a butterfly stirring the air today in

China might well affect the weather somewhere else in the world.

So when the birds are restless and chatter on the telegraph wires, and when the tide pulls crazily to one side of the beach creating dangerous little whirlpools that eddy and suck, it means that in spite of fine weather forecasts, those butterflies in Beijing might well be responsible for the storm clouds over the coast where I live. This is mysterious and humbling stuff.

Unfortunately, over the centuries, we have denied and abused our relationship with nature, at the same time abusing ourselves. We have ripped the guts out of the earth, soiled its waterways, degraded and threatened our planet. Global warming is already a reality, political and economic systems no longer support the people they are supposed to serve, the gap between rich and poor grows ever wider, and although violence has always been endemic to all civilisations, the rate and nature of killing this century appals.

At the same time, we are buffeted by unprecedented social and technological change. We cling to our life-rafts, not recognising that we need a different kind of vessel if we are to stay afloat.

In his provocative but inspiring book, Robert Theobald impels us to realise that fundamental shifts in reality mean we can no longer depend on our current institutions and on our expectations from the past. He points out that our concentration on economic growth and our reliance on technology as the solution for all our ills cannot continue into the twenty-first century without disaster. Somehow – in the immediate future – we have to find the courage and wisdom radically to change our whole way of living and being, something that becomes more difficult the longer we fail to confront the challenge.

Before we can think and act creatively, we need 'courageous realism' – Theobald's words – the capacity to see the whole landscape as it is, and not as we would like it. His are the views of an enlightened economist, someone who has spent a lifetime working on the leading edge, arguing that only radical shifts in our visions and pathways can prevent massive and imminent breakdowns in the world. Quality of life is a more relevant goal for the twenty-first century than the accumulation of goods and wealth – particularly when that accumulation rests in the hands of only a few, and where people are treated as objects for economic ends.

His writing is thoughtful and wide ranging as he takes us through all the reasons why change is so urgently required. But he does not bring a message of gloom and doom. Far from it. Theobald is optimistic about our capacity to find a way through, believing there is overwhelming evidence to support the capacity of individuals to grow and to help one another. I would support this most strongly. My own experience is that, too often, we deny or dismiss the intelligence and resilience of human beings.

One of the major strengths of Robert Theobald's work is that he gives a sense of empowerment. He does not offer prescriptive solutions, but rather suggests joining together and using our collective wisdom and our common sense in dealing with issues such as ecological integrity, the destructive nature of adversarial politics and leadership which is based on power and manipulation, rather than on knowledge and skills. He is also not afraid to use words like love and compassion.

Given the vastness of the task, nothing less than a fundamental shift in values is likely to bring about change. Change has to take place at the deepest level of our consciousness. Values can be taught, but are better experienced and observed. We are what we do, and not what we say.

These are simple messages but profound, if we are to restore balance to a scarred and depleted world. Almost certainly we are further along the paths of change than we realise. Tiny invisible forces are at work, denoting a restlessness within and without, a life-preserving move away from 'what's in it for me?' to 'what's best for the common good?' Our very state of global crisis is already transforming human consciousness. Could we be growing up?

Anne Deveson, Sydney, 1999

Preface

The pervasive statement from academics, media and politicians that "there are no choices" about the way we live is based on an extraordinary failure of nerve and imagination. If we actually are unable to change current patterns, then we have to be willing to accept that the gap between the rich and the poor will continue to widen. We shall have to tolerate ecological degradation. We shall be driven by the inertia that threatens massive breakdowns in the social order. Businesses, institutions and cultures will die and individuals and families will find themselves living in an increasingly destructive and hostile environment.

As soon as we broaden our vision, however, we discover there are indeed many other options besides continuing current destructive dynamics. The fan of possibilities has never been so large; we do not need to be constrained by current economic dogmas. One of the advantages of being trained as an economist is that I know that the current dominant pattern of thinking is nonsensical. Market forces should make choices about *how* things are produced – they should not dictate *what* is worth doing. The "what" should be determined by society. This is the political challenge we are badly failing to meet at the current time.

All too often, we narrow the art of collective decision-making down to elections and law making. Today, citizens are profoundly alienated from this whole process. In most countries, people see both parties as accepting current dynamics and failing to deal with the issues that are directly relevant to them. The real challenge of the current moment is to discover how societies can move new issues

1

onto the action agenda and then resolve them without falling into adversarial traps.

In order to revive politics as the highest art form, we have to see society as primary and the economy as secondary. While many people wish for this outcome, they fear that current dynamics are so strong that fighting against them is a waste of time. There are two positive levels of response to this feeling. First, the extreme free-market dogma that dominates governments today was put in place by a small group of people in the seventies and the eighties. If this past pattern of propaganda could convince so many people that they should accept ideas that contradict their self-interest, then we should be able to convince citizens that more humane and compassionate ideas will meet their deepest needs. And we should be able to do this in a much shorter time. This book proposes steps that resonate deeply with the widespread sense of a need for a values and spiritual revival. Many people are obviously yearning to make meaning out of their lives.

The second response to the belief that nothing can be done is to point out the wide range of evidence suggesting that we are much further along in making the necessary changes than we realise. If we look below the media coverage, we find that an incredibly wide range of ideas and actions already exists to challenge the current dominant patterns. Unfortunately, the emergent dynamics are still fragmented and this makes it very difficult to get a sense of the extent and depth of the movement that already exists.

I can provide a great many examples of this energy. One of the most fascinating developed at the annual meeting of the Australian Institute of Company Directors in 1999. The speakers provided a mix of conventional economic analysis and more creative thinking. It was obvious from the reactions that it was the out-of-the-box presentations that caught the attention of those attending. These challenged people to look beyond profits to the triple bottom line – which includes society and ecology – and to recognise the importance of values in corporate decision-making

The thrust of my work over the last 40 years has been to encourage people to become part of the dialogue and action about the new world, which is so rapidly developing around us. Once we recognise the shifts that are already developing, the challenge that lies ahead of us inevitably seems less daunting. Let me start from the beginning of the argument. Logic and mathematics have dominated the Western world and particularly the Anglo-Saxon culture. We have been convinced, for example, that one plus one always equals two. But our new ways of thinking show us that one plus one can equal three or zero. It all depends on the synergies or entropies that occur when two people or groups interact.

If you, the reader, still believe in the logic of mathematics and cannot see beyond it, you will live in a world where cause and effect are clearly joined, where logic is a primary tool, where you feel sure of the results of your actions. If you understand synergies and entropies, reality seems totally different. You will be aware that your attempt to achieve a particular result through your actions may have consequences that are profoundly different from what you expected. Interestingly, people are increasingly aware of this reality in families but all too often it is down-played in workplaces. In communities and at the global level, we often seem to totally ignore the fact that the indirect consequences of our actions are more dramatic than those we directly intended.

This is the clash that CP Snow discussed in much of his work: the profound difference between the arts and the sciences. Fortunately, the gulfs between the sciences and the arts, between the intellectual and the theological, the systemic and the religious, are closing. While each of these ways of thinking still uses its own language, the conclusions they are reaching today are remarkably similar. A new world-view is coming into existence and it requires us to change the ways we have thought in the past.

One of the results of this emerging shift is that we are beginning to recognise the way that our world-view determines the realities we are able to see. In addition, our world-view inevitably becomes incorporated into our built environment and thus constrains our behaviour. Winston Churchill caught this reality in his statement: "We build our buildings and then our buildings build us." The consequences of a world-view are actually even wider for they also create social institutions which then demand certain forms of behaviour from those who live within them and inhibit other patterns.

The industrial-era mindset and world-view within which we are currently enmeshed does indeed provide no choices. The new knowledge, which is developing so rapidly, shows that we do not have to continue to accept the premises that have brought us to this point in history. We can discover a profoundly different future that will promise us a high quality of life while using resources far more effectively.

Real choices emerge at a very different level than those that are currently being discussed in most places within the culture. But they can only be realised if we develop an extremely different world-view and paradigm. The issues to which we pay attention must be profoundly changed from those of the past if we are to benefit from the extraordinary technological and knowledge potentials that are currently available to us.

There are, in fact, two competing visions of the future, which are struggling for attention at the current time.

One is the message that dominates the formal communications channels of our society. It assumes that we must continue the dynamics of the industrial era, proposing that twentieth century commitments to maximum economic growth policies and a belief in technology as the solution for all problems should extend into the third millennium.

There are two variants of this view. One of them believes that we need to move even further into the capitalist and free-market models: that the problems we currently face result from failing to follow the logic of our current system fully. It is this view that the United States is pushing most strongly. When it is introduced into countries that have no suitable infrastructure it results in a form of "thug" capitalism which the currently developed countries would totally reject.

The other argues for "capitalism with a human face" and therefore attempts to bring about marginal changes in systems. The consequent proposals ignore the fact that we have reached the point at which we have essentially unlimited productive and destructive power. In these drastically changed conditions, only a radically changed set of patterns can ensure the long-run survival of the human race.

Dominant political parties – those both in power and in opposition – have bought into one or other of these approaches. I reject these views of the world for several reasons.

- The most critical is the environmental and ecological pressure that will emerge if populations and standards of living continue to increase throughout the world. There are very few analysts who believe it is possible for the earth to support a population of 10 billion people at even current developed-country standards of living. There is no chance that we can meet the needs of the poor world if the rich countries remain committed to rapid increases in their own standard of living.

- Current economic and market strategies are increasing the gap between the rich and the poor and there is plenty of evidence to show that this trend will continue. This will lead to massive tensions and strife within, and between, countries.

- Our increasing technology and knowledge requires radically different governmental strategies than those that exist at the current time.

The second scenario accepts that we are in the middle of a radical and fundamental shift in all of the ways we think and act. It recognises that the lives of individuals, families and institutions are being stressed seriously by the many driving forces of our time. There are nevertheless two very different reactions to this recognition.

Many of the people who recognise that the future has to be different from the past are still unable to see the size of the shift that we are called upon to make. Jack Murphy, a colleague, talks about the fact that many of us are only 25 per cent ready for change. We often want to alter the world in which we live without facing the fact that our lives also need to change. We do not ask the hard questions: "How does poverty benefit those of us in the upper and middle class?" or "Does the concept of retirement make sense in the twenty-first century?"

If we are to be really effective at the current time we shall have to abandon attitudes and values – that have been developing ever since we moved from hunting and gathering towards agriculture – and reintegrate ourselves into the natural order rather than continue to dominate it. We shall have to create a new form of spirituality that recognises how the world in which we are embedded actually operates.

Fortunately the new conditions we need are already developing around us. They will encourage diversity and pluralism, where each person and group can have wide degrees of freedom within a basic set of agreements about values. They will support organic thinking rather than mechanical thinking. They will encourage partnership rather than dominator models and a belief in original blessing rather than original sin. Listening to the views of others will be seen as central. The values of honesty, responsibility, humility and love will be restored to primacy but we shall also note the hypocrisy that has often proclaimed the importance of these values while acting in intensely destructive ways.

The twentieth century has been a time when we moved towards understanding our need and ability to see ourselves as separate and with the capacity to be individually creative. The twenty-first century requires that we learn to work with each other, to be collaborative. We are moving towards a period when we need to recognise the many obvious and subtle ways in which our energies are inevitably interconnected.

The world we are entering is not one of slick and easy answers. Rather, we are forced to open to each other. It is a world where the future is uncertain and we must all be ready for the twists and turns of life. It is a world where we are all required to be part of the process so we can co-create a desirable set of conditions for ourselves and for our children and grandchildren.

Fortunately, we know a great deal more about this desirable future than is generally acknowledged. We are further along in developing new models of behaviour in all sorts of institutions than we have so far been able to communicate. Note some of the emerging agreements.

- Work will need to be more engaging and fun: this will be required to ensure creativity.
- Relationships will be seen as one of the prime creators of value.
- We shall see that people need to learn throughout their lives.
- We shall move from a medical model to a health model.
- We shall recognise that litigation imposes an immense cost on individuals, institutions and the society.
- We shall understand that young people must be nurtured, particularly in the first five years of their lives, so as to break the cycles of dependency and abuse.

So how than can we achieve the fundamental change for which my vision calls? There are two possibilities. One of them would change the responsibilities that existing institutions accept. Politicians and business people, union members and educators, religious leaders and those in the non-profit sector would come to realise that they need to be concerned with creating a new way of thinking and acting. Given the growing volatility and turbulence in society, they would commit to finding ways to treat long-run concerns, which are all too easily forgotten in the hubbub of day-to-day decision-making. They would agree to bring underlying issues onto the agenda.

Business would take on particular responsibilities given its current dominance in terms of economic and political decision-making. Companies have been in the forefront of the movement that has denied the legitimacy of much government activity and there have been many gains from advancing this point of view. It is increasingly clear, however, that this strategy is leading to a highly dangerous vacuum in many areas of social decision-making. Companies therefore need to move into areas they have previously avoided.

There is, in fact, a major need for the public to understand how far companies have moved in their perception of how they should behave. Few people recognise how rapidly business is shifting both its concerns and its styles. Treated properly, companies could be an ally in the process of positive change rather than its enemy.

This leads me the second possibility for dealing with fundamental issues. We might radically reconceptualise how politics actually works in the twenty-first century, understanding that the critical part of the political process does not concern how issues are decided but what issues get attention. The Internet and the World Wide Web are dramatically changing the rules of the political game but few of us have yet understood the implications of this shift. The ability of the public to determine the agenda has never been so great.

It may well be that governments, as presently constituted, are increasingly irrelevant to the process of political decision-making. They still have the power to waste resources and to make destructive decisions. They seem increasingly unable to recognise leading-edge issues or the extraordinary shifts in underlying patterns of thought that are currently taking place. The creative energies of cultures around the world are actually flowing in other channels. It is only as we acknowledge this extraordinary shift that we are going to be able to grasp what is really going on in the world.

I believe that the real dynamics of our global culture are largely invisible to us. I have attempted in this book to shine the light on them, and my discussions are more about what is going on around us than what should be created. I believe that today's key skill is discernment. We need to look at how people and organisations are already responding to the dynamics of our time. As we do so we shall discover our extraordinary potentials.

Is it possible to summarise the drives that are developing? The following statements seem to me to contain the core shifts.

- We are recognising that the drive towards a higher standard of living for everybody in not sustainable and that we need to concentrate on the quality of life. Achieving a high quality of life is only possible with commitments to:
  – social cohesion, which requires reducing ethnic violence and the gap between the rich and the poor
  – ecological integrity as the underlying necessity for the survival of the planet and everything that lives on it
  – effective decision-making to deal with long-run and complex issues.
- It is increasingly certain that these goals can only be achieved on the basis of a values and spiritual understanding.

We Do *Have Future Choices* aims to enlarge these understandings, but I need to make it abundantly clear that neither I, nor anybody else, has an unclouded crystal ball at this stage. We all see through a glass darkly. It is my hope that some of the ideas I put forward will spark new understandings for you and enable you to see actions that will make a difference in your own life and those of others.

The text you will read represents a substantial revision of *Turning the Century* published in 1992, which, like so much of my work throughout my life, was ahead of its time. I once wrote an autobiography called *We're Not Ready For That, Yet!*, which addressed the fact that my ideas were often considered too dramatic. Indeed, I was once told by a Supreme Court Justice that there was "nothing so dangerous as a man too far ahead of his time". I hope that the years that have elapsed since the initial book was published will have lent relevance to my ideas. As always, I shall learn from the feedback I receive.

The book is in four sections. Chapters 1 to 3 provide an overview of the challenges that confront us. They provide few new concepts, although there are, of course, a number of novel ways of presenting old points. Chapters 4 to 6 examine the economic issues. They show that we must abandon the goal of maximum economic growth and labour-force participation and suggest measures which will move us towards a higher quality of life. Chapters 7 to 9 explain why we must move from our current educational systems to a commitment to learning-to-learn on a lifelong basis. Chapters 10 to 12 look at collective decision making, or politics. It is suggested that our national sovereignty models will require substantial change and that majority rule is not a satisfactory model for the compassionate era.

I have not included the standard list of acknowledgments in this book because I have learned from so many people. However there are a few I must thank particularly. First, Anne Deveson, who not only wrote the foreword to this edition, but continued to challenge me to develop both my thinking and my action patterns. Amanda Butcher, who drew my attention to flaws and weaknesses in my arguments. And the whole crew at Southern Cross University Press, who made a totally unrealistic schedule work.

As stated, I benefit from feedback. Positive is pleasant, but I probably grow more from intelligent negative comments which show where I have more to learn. There are no experts in this work – we are all learning to tell a new story and we all need to listen to one another with care and courtesy.

I can be reached at theobald@iea.com or 202 East Rockwood Boulevard, Spokane, WA 99202, USA.

Chapter 1

The Revolutions of the Twentieth Century

"May you live in interesting times." The Chinese are said to view this as a curse, and if we share their negative perceptions about periods of fundamental change, we shall see ourselves as fated to live tragic lives. Alternatively, each of us can decide that we are immensely lucky to be alive at a time when the human race can grow up and become part of a positive evolutionary process, working with – rather than against – natural forces.

Today's pace of change is without parallel in human history. The ice floes that accumulated during the Cold War have broken up. Events are moving faster than we can understand, let alone manage. The survival of the human race demands larger changes than our media, our academic systems and our politicians have so far been willing to consider.

The real clash today is not between differing facts and data but between "stories". Each of these stories has its own style. The old story was one of heroes who, working alone, made the world profoundly different. The new story I am telling has no single hero or heroine – it rests on a call to all of us to play our part in building a new society so as to reach a very different era that I choose to call "the compassionate era".

Interestingly the 2000 Presidential campaign in the United States is going to be fought around the issue of compassionate conservatism. Governor Bush of Texas is making this his rallying call and it will be interesting to see what content he gives to this slogan. Will it include a recognition that today's institutions and systems have been made obsolete by our changing knowledge structures and growing technology? Or will it be a cosmetic makeover which proposes "cut-throat capitalism with a human face"?

Hopefully Bush will challenge the United States to tackle the issues of our times with courage, imagination and joy. This would make it easier for other countries to break out of the current cultural trance which dominates politics throughout the world. There is a route into the future that will continue the human adventure, rather than end it. In these turbulent times, our individual and group choices do make a difference. None of us can change the world by ourselves, but the sum of our decisions does decide the way the world evolves. The tides of history are running with us if we are smart and committed enough to discover and move with them. A profoundly new vision and story is already emerging all over the world.

We are living through an extraordinary change in conditions which requires that the human race leaves behind its adolescence. Fortunately, there is a natural tendency to examine the future as we reach the end of a century – and more so at the conclusion of a millennium. Asking fundamental questions as we approach the twenty-first century is therefore inevitable.

In order to understand our times we must look at four primary driving forces which are changing global systems rapidly. I list them below in order of their understanding and acceptance in Western cultures. Some of them are already relatively well known: others are only now beginning to be recognised. While much of the material I set out in this chapter will be familiar to you, I often reach significantly different conclusions than those that are predominantly accepted. If you have kept up with the debate about fundamental change, however, you may want to skim or skip the rest of this chapter.

Beyond violence

Violence has always been a major part of the human experience. It is a deeply personal issue as well as a major danger to the continued existence of the world. We all know people who have been mugged or abused as children, even if we ourselves have not suffered these experiences. We are all aware of the casual violence of adolescence that in many places seems to be mutating into something far more dangerous. The combination of available weaponry and frustration raises the level of threat significantly.

We are all aware of the dangers of war – the most visible form of violence. Immediately after the atomic bomb was dropped on Japan in 1945, a few people recognised that it had become too dangerous to use all available weaponry. The twentieth century therefore saw the development of a huge paradox: as weaponry became more destructive, its ability to determine the shape of events declined. America and Russia were unable to win wars despite their superior might. The struggles in Korea, Vietnam and Afghanistan resulted in stalemates or withdrawals. While the enemy could certainly have been defeated if nuclear weapons had been used, the cost in terms of internal and external public opinion was perceived to be too high and the risks of escalation too dangerous.

The Gulf War seemed, at first sight, to have created a very different pattern. Advanced weaponry systems provided an overwhelming advantage to the United Nations. A quick victory was achieved with very low loss of life on the UN side, and because America had dominated the coalition, the initial reaction was that America could stand tall again. There was little courage to raise the tough issues which victory swept under the rug. We left behind a peace which implied the ousting of Saddam Hussein but was unable to ensure his fall. The sanctions on the country that were meant to have led to new leadership, have instead caused the death of many people, particularly children.

The real issue posed by the Gulf War and the attack on Kosovo lies deeper. Barbara Ehrenreich caught some of the issues in the following quote from her Time magazine essay 'The Warrior Culture', published on October 15, 1990.

> "You must understand that Americans are a warrior nation," Senator Daniel Patrick Moynihan told a group of Arab leaders in early September, one month into the Middle East crisis. He said this proudly, and he may, without thinking through the ugly implications, have told the truth. In many ways, in outlook and behavior, the US has begun to act like a primitive warrior culture.
>
> It has not yet penetrated our imagination that in a world where the powerful, industrialized states are at last at peace, there might be other ways to face down a pint-size Third-World warrior state than with the massive force of arms. Nor have we begun to see what an anachronism we are in danger of becoming, a warrior nation in a world that pines for peace, a high-tech state with the values of a warrior band.

The Gulf War and Kosovo did not change realities. War is still obsolete as a way of settling disputes. These wars were aberrations, not the beginning of a new world order. This is the lesson that must be learned if human survival is to be possible. The apparent low cost of a high tech war to the victors conceals enormous damage when the picture is drawn more widely. It was the decision to go to war that led to the massive ecological damage and the large-scale loss of life. There were alternatives but the US did not have the patience or creativity to work them through. These alternatives would certainly not have been costless, but would clearly have been less damaging than the war.

Let us assume it was desirable to intervene in both the Gulf and Kosovo. Then let us ask whether we could have bought better outcomes with the amount of money we were prepared to spend on the two wars. From my perspective, that money we spent on destruction would have yielded far more positive results if used to promote peaceful outcomes.

One of the primary arguments of those who reject war as a method of settling disputes is that they almost always leave the world more unstable than before and, all too often, sow the seeds of future violence. The reparations demanded from Germany after World War I, made World War II essentially inevitable. There was no way that Germany could create a viable society if it had to make large-scale reparations. The Allies in World War I therefore planted the seeds from which Hitler inevitably grew. A few far-seeing individuals understood the dangers but the desire for vengeance was so great that their voices were drowned.

After World War II, on the other hand, America seemed extraordinarily generous. General Marshall was able to convince the President and Congress that it was in the best interest of the US to rebuild Europe and Japan. Nevertheless, while American aid was given freely, we need to remember that one of the primary motivations was to block the perceived danger from the communist world. The Cold War developed as early as 1946.

Once again, the seeds of a new world war were sown – this time in World War II. The tension between the East and West became so great that, if nuclear weapons had not existed, Russia and its allies would have fought with the members of the North American Treaty Organisation at some time during the second half of the twentieth century. Despite the fact that we hate to admit this reality, nuclear weapons were "peacemakers".

The nineties have produced a situation without parallel in human history. The former Soviet Union, which was once seen as a "great power", has now been revealed as an economically under-developed area of the world where most people face hunger, and many starve. In the past, this type of pattern led to the rise of a dictatorship that enforced the discipline by which economic viability could be reestablished. The most recent major example was the rise of Hitler in Germany.

Avoiding this danger should be the primary issue that preoccupies the leaders of the West in their dealings with Russia and the republics that formed the Soviet Union; all other questions should be subordinated to it. One of the most disturbing implications of the Kosovo dynamics is the hatred towards the United States which has developed in Russia.

The fear of nuclear holocaust prevented the development of a major war for over 40 years. It also helped control many areas of smaller-scale violence between countries and between ethnic groups within countries, for both the great powers were afraid that dynamics might get out of control. New and profoundly difficult questions are emerging now that the stabilising power of the Cold War has been removed. How do we prevent the development of regional bullies? How do we deal with the rise of ethnic energies? How can the export of arms be limited so the capacity for violence within and between smaller countries is reduced?

We shall not understand the issue of violence, however, until we ask when conflict causes violence and when it does not. Conflict is inevitable in all societies, and emerges from the differing perceptions and attitudes that always exist in a pluralistic world. There are, however, two very different possible reactions to divergent views: one is to argue that the other group is wrong and that force and violence should be used to subdue it, while the alternative is to recognise that although there will always be clashing goals, more positive results can be achieved through creative problem-solving than by forcing agreement through coercion.

Conflict has highly positive aspects. The fastest way to learn is to discover a person or group that reaches totally different conclusions to your own when looking at the same reality. As you examine alternative views, your own understandings are inevitably enriched. You may not change your conclusions but you will certainly become more aware of factors you have previously overlooked. This is the key towards new approaches to violence.

Conflict is inevitable. At its best, it is a sign that people know what they want and need and are willing to challenge others to make sure their rights are respected. It becomes dangerous and violent when groups believe that their rights are more important than those of others and that they should impose their desires.

In this context, we need to recognise that much of the debate following Iraq's invasion of Kuwait centred on a clash between industrial-era and compassionate-era rhetorics, although it was seldom defined in this way. Many of the world's leaders concentrated on the issue of responding to aggression or regaining access to Kuwait's oil. They wanted to "win". On the other hand, a few senators adopted a compassionate-era viewpoint, recognising that there was no easy solution to a complex situation.

They pointed out that there were other nation-states which were interested in dominating the region and that the lessening of Iraq's power might well give Syria and Iran a freer hand. They reminded people that the only reason that Iraq had become such a threat was that the nations of the world, particularly America, had built it up to prevent the victory of Iran during the eighties war. Evidence which emerged after the war shows that the Bush administration was one of the major supporters of Iraq right up to the time of the invasion of Kuwait.

In Kosovo, the situation was even more complex. Opposition to Slobodan Milosevich was already developing and there was a possibility of his overthrow through internal pressure. The causes of the conflict go back literally hundreds of years and there was violence on both sides. As always, the first casualty of war is the truth. The media were all too willing to present a one-sided view of the issues – and as a result, war was a popular scenario, with the Serbs as the villains and the Kosovars as victims.

It was a war that hardened lines, making it far more difficult for Serbs and Albanians to live together. The war moved Albanians out of their homes – the peace did the same to Serbs. Serbia believes that it has been unfairly treated and many countries around the world agree. The Balkans are even more unstable than they were before the intervention.

The debate around the Kuwaiti invasion and the NATO attack in Yugoslavia was, in part, an argument between the past and the future. Those who argue for the future believe that dialogue is always worthwhile. They are convinced that the way to work through an issue may emerge anywhere and that it is only by truly listening to all those involved that a deadlock may be turned into hopeful movement. They believe that the range of circumstances in which power and force are seen as acceptable models for bringing about change must be dramatically reduced. It is only as this pattern becomes established that the waste of resources on weaponry will be significantly diminished.

One of the wonderful aspects of the twenty-first century is that human and environmental survival requires the progressive elimination of violence. The fact that we can only flourish if we move beyond violence does not, of course, mean that we shall take this step. We have a choice. We can decide to perpetuate historical patterns at immense cost to the human race or we can accept the challenge of moving forward, learning to live by spiritual values.

I am increasingly convinced that we shall achieve a positive future if we can abandon our ideologies and biases and learn to listen to each other. We must come to understand why individuals and groups see the same situation differently. If we fail to do so, the pace of technological change will drive ethnic groups and nations apart and cause a total breakdown both inside countries and between them.

This is one example of the pattern that will run throughout this book. Situations look totally different depending on the patterns of thinking one chooses to adopt to understand the world. If one works within a violence model, then there are no choices. If one works with dialogue, then even the most intractable situations may yield. Nineties' dynamics in Ireland and South Africa show what can be achieved. While there are still huge dangers in both nations, extraordinarily positive changes have been made.

Ensuring long-run ecological balance

It is now generally agreed that human beings are altering planetary ecological systems in unpredictable ways. The consequences of the increase in carbon dioxide, the thinning of the ozone layer and the effects of acid rain all have global impacts. As Australians are all too well aware the depletion of the ozone layer can lead to major increases in skin cancers.

Although nobody knows how to model the planetary ecological system, the dominant opinion among specialists is that global warming is inevitable. Meteorological observations show that the nineties have been hotter than any decade in recorded history. Climate catastrophes have become more and more serious in recent years: the costs in 1998 reached a new peak, according to figures from insurance companies and the International Red Cross.

While the reality of ecological overload is obvious, global warming is not the only possibility. Some fear that a new ice age can be triggered. Because we have essentially no knowledge about how major climate shifts take place, we should be extraordinarily careful when making specific projections. On the other hand, the growing evidence that sharp breaks in climatic patterns have taken place "rapidly" in the past should increase our determination to make intelligent decisions as soon as possible. Chaos theory shows that sharp breaks in trend often take place.

The highly dramatic consequences of atmospheric trends have drawn attention away from the excessive stresses on our land and water systems. These dangers are also critically important, however. The viability of the "enclosed" Mediterranean and Caribbean Seas is threatened by pollution. Underground water supplies are being infiltrated by surface run-off, community and industrial waste, pesticides, herbicides, fertilisers and deep-well injections. Chemicals and other noxious products are being exported to poorer countries and doing untold harm there because storage techniques are inadequate to the types of material they are receiving. Once water has been polluted, recovery to a viable state may take decades and even centuries. Rivers, lakes and even internal seas throughout the world, particularly in Eastern Europe and the countries of the old Soviet Union, are dying. Countries try to export chemical and nuclear wastes to other countries: this is a serious danger even in rich nations like Australia.

As a result of the growing damage, water quality and supplies will dominate economics and politics in many parts of the world in the twenty-first century. Indeed, they could create greater problems than the availability of oil. Already, supplies throughout the Middle East are inadequate to immediately foreseeable needs. Behind the territorial issue, which dominates discussions between Israel and the Arabs, lurks the problems of allocating water supplies more fairly. In the US, the future of the water-shortage states, such as California and Arizona, is increasingly doubtful. Because rainfall is not regular from year to year, major droughts in various parts of the world will cause havoc when they inevitably occur. In Australia, climatic variability may well determine the maximum feasible population for the continent.

Intensive cultivation of land throughout the world has led to the loss of much surface topsoil. Salinisation of irrigated land is also a growing problem in many areas. Attempts to use European production techniques in Australia have led to such severe problems that much of the land now producing cereal crops will have to be abandoned. Worldwatch, an organisation which has been tracking trends for many years, is increasingly concerned about the ability to raise food production fast enough to keep up with population increases. This reality is hidden by the fact that the rich countries are overproducing, many poor countries cannot however afford to purchase what is available.

Individuals respond in a variety of ways to this growing evidence of major long-run ecological stress. At one extreme, people deny that the problems are urgent, or indeed really significant. Those who react in this way believe that while there is certainly a need to limit environmental damage, there is no requirement to change the whole structure of our thinking and actions. This leads to a belief that it is possible both to preserve the environment and continue maximum growth strategies.

Most governmental and United Nations' thinking is still along these lines: the UN Brundtland Report, which is the current "bible" on the issue, supports this thesis. When the leaders of the major powers get together, the emphasis is almost always on maximum economic growth. Social and environmental issues are seen as secondary. While the balance is shifting, it is doing so far too slowly.

The opposite view sees humanity as a plague on the face of the earth. Some individuals have gone so far as to welcome AIDS as a way to decrease population. It is also suggested that Gaia (a mystical concept for the earth as a living organism) knows what is required, and will therefore move in foreordained ways to achieve appropriate goals, regardless of the actions of humankind. According to this theory, trends will develop to limit the number of people who can live on the planet.

I am convinced that both of these extreme views are wrong. I believe that we must recognise that human beings are now one of the primary forces changing the planet and they will continue to play this role in either a positive or negative way. I am sure we can discover what we should be doing so long as we are willing to give up our attachment to old ways of thinking and past moral codes which developed when conditions were very different. Human beings must learn to live within ecological realities. Denial of this fundamental requirement will continue to worsen our situation. Humanity must find directions that will lessen the stress on people while also ensuring ecological and social viability into the indefinite future.

One of the primary immediate needs is to recognise that megaprojects are often too dangerous to build. We do not know how to model the impact of major changes – particularly when they may change Earth's ecosystems drastically and dangerously. For example, the building of the high dam on the Nile has fundamentally altered, and damaged, the Mediterranean ecosystem.

Unfortunately, there are still places on earth which are sufficiently far away from attention that megaprojects are still being planned and sometimes constructed. Many of the most serious past errors have been in the Soviet Union and Eastern Europe. Notable among future dangers are projects in the north of Quebec, Canada, which aim to produce huge amounts of electricity and are even considering transporting large amounts of water from the north of the American continent to the south. Alaska is now considering a project on a similar scale. China is also working to create huge dams which are widely agreed to be dangerous.

It is now clear that we have to pay far more attention to ecological matters. Fortunately, we do not need to know the exact shape of future dangers before making appropriate changes in direction. Cutting back on levels of production and waste will provide benefits whatever the shape of the specific problems that may confront us. We need to quit arguing and move forward. The Natural Step, which originated in Sweden and has now spread around the world, provides a basic set of understandings which makes it easy to see the fundamental agreements which are emerging around ecological issues.

A growing number of institutions and companies are adopting the idea of the Triple Bottom Line. In addition, to their traditional financial responsibilities, they are committing to looking at their ecological and social obligations. Firms are recognising that waste can be a profit centre. They are also grasping the fact that people are their most important resource. This is shifting our understandings of the issue of human rights and responsibilities.

Human rights and responsibilities

The Bill of Rights is seen by a large number of thinkers as the crowning glory of the American Revolution. It reflects the true driving force which gave the revolt against Britain its edge. There was a fierce desire to curb the use of authoritarian and often arbitrary power expressed in the Revolutionary motto: "Live free, or die."

People wanted the right and the ability to make decisions for themselves. Strong individuals populated North America. Those who were willing to abandon hearth and home for the risks of crossing the Atlantic and homesteading a strange land at the other end of their journey came to the new continent. It is not surprising that they demanded the right to set their own directions.

De Tocqueville, the great French writer, saw and caught this mood when he visited the US in the early nineteenth century. He understood that the cultural style of the country was very different from Europe, despite the fact that it had been populated from there. The people who had moved were significantly different from those who had stayed home. Science-fiction writers have explored this same theme. Many stories are based on the belief that if human beings do gain the ability to travel to the stars, it will once again be the imaginative and the courageous who choose to travel. The fearful and the lazy will stay behind.

One of the fascinating areas of speculation is the reason why countries colonised from Europe developed such different national characters. The individualism of the United States contrasts strongly with the commitment to social cohesion which is far stronger in Canada and Australia.

Some of the differences emerged around the drive towards individual rights in the eighteenth century. The power of the state and the church needed to be broken, and the rights of the individual needed to be affirmed and reinforced. The emphasis had been completely one-sided in the Middle Ages, with the collective being seen as far more important than the individual. Despite this obvious imbalance, the intellectual giants of the eighteenth century did recognise future issues with remarkable prescience. They aimed to honour both the power of the state and the rights of the individual.

Unfortunately there was one force which could not possibly have been grasped at the time they were working out their grand schemes; they were not aware of the corrosive effect that capitalism would have on societal commitment. In their time, economics was very much a creature of the state, designed to serve state purposes.

The idea that it might break free and become the driving sector of society, rather than being subordinate to the power of the state, would have seemed the wildest fantasy to the founding fathers. Adam Smith, an eighteenth century Scottish economist, who is often used as the justification for current directions, would reject them out of hand if he were living today. While Smith did believe that an invisible hand caused firms to do what was needed, he never thought for a moment that economics should drive all decision-making processes and did not consider the possibility that such a situation would develop.

Most people still saw themselves as embedded in their communities in the eighteenth century. The idea that individuals should do what seemed best to them – regardless of consequences for neighbours and employees – developed in the nineteenth century, as Adam Smith's idea of the invisible hand taught that social good is created out of individual self-interest. Many people came to believe that competition was beneficial. It was therefore all right for some people to be hurt, because the overall impact of selfish behaviour would automatically be positive.

This approach to economics really took hold in the mid-nineteenth century when lawyers decided corporations were permanent entities with rights similar to those of individuals. Most of the larger-than-life figures who ruled their companies believed they had the right to make the largest possible profit. One of the most powerful of these tycoons, William Henry Vanderbilt, when challenged about his behaviour, made it clear exactly where he stood. He announced without any hesitation: "The public be damned." The anti-trust legislation of the late nineteenth and early twentieth centuries that aimed to control predatory capitalism was the direct result of his type of attitude and actions.

Unfortunately, the anti-trust bills did not tackle the central issue: business' claim that it could do what it wanted in the economic field without considering social consequences. Joseph Schumpeter, a great Austrian economist who has never received the attention which was his due, showed that the emphasis of the corporation on profit, and the desire of individuals to serve their narrow self-interest, would destroy the ties required for any society to function.

Schumpeter was very aware that societies can only flourish if there is a strong sense of interdependence. His fears that this sense of mutuality would be destroyed by capitalism have been proved true by developments. The most obvious evidence of this reality is the language we use as we pitch capitalism to the poorer countries and Eastern Europe. We inform them that it is only if people are permitted to gain great wealth, and others are thrust into poverty, that the capitalist system can be expected to function properly. We propose a form of capitalism to them that we would reject in our own countries.

We have become so used to this way of looking at the world that we fail to recognise its essential injustice. It is certainly true that absolute equality is not possible or desirable, but it is equally true that the degree of income disparities that have developed, particularly in the eighties and nineties, are destructive for our future. As people become aware that they are being left behind in the economic race, they are responding by demanding their rights. More and more groups believe that they are being treated unfairly.

The demand for equal rights was essentially started by the blacks during the sixties, with feminism's "second wave" push for equal rights for women soon following. Now every group has adopted the same strategy. The easiest way to understand the danger of this approach is to note that many whites and males are now organising to counter the claims of other groups. They increasingly see themselves as being unfairly treated because of the perceived advantages that minorities and women are being given.

The essential difference between the emerging white movement and the social pressure created by minorities is that the former can win at the polls because it is in fact a majority, even though it defines itself as a mistreated minority. Non-whites must rely on whites for justice; whites can dominate the system and exclude others. Pushing whites to the point where they feel that they are being mistreated is therefore counterproductive, for they can prevent the essential movements toward social justice.

Central to any new way of viewing the new social contract must be the understanding that there can be no rights without responsibilities. One of the easiest ways to grasp this truth is to look at the way in which the discussion about weapons has been so greatly abused in the United States. The second amendment to the Constitution, on which the debate is based, states: "A well-regulated militia being necessary to the security of a free state, the right of the people to keep and bear arms shall not be infringed." The National Rifle Association has used this amendment to claim an absolute right for citizens to possess any form of weapon. They ignore the obvious truth that the right of the people to bear arms is clearly subordinate, in the original amendment, to the security of a free state.

Different countries react differently to mass murders involving firearms. Australia and Britain have reacted by cutting back dramatically on the rights to own guns, while in the United States, public outrage has not yet overcome political lobbying.

Modern weaponry has changed the nature of the world so profoundly that having modern weapons in the hands of citizens damages the security of a free state rather than enhances it. People need the ability to prevent the abuse of power but the dangers of the late twentieth and early twenty-first century cannot be controlled by weapons – rather, that control will be possible through the force of ideas and personal courage.

It was not weapons that changed the course of history in Eastern Europe: it was the will of the people. The movement into the future has to be driven by a new covenant between all those who live on our small and overcrowded globe. The story which supports this covenant will have to provide us all with rights and demand that all of us fulfil our responsibilities.

The United States currently acts as though its current economic and political thinking is always relevant to the rest of the world. If massive destruction is to be avoided in the twenty-first century, American patterns of thought and behaviour are going to have to change dramatically. The current emphasis on rights must be abandoned. There is a need to balance rights and responsibilities.

Impact of new knowledge

It may seem strange to place new knowledge so far down the list of driving forces, given that I stated at the beginning of this chapter that I would list them in order of our degree of understanding. After all, people are increasingly aware that computers and robots, bio-technology and nuclear energy, engineering and medical skills, and information and communication technologies have been changing the world in which we live throughout the second half of the twentieth century.

Harold Linstone, editor of the journal *Technological Forecasting*, wrote in the late eighties:

> Technological advances continue to trigger much change. Information technology is moving at a remarkable pace. By 2000, information will be processed by computers a thousand times more powerful than our current ones ... Other fields of rapid technological change include production automation (robotics), the creation of advanced materials (ceramics, bacteria-based polymers, genetically engineered drugs), the use of superconductivity to improve magnets and fossil fuel substitutes.
>
> We recognize that this unprecedented pace of change is not matched by social rates of change. Indeed, the gap between technological and societal rates of change is becoming ever wider. The US is approaching the twenty-first century with a 19th century institutional structure while subject to a dizzying pace of technological advance.

Owen Paepke has developed another way of raising the same critical issue. He notes that 60 per cent of the labour force used to be needed to produce food in the developed countries, and the number is now down to five per cent or less; further decreases will not be really significant. He then notes that, used effectively, only a small proportion of the lifetime of each person is required to produce goods and services. Human beings need not be tied to production as they have been throughout human history. This is true not only in the rich countries, but in the developing world. Modern technology decreases the demand for labour and makes an economic development strategy based on full employment impossible.

This type of understanding is increasingly common. We have, however, concentrated our attention on the ways in which this increased knowledge could provide a higher standard of living through dramatic increases in productivity. We are only now looking at the social and political implications and beginning to understand the inevitable shifts in the styles, approaches and systems by which we have lived during the industrial era.

One of the most extraordinary, and invisible, shifts in dynamics during the latter half of the twentieth century has been the shift in our attitudes towards time on the job. Until World War II, there was an implicit agreement that improvements in productivity would result in both higher standards of living and shorter work lives. Over the last 50 years, all the emphasis has been on the accumulation of stuff.

This pattern is now shifting. France has brought in a law limiting hours of work in order to reduce unemployment. The problem, of course, is that policing such a policy is essentially impossible. There is a need for a shift in social priorities if the amount of time spent on the job is to be effectively controlled.

It is the implications of computers and robots, as well as ecological realities, which will force us to shift our patterns of thinking. The basic reality is that if the nature of a task can be fully defined, then it is possible for the activity to be taken over by a computer, or a machine controlled by a computer. When judgment or intuition is required, then computers, at least as currently structured, cannot take over from human beings.

The challenge, therefore, is to educate people so they can do more than computers or machines controlled by computers. This means that educational goals that aim to turn people into "efficient" workers are counterproductive. Students are still taught to do what they are told rather than to learn to think for themselves. The creativity they need to be full human beings, and that is required to enable our institutions to cope with rapid change, is therefore stifled. We can only deal with this danger by committing ourselves to developing learning-to-learn systems that encourage imagination and creativity.

Will this be enough? Many leading-edge thinkers believe that computers will develop the skills to deal with unstructured situations in the twenty-first century. This naturally leads to the fear that human beings will be unable to keep up with

30

computers and will ultimately be replaced by smart machines. This fear is only valid so long as one remains caught in industrial-era patterns of thinking.

There is no "absolute" set of understandings which can be learned by a computer, which will permit it to operate without error or ambiguity. If computers gain the skills to deal with real, complex situations, they will be no more certain of the results of their actions than human beings are able to be. The idea that there can be an all-knowing computer died when we realised that knowledge is not objective but perceptual. The results from computers will be no more certain than the results obtained from human judgment.

There is another area where our growing knowledge is changing our norms and standards rapidly and dramatically. Growing medical and biological information is shifting the way human beings think about their bodies. It is also challenging our beliefs about life and death in ways which are deeply troubling. Referendums have been held in many parts of the world around the right to die: the resulting solutions have not satisfied anybody.

Death is obviously a part of the lifecycle, but this reality has been denied in Western countries and particularly in America. In primitive societies, however, there was no way to practise the deceptions that are now so common. For example, in the traditional Eskimo culture, where survival was always in doubt, the individual who could no longer support the tribe was expected to choose death in order to ensure the survival of the group when scarcity threatened. Similar patterns existed in many societies where life was always marginal.

The development of medicine set us off on another track. Doctors took an oath to support life; so long as their powers were limited, this oath was essentially benign. People were enabled to live longer and the quality of their lives was improved. The developments in medical technology in the second half of the twentieth century have shifted the situation dramatically. Today, death has to be chosen by more and more people and we have developed new tools such as living wills to ensure that people are not kept alive on life support if they choose to reject this option.

Society is still trying to keep the complex issues around the end of life at bay by defining death as the ultimate enemy. We need new definitions if we are to make sense of today's patterns. I would suggest that life is the ability to develop and help others to develop, and that death occurs when this is no longer possible. I am arguing that we can only make sensible choices if we adopt a subjective definition of life and death rather than the objective measures of the failure of heart and brain which we use today.

I am, of course, aware that we shall only be able to benefit from this new definition if we can develop a far greater level of personal and group maturity than in the past. We must learn to value life, helping those in unreasoning despair to move beyond their darkness – whether it results from their teenage fears, the aftermath of pregnancy or the fear of old age. We must also recognise that a time does come when death is an option that can be welcomed as the appropriate end to a good life.

The cross-cut between medical and societal challenges is even more complex. We are now in the process of deciphering the genetic code. We shall be able to determine the types of diseases that are genetically based and likely to be passed on to children. A growing number of people therefore argue that it will be possible to delete a dangerous gene from a human being so that the quality of life of their children will be better.

The problem with this approach is that we do not know, and will perhaps never totally know, the linkings between genes. We may aim to improve the qualities of the next generation but introduce, instead, new problems. As options of this type increase, how should parents make these choices? Indeed, there may be a prior question: will the state try to take away the freedom of people with inheritable serious diseases and deny them the right to have children?

Some people want to go still further and start programs to "improve" the human race. They argue that the human race should be bred to achieve certain patterns, but just what patterns should we choose? Some would want longer life, but do we know that older people can maintain a high quality of life until their death? And what would dramatically longer lifespans do to already acute population problems?

Others might want to choose intelligence as their goal, but this is a tricky concept. Do we mean the ability to absorb book learning, or should we be interested in creativity? These are not necessarily linked and, indeed, may require very different qualities.

Human beings have been successful because of their diversity. They have not specialised like animals into a specific niche. Some people have therefore always been able to see the advantages of new directions, and a genetic program that worked to decrease diversity might well prove to be a severe disadvantage.

Finally, it is useful to look at the impact of communication technologies. Only a hundred years ago Carnegie built libraries in many cities. These libraries provided people with a chance to enter the world of ideas for the first time. Today, our problems are totally different from those of the past. We are besieged with more messages than we can possibly absorb or process. We are overloaded with information. And more and more of this information is designed to manipulate our thinking rather than help us see clearly. Indeed, we can now see that as information doubles, knowledge halves and wisdom quarters.

The majority of the messages we receive today are screened by others before we receive them. Many of us have had the disconcerting experience of being at an event and then watching it on the news and feeling that what was reported did not reflect what we experienced. Part of the problem comes from the fact that each observer sees a different picture. In addition, the media knows what "news" is and inevitably distorts what goes on so that it fits this dominant perception.

This problem is going to worsen in the immediate future. New technologies such as "virtual reality" which enable people to act within a totally created world, will further challenge our abilities to understand and make decisions about our lives and societies. It will only be as we understand why it is important to help people learn to learn about reality, and as we can provide

33

ourselves with a story which makes sense of current conditions, that we can hope to break out of current confusions and frustrations.

The Internet and the World Wide Web hold enormous promise for creating a profoundly different and potentially more attractive universe. It permits far broader access than ever before, but it also enables distorted information to be disseminated in ways that are very convincing. And Internet users can be subjected to pornography and other similar material without their consent.

The Internet is also threatened by various forms of worms and viruses. If a disease that affected human beings or nature was deliberately let loose, there would be broad agreement that this was totally unacceptable behaviour. Those who aim to damage the Internet and the World Wide Web have so far been treated largely as pranksters, but as we come to recognise how much we depend on our electronic connections as the nervous system for society, this will necessarily change. We have created a nervous system for the human race, and its disruption in intolerable.

It is argued that we have moved into an information age, but the real opportunity of our time is to context our superabundance of information so it provides us with knowledge. The working patterns that are required to develop knowledge are very different from those needed to produce information. Overworked people can be effective in an information system, but only balanced individuals can context knowledge and perceive wisdom.

The capacity to produce artificial worlds is being increasingly explored in films. Both *The Truman Show* and *Matrix* considered the possibility of manipulating reality – indeed, they encouraged many of us to ask: "What is reality?" As we recognise that reality is malleable, we are all challenged to discover what role our own actions play in determining the personal, social and global realities within which we live.

Looking forward

The primary forces that are currently driving our world emerge from past commitments. People decided that they wanted to achieve certain goals and they often succeeded in doing so. The human race has not failed – it has succeeded. It is therefore difficult to understand the grim despair which controls so many who propose fundamental change. Those who deny the capacity of people to deal with present crises are turning their backs on the overwhelming evidence that proves that individuals can grow and help others to grow. They are denying the intelligence and resilience of human beings.

My frustration at the negativity of many professional change agents is only equalled by my disagreement with those who believe that because one has been successful in the past it is possible to continue in the same direction forever. The mindless optimism of growth-oriented economists and politicians, which denies all the obvious evidence, is deeply depressing. The unwillingness to face any of the major questions of the day, opting instead for diversionary issues, makes it easy to despair.

Fortunately there are millions of people who operate in a quite different mode. These courageous realists look at the changes going on in the world and do what they can, in their own situations, to improve dynamics. They are well aware that positive directions do not develop as a result of orders from the top of the society, but rather emerge as a large number of people do a wide variety of things a little bit differently.

This group appreciates the viewpoint of William James, the well-known author.

> I am done with great things and big things and great institutions and big successes, and I am for those tiny invisible molecular moral forces that work from individual to individual, creeping through the crannies of the world like so many rootlets or like the capillary oozing water, yet which, if you give them time, will bend the hardest monuments of human pride.

When operating as a courageous realist, one sometimes sees oneself as a salmon swimming upstream against a current which is too strong. To break out of this discouraging feeling we need friends and colleagues, and the purpose of this book is to help courageous realists find each other. We need to understand that the core disagreement is between those who are prepared to recognise that fundamental change is already taking place and those who want to maintain a status quo which is more and more dangerous.

We have moved into a world with essentially unlimited productive and destructive power. The patterns of thought and behaviour we have inherited from the past are therefore counterproductive. Fortunately, we know a great deal about the directions in which we can move – and indeed are already moving.

Chapter 2

Changing Success Criteria

Individual and group survival in the twenty-first century requires fundamentally different behaviour to that which was required in the twentieth. All of us need to rethink our current understandings of the world and learn to see it in new ways. This is the only way life can be attractive in today's conditions.

Traditionally, many of us aim to outdo others using the success criteria of the past. We try to go beyond our ancestors – for example, during the industrial era it became the norm for people to aim for greater wealth (and 25 per cent more than what one currently possesses is still the goal of many people). But now it is being realised that this goal is obsolete because ensuring maximum rates of economic growth is no longer desirable. Rather, we need to ensure ecological balance for as far into the future as we can see.

Changing our success criteria is always a challenge but there are parallels from the past. People had different goals in hunting-and-gathering societies than in agricultural times. Similarly, the desires of individuals and groups were different in the agricultural period as compared to the industrial era. Now we must move out of the industrial era into the compassionate era.

The need to change success criteria is therefore not new. The fact that each of us has to change our success criteria within our lifespan is, however, totally novel. The current moment of choice is unique. Every previous generation was constrained by the need to toil for a living. Today, the necessary amount of work can be greatly reduced. We have developed effectively unlimited productive and destructive power, but we also have the ability to choose life or death for ourselves and our beautiful planet. Each of us influences the route our culture will take by our thoughts and the decisions we make.

Future generations will envy those of us who have the opportunity to be involved in this process of choice. Our grandchildren will not understand if we "sleep" through this extraordinarily exciting moment in history. They will wonder how we missed the opportunity to be involved in the creation of a new order.

Patterns of change

I have been discussing the issue of change for almost 50 years. One of the most common responses to my ideas has been that I'm saying nothing new because change has always existed and is, indeed, the only constant of human experience. At one level, this is absolutely true. Even hunting-and-gathering tribes had to cope with seasonal fluctuations and varying weather patterns. Nevertheless people lived out their lives in a known environment where patterns changed slowly because existence was controlled by natural forces and stable cultures.

City-states, based on agriculture, began to have more options. Priests and kings gained power and the lives of the masses were subject to increasing upheavals. But the underlying rhythm of the seasons remained and the sense of vulnerability to natural forces persisted.

The industrial era was based on a fundamentally different concept of change. The idea of controlling nature developed. People began to see how they could benefit from supporting and investing in new ideas and technologies that would alter the conditions in which they lived. A growing gap developed between the young who saw the new conditions as desirable and the old who wanted to preserve the past. Shifts took place as the old died and young people with new ideas took their places. This process was able to keep up with shifting realities because life expectancies were still short and older generations died off before their blocking became too destructive.

This industrial-era generational pattern of change can no longer respond to today's dynamics. Lifespans are now far longer. Much technological development occurs in months rather than years, let alone decades. You and I can therefore no longer complete our lives using the ideas we learned when we were growing up. This is one of the fundamental revolutions of the current period of history. It is also the reason why we must all continue to learn throughout our lives.

An image will help us understand why the nature of our challenges is altering so profoundly. Think about the eye of a hurricane. On one side of the eye, the storm hits from a particular direction. If a craft passes through the quiet eye, the wind then hits it from the opposite side as it moves into the turbulence again. We can think of our culture as passing through the eye of a cultural hurricane. Approaches which were suitable for creating the maximum growth strategies on one side of the eye become counterproductive on the other when we need to move toward profoundly different goals.

The industrial era created a storm of modernisation and materialism. The eighties and nineties were the eye of the hurricane. Maximum economic growth, national sovereignty and the importance of weaponry were supported most strongly just as their realities were fading away. This is not unusual. Frequently in history a set of beliefs is most discussed, and used, when it is losing its vitality. People cling to old beliefs and action patterns when they feel they are being overwhelmed by new realities.

The world is now moving out of the eye onto the other side of the turbulence. The commitment to maximum growth is being replaced by a desire to increase the quality of life and to preserve the environment. The danger of the growing split between the rich and the poor, within and between countries, is increasingly perceived as both intolerable and highly dangerous. The gender gap is growing as more women than men sense that the time has come to abandon violence against other people and the environment. This gap is increasingly visible in voting patterns.

There is also a growing sense that our decision-making mechanisms are failing us. The adversarial models we have inherited from the past cannot cope with the complex issues that are emerging at the current time. More and more people agree that adversarial structures are ineffective in today's conditions and must be replaced by a search for consensus and common ground.

The real difficulty of our times is that the needed changes have to take place at the deepest level of our consciousness. Some talk about a religious revival that would bring the core messages of all faiths together. Some believe that spirituality is a better way of thinking about the issues. Some choose to work from the emerging intellectual understandings in system theory and around chaos and complexity.

Given these fundamental alterations in perception, many people are now looking for shifts that will move us in the opposite direction to those which are still being proposed by almost all academics and politicians. Most intellectual and establishment decision-makers have not adapted to the fact that the move through the eye of the hurricane is essentially complete and that we are playing catch-up with trends that have already emerged. They are still proposing directions that were appropriate in the past.

One of the profound issues we face at the current time is how to link the positive energies that are emerging so rapidly. Given the many groups that are now active, one of the crucial questions is why they have so little impact on the inertia of systems that need to be changed. One of the reasons, I believe, is that much discussion is conducted at a very high level of abstraction. All too often their arguments are stated in ways which make the general public feel incompetent to grasp the realities of our time.

I use a very different style. As I have grown older I have recognised that the way I live is far more critical than the actions I take. People decide whether or not to listen to me in terms of whether they find me credible. Fundamental change in thinking is not triggered intellectually: it results from trust and a positive emotional charge.

The stance I take is obviously related to the way I see the world. I do not believe a small elite group can manage the change process. I am convinced that a much broader range of leaders must be willing to support the new directions society so urgently needs. I am deeply in tune with a sentiment I heard many years ago: "At the end of every intellectual journey lies common sense."

This position has significantly affected my life in a wide variety of ways. The most dramatic case came when I was asked by the Canadian Broadcasting Corporation to give the Massey radio lectures. This was a prestigious opportunity to set out my ideas and I engaged in an extensive process of consultation to prepare these lectures, intending to speak in a way that would reach as many people as possible.

Shortly before the planned broadcast date, CBC cancelled my invitation, arguing that the talks were insufficiently intellectual. Later, when the Australian Broadcasting Corporation played them, the response was extraordinary. From the ABC's perspective, I had managed to create "resonance". People did not feel that the ideas were dramatically new but they heard their own ideas being played back to them in ways that encouraged them to own their own passions.

My primary purpose in life is to encourage people to develop new leadership styles based on knowledge and skills rather than power and manipulation. This work has been immensely rewarding at one level because I have seen people develop and grow – at another level, it has often been frustrating because all too often those with whom I have worked have chosen to remain on the margin of the society rather than impacting on its core dynamics. The need to become involved with the mainstream is growing rapidly as the scope of crises continues to broaden.

The end of this millennium, coupled with specific Y2K issues, has given us the opportunity to open up questions which have been of critical importance for decades. They have been hidden because they would disrupt current structures, but today we are realising that continuing past patterns is more dangerous than the disruption caused by the search for new directions.

An historical perspective

One of the major surprises of the coming compassionate era is that there is a real similarity between the views of people who lived in hunting-and-gathering societies and those we will need in the future. The common thread is that we are necessarily embedded within the natural order.

In hunting-and-gathering societies the natural order was viewed as permanent. It was believed that nature should be propitiated and its functioning could be influenced by the proper activities of shamans, or witch doctors. Life was dominated by tradition. The cult movie classic *The Gods Must be Crazy* explored what happened when a Coke bottle was found by a primitive tribe. In a world where there were stable patterns, and everything was shared, the bottle disrupted a long-running balance among individuals and groups in the tribe and therefore had to be destroyed, despite its utility. The comedy in the film came from the adventures and misunderstandings that developed as primitive and modern mind-sets came into conflict.

Industrial-era human beings, on the other hand, began to believe they could overwhelm nature. Our existing buildings, agriculture, and our very way of life proclaim the belief that human beings are invincible. Nature was squeezed out of the picture until Rachel Carson, author of the sixties book *Silent Spring*, started its renaissance.

As we move towards the twenty-first century, we are recognising that natural forces are far more powerful than the most massive of humanity's efforts. Earthquakes and hurricanes dwarf the power available to human beings even today. The growing instabilities in weather are proving immensely costly and damaging, with 1998 being one of the worst for weather-related catastrophes worldwide. We are slowly learning that we shall either collaborate with natural forces or the feedback from them will prove increasingly disruptive and destructive.

Societies are slowly coming to grips with a reality that we largely ignored during the industrial era. We are learning to deal with the pervasive implications of the fact that human actions can affect the direction of events but not control them. As we do so, we are becoming aware that limited triggering events can have huge consequences when the time is ripe. Large efforts, on the other hand, may have no significant impact if they aim to overcome dominant trends. These modern views are totally incompatible with the mechanical cause-and-effect universe which dominated the industrial era, where a given cause was always assumed to have the same impact.

Order was preserved in the industrial world by the belief that the people at the top of systems were knowledgable and could therefore be trusted to do what was right. So long as people accepted this way of thinking, the system was functional. The people in charge made mistakes but most of them were never visible because the Establishment held together and covered up its weaknesses and its mistakes. This level of power caused much injustice but the model worked at the time. Fortunately we have moved beyond it but we are still trying to come to grips with the profound shifts that have occurred.

One can see the differences between today and the past by considering how differently important people used to be treated. President Roosevelt was hardly ever photographed so that his wheelchair was visible: it was thought by all concerned that this decreased the dignity of the office. Today the media dramatises the failures of every public figure, from their sexual behaviour to their tumbles down aircraft steps. We are caught between our desire for our leaders to solve all our problems and our recognition that these people are only human.

We have therefore reached – to use Beth Jarman's and George Land's term – a "breakpoint". The approaches that served us in the past can damage us today. What then is the way forward, given that many current models and approaches are not only obsolete but destructive? The first step is to acknowledge that in any given situation people will inevitably approach a subject from many different viewpoints. Nobody ever has all the truth.

Our views are determined by our past, our genes, our sex, our age and many other factors.

One of the emphases of our time must therefore be on helping people listen to others rather than just wait for the moment at which they can get their own ideas into the debate. This change of style is of course difficult because most individuals and groups are more interested in supporting their directions than in searching for the truth. The need for this shift is, however, inarguable.

A far more difficult question emerges from the fact that everybody's perception is not of equal relevance. Dialogue requires more than a search for consensus; it demands a drive to find the truth. In all groups, some people do not have the experience to make an informed judgment. There are many reasons for this difference in skill levels. Two of the most important are that some people think in cause-and-effect terms rather than the system style which is required for clear understandings. Some ignore the fact that "wishing does not make it so".

While dialogue styles are indeed essential for the future, they can nevertheless lead to all sorts of dangerous errors. The two most destructive lie at different ends of a continuum. At one end, it is argued that all perceptions are equally valid – that there is no way of distinguishing between the relevance of ideas. This first pattern of thought leads to the belief that all attitudes and beliefs must be accepted. Visionary planning becomes impossible. We become lost in a maze of individually expressed thoughts, none of which seems to have any greater meaning than another. Purpose and vitality are lost beyond recall.

The other danger results from people who accept that all reality is perceptual but then claim that their own perceptual ability is always superior to that of others. This approach may seem innately contradictory but I know of many people who believe it is valid. Effective dialogue is also destroyed by this approach because one of the people in the group claims the absolute right to decide how the discussion should progress.

Dialogue styles are difficult because those who practise them need to walk a tight-rope. Each person needs to accept that their ideas may be wrong but that they need to advance them until they are changed by better input. The people who are most skilled in compassionate-era activities are therefore confusing and threatening to those who use industrial-era styles, because the two groups see the world totally differently. Industrial-era leaders believe they must control people and dynamics. Compassionate-era leaders are most effective when they support people who are ready and willing to be active. They nudge and encourage, rather than force, positive directions whenever possible. They invite rather than coerce.

Each of us who aims to support dialogue necessarily walks a tightrope. There are two dangers. One is insisting on one's own point of view to the exclusion of those of others. The other is permitting people with lesser knowledge and skills to make decisions although one is aware of what will work better. I have tended throughout my life to permit bad decisions to be made in the name of dialogue – I continue aiming to achieve a better balance.

It is extremely difficult to write about the shift from the industrial era to the compassionate era without seeming to imply that the industrial era was an error. It is therefore important to state specifically that the industrial era was not "wrong", any more than adolescence is wrong. Nevertheless, our new stage in human evolution requires the abandonment of industrial-era ideas and their replacement with more complex thought patterns. The simplicities of the past are inadequate to the realities of the present.

To be effective in the future, society must abandon the conventionally easy responses which are used when actions do not achieve desired results. One common pattern today is to put more energy behind the same actions. For example, nearly everybody now agrees that the schools are not meeting the needs of students but the response in almost all areas of the world has been to affirm existing systems and to do more of what has been done in the past. Another common response is to put "bandaids on cancers" which are, after all, depressing and ugly! Small, cosmetic changes are made but the breakdowns continue to expand in scope because the real difficulties are being ignored rather than faced.

We need to distinguish in our minds between two very different styles. One aims for marginal shifts in patterns and hopes that they will be sufficient. It assumes that the current set of ideas can be maintained – jobs, retirement, schooling, etc. The other accepts that we are going to need totally different systems and that the words and images we have inherited from the past are getting in the way of our creativity.

Here is an old story which is helpful for understanding this point. The people of a town kept finding bodies at the bottom of a precipice, and the community reacted by dividing itself into three groups with three very different approaches to the problem. The first one wanted to improve the response times of ambulances. The second wanted to build a fence around the cliff so people could not fall over by mistake. The third favoured changing peoples' attitudes and skills so they would not be tempted to play near the cliff nor to climb it without adequate skills.

Only the third approach holds any real hope for the future. Societies need to enhance everybody's capacity to make decisions for themselves.

Today's industrial-era planning is based on data and information. Actions are determined – in theory – by objective approaches. The dominant appeal is to logic and rationality. The first step in the transition to the compassionate era is to accept the importance of intuition and passion. One discovers what seems worth doing as an individual or group and then puts together the skills and resources to move from visioning to reality. In doing so, people recognise that they are themselves part of a solution.

I remember talking to a group of school superintendents in Wisconsin. One of them, in particular, had given up hope despite the fact that he had been a "radical" in the sixties. Facing the reality that positive visions were possible was very difficult for him. He had to abandon the despair which had governed his life for years (and, indeed, made it tolerable!) He

46

had built his life around attacking others for their failures rather than thinking about what he, himself, could do effectively.

If I am right in my belief that many people are ready for fundamental change, why does so little seem to be happening? Many positive shifts are actually taking place but our culture is looking at the negatives, particularly in media attention. For many years I have been promoting the idea of a news segment called 'It's Working' and a number of communities have picked up on this concept on a local level. Reporters comment on what is going right in the community rather than reporting on the breakdowns, the rapes and the murders. Typically, there is a front page story each day with reporters being given the opportunity to write a by-lined article for the space.

We are suffering today from the problem of "the competent, but isolated, many". Most people feel alone in their efforts to improve the functioning of society. This makes them less willing to take risks and reduces the overall effectiveness of the movement towards new attitudes and directions.

A useful image for understanding how change could take place in these circumstances is to imagine contemporary society is a forming crystal in a super-saturated chemical solution. The crystal can grow rapidly under these circumstances, but unless conditions are exactly right, additions to the crystal will not take place, or they will be flawed. Organisational processes for fundamental change activities must therefore be planned very carefully in their early stages if they are to attract the people who know enough to support the desired goals, rather than disrupt them. Later on, the process becomes almost automatic and self-generating.

As we leave the twentieth century, a large number of initiatives already exist. The primary challenge is to connect them so that a critical mass will develop.

Beyond the American dream

Where do we go from here? One of the most important shifts is to commit to environmental balance rather than economic growth. Many problems can be reduced by limiting the usage – and above all, waste – of energy and materials. The more we invest and consume, the greater the impact on the environment. The less we use and waste the better.

EF Schumacher made this point clearly in his influential book, *Small is Beautiful.*

> An attitude to life which seeks fulfilment in the single-minded pursuit of wealth – in short, materialism – does not fit into this world, because it contains within itself no limiting principle, while the environment in which it is placed is strictly limited. Already the environment is trying to tell us that certain stresses are becoming excessive. As one problem is "solved" ten new ones arise as a result of this first "solution". The new problems are not the consequences of incidental failure, but of technological successes.

Perhaps the most visible challenge is the ever-increasing use of the automobile. I am old enough to remember when the first dual-track roads were introduced into Britain just before World War II. We all marvelled at the potential for car ownership and higher speeds. Today, roads continue no be built although there is clear-cut evidence that traffic increases to fill the available road space and than the average speed of automobiles continues to fall in cities.

The automobile was originally a luxury that quickly turned into a necessity. Now it is becoming a burden. The Los Angeles area has faced up to this evolution and begun to come to grips with the realities of both limited energy resources and ecological threats. Unfortunately, cities and suburbs have been built in a way that relies on cars. It will take a very long time to change habitation patterns so that people can once again live in their neighbourhoods, only leaving when they want to do so or for major events, rather than because what they want for everyday living is not available within walking distance.

California has the excuse that their major choices of habitation patterns were made before traffic patterns were really understood. The Seattle area, on the other hand, is doing most of the damage after the costs are far better known, and the city is moving towards gridlock throughout the metropolitan area.

Citizens complain but politicians seem unable to come to grips with the issue. They are, indeed, more or less powerless given current attitudes.

At a recent meeting in Sydney, I was informed that the average number of people in a car is 1.1 – that despite the creation of express lanes for those who car pool, people still travel by themselves. The person who presented these facts argued that there was nothing to be done: that we simply had to accept that there were no alternatives to continued road expansion.

The thought that mobility might have to be limited to preserve the quality of life would have seemed ludicrous at the beginning of the twentieth century. It is only today that we are beginning to recognise that densities may become so great that they could destroy that quality of life. Oahu, the most populous island in Hawaii, provides a perfect example of the dilemma. In addition, the major fires in Santa Barbara and Oakland, California, confirm the dangers of ignoring ecological limits. The continuing drought has made deathtraps of desirable homes.

Let me now move from the large-scale issue of system design to one where each of us can make an immediate difference. There is today a major controversy as to whether paper sacks or plastic in landfills are more dangerous to the environment. A case can be made by both sides. The extraordinary fact is that few people have yet realised that both paper and plastics are far more destructive than an available alternative. Most Europeans carried cloth bags or wicker baskets in the past, and a large number still do, thus reducing the need for either plastic or paper.

This raises the broader issue of packaging. All too often packaging is bulkier that the product – and sometimes seems more valuable. There is a need to rethink the way in which goods move, how far they move and how much protection they really require. Those who are going back to buying in bulk are discovering just how much the cost of groceries reflects the excessive cost of modern packaging.

Waste is currently so much a part of our lives that it is often invisible. One major reason for unnecessary use of materials is accelerated obsolescence – products are not made to last the optimum length of time. Even when they are, advertisers will often try to convince people that the "new" model makes it essential for them to replace their current one earlier than is required from an economic or technological viewpoint. Fortunately, this pattern is changing. The snoozing Maytag repairman on American television waiting for a call used to be an oddity – now the advertisement reflects the reputation many firms would love to possess. More and more cars are boasting of their higher quality and the increased resale value due to their longer life.

People are becoming more and more aware of the problems associated with excessive waste. As landfills close and water supplies are threatened by chemicals, there is increasing understanding that it makes sense to throw less away. Cities such as Seattle are charging households on the basis of their garbage weight. People are encouraged to be more careful in creating waste and even to take pride, as citizens did in earlier generations, in how little they have for the garbage collector.

Municipal waste is, however, only a tiny proportion of the total waste stream, maybe less than two per cent. Real recycling progress depends on changing the behaviours of producers, and fortunately, shifts are developing here also. The idea of productive processes with zero wastes is being spread by the Natural Step, which is gaining increasing attention in countries around the world and particularly Australia.

The real issue, of course, is changing the underlying habits, principles and values by which we live. Most of us have been brought up to believe that we always need 10 to 25 per cent more than we already have or can afford! We are always striving to do more, to have more, to travel to new places. The brass ring is always just out of reach but we "know" it can be obtained if only we try a little harder, or are lucky. So long as we hold this view, production and waste will inevitably increase.

The American dream of ever-greater wealth continues to spread throughout the world. When people complain that it is no longer available, this statement usually means that they are unhappy about the slow rise in the standard of living and, in many cases, its decline. We are still encouraging young people to believe they can "have it all" despite the contrary evidence and the fact that many teenagers already recognise that they will not be any wealthier than their parents.

EF Schumacher has also caught the heart of this issue.

> The cultivation and expansion of needs is the antithesis of wisdom. It is also the antithesis of freedom and peace. Every increase of needs tends to increase one's dependence on outside forces over which one cannot have control, and therefore increases existential fear. Only by a reduction of needs can one promote a genuine reduction in those tensions which are the ultimate causes of strife and war.

We have to learn to live with "enoughness". People had a different vision of "the good life" – or, perhaps, the feasible life – before the coming of the industrial era. Most people did as well as they could with what they had available to them. The idea of finding the pot of gold at the end of the rainbow emerged during the nineteenth century. Today the idea of "enough" is usually perceived as constraining freedom, forcing people to give up their dreams, to settle for less, to fail to reach one's potential. But there is another far more positive side to the concept of "enoughness". It can be a way of reducing the clutter in one's life, of deciding what is truly important and working to attain it.

Overload patterns, which frustrate us increasingly, develop because we want it all. But are we really better off always rushing after the latest sensation rather than enjoying the tried and the true? Surely moments of quiet are worth struggling to maintain through all the busyness which our culture thrusts upon us. Is it good for kids to have everything they want at an early age and to discover later how difficult it is to maintain these high standards for themselves?

Around the world, people are choosing to cut back. Dennis Hammond, an e-mail colleague from Minneapolis, put it this way:

> All humans of every colour seek happiness, but most of us don't know what it is or how to get it. Happiness is ... not

51

having and having and having. There's nothing wrong with goods, but they've become the focus, and the spiritual aspect is more important if we want to know peace and contentment.

Enough is not scarcity. Nor is it excess. Enough lies at a quiet balance point which each of us must find in the light of our own energies, lifestyles and the overall resources of the world in which we live. The vast majority of those in the rich countries will have to learn to live with less as we move through the twenty-first century. On the other hand, the poor in the rich countries and the vast majority of the people in the poor countries must be able to move out of the extreme scarcity which destroys so many of their lives. The World Bank has estimated that as many as a quarter of the world's population are living in extreme penury and that in the late nineties, the Asian collapse increased the number by some 200 million.

If we are to achieve the necessary balancing of income and wealth, the process of learning must inevitably go both ways. The wealthier countries must discover how the poorer countries manage with what appears, from the outside, to be totally inadequate resources. The poorer countries can benefit from the knowledge created in the technologically advanced world without dreaming they can adopt lifestyles that cannot be sustained in the long run. All of us can then have a higher quality of life. We can learn to value other experiences besides consumption and live by a different set of values than those that dominated the industrial era.

Avoiding breakdowns

There are two options for bringing about change. One is to enable people to educate themselves so they can keep up with the changing needs of the world. The alternative route is to reinforce the current legal structures and make them increasingly draconian. For example, the government in China imposed population control because densities are already so great that further increases would clearly decrease the quality of life.

Open systems are more desirable and effective over the long run. But they only work if people understand the realities of the time and are willing to make the hard choices necessary for survival. Maintenance of free and open systems will be impossible if the strain on human, energy and ecological systems is so high that people are unable and unwilling to learn new ways of looking at the world. Indeed, this is the central danger of our time because most people are so overstressed that they feel that the problems we face are insoluble.

Perhaps the most urgent and difficult issue is the need to shift our perception of success. The wealthier countries have come to define success in terms of greater production and consumption, but in an ecologically limited world, this vision cannot be maintained. These countries must cut back in order to make space for greater production by their poorer neighbours.

It is easiest to demonstrate this issue in the field of energy. It is still believed by many that because total fossil fuel energy reserves in the world are high, there will be no energy problem for centuries. It is also argued that technology will inevitably develop new energy sources during the time that is available before fossil fuel resources run out.

There are two profound flaws in this style of thinking, which, taken together, demand radical changes in analysis and action.

First, the relevant concept with which society must deal is not total energy reserves but rather net energy reserves. It always costs energy to obtain energy. The deeper the wells and the tougher the environment where wells are dug, the smaller the net energy which will be generated. The decline in net energy yields in the US has already been dramatic.

When looking at potential production, it is first essential to remember that some fossil fuels are present in forms which are unlikely to yield net energy at any time in the future. Oil shales, for example, which were seen as a possible saviour for the energy hunger of the Western world in the seventies, now seem to hold little potential. The amount of energy needed to free the oil shales from the rock in which they are held is so great that past experiments have expended – rather than gained – energy. Indeed, even if it were possible to produce net energy, the effective use of these "resources" remains very unlikely because their processing is water-intensive and deposits are located primarily in the West where surplus water is almost non-existent.

The net energy ratio will therefore continue to worsen over time as oil and gas have to be sought in less and less favourable conditions. A similar, although less dramatic, pattern exists for minerals, although there will still be untapped reserves of some of them for many centuries to come. Nevertheless, the richest and most easily accessible ores have already been used up – an issue which again relates to energy. If there is less net energy, and if the cost of working minerals is also rising, then the ability of societies to afford the extraction of metals will decline.

Free markets do not reflect the long-run value of supply but only the current balance of supply and demand. Thus the cost of oil and minerals has been dropping over recent years. This has been argued by some people to show that any concern about shortages is naïve. Others, like myself, recognise that we are seeing a fatal flaw in current market patterns. Indeed, the perverse impact of market forces is often enhanced by tax policies which encourage extraction rather than limiting it.

The other reason for limiting fossil fuel usage is the danger of atmospheric degradation and climatic change. Cutting back on global levels of fossil fuel usage will, however, be very difficult. Any reduction in use in the rich countries will be swamped by increased needs in the poor country unless patterns of development change dramatically. The dangers are increased because most poor countries are still not widely aware of the necessity of planning in ways which reduce the dangers from fossil-fuel emissions.

The potential problems are demonstrated in a decision by the Chinese to provide families with refrigerators. Unfortunately their design was extremely inefficient and required the burning of far greater amounts of coal to produce energy than was theoretically necessary. Because China's coal is extremely dirty, the consequences for the atmosphere of China, and indeed the whole of the world, will be very serious.

The Kyoto Conference On Global Warming shifted the debate on this topic dramatically. It was recognised that limits would indeed need to be set. But the treaty developed at this time has not been signed by many key nations, including the United States. Indeed, it is unlikely to be until there can be greater understanding of the current gaps between the income of the rich and the poor world and the ways to close the gap.

Worldwide decisions to reduce fossil fuel usage would raise two central questions. First, how much can energy usage be cut while maintaining or improving the quality of life? We are beginning to understand that better results can be achieved using less resources. Analysts such as Amory Lovins have shown us that we are wasting huge amounts of energy. There have already been extraordinary gains in energy efficiency following the oil shocks of the seventies; these show what can be achieved. A study of energy use at the Lawrence Berkeley Laboratory found that "energy use in the US per unit of activity or output fell 21 per cent between 1973 and 1987". Similar results have been achieved in other pasts of the world.

We should certainly use the knowledge that is being developed by the Lovinses and others to limit throughput. (Throughput describes the total amount of energy, materials, goods and services which flow through the economy.) Indeed, as one broadens one's perspective, it becomes clear just how significant the reductions could be. For example, if people decided to live on a vegetarian diet, the usage of fossil fuels would decline dramatically. It has been estimated that it takes 78 fossil fuel calories to get one calorie of protein from beef, as opposed to only two fossil fuel calories to get one food calorie from soybeans, a food which is also high in protein. Movement in this direction will increase as people recognise that they can be healthier if fewer of their calories come from a meat diet.

A great deal can therefore be done by increasing efficiency and changing lifestyles. But there is still a second, very difficult, issue. So long as we maintain a commitment to maximum economic growth strategies, any gains in efficiency will be overwhelmed by the impact of increased production. Dr

Len Brookes, former Chief Economist of the UK Atomic Energy Authority, articulated the dilemma.

> One has to be absolutely clear about whether one is trying to improve economic performance or whether we are acting to reduce carbon emissions to avoid a global catastrophe. If we are trying to reduce carbon emissions, then we will have to reduce economic activity on a worldwide scale. Don't kid yourself that an easy solution like energy efficiency will reduce the total demand for energy, it just doesn't work this way.

So long as our current economic system continues, the energy which is saved in one part of the system will be used elsewhere.

Significant progress can only be made after we recognise that a commitment to balancing ecological systems cannot coexist with a continuance of maximum economic growth policies. The Brundtland Report to the United Nations on the environment failed to address this reality. We shall therefore have to examine which of the activities and structures we created in the industrial era can be supported in the future.

In order to make these choices, we must make realistic assumptions about the maximum amount of energy which will be available to support each human being in the future. Currently the three major visible alternatives to fossil fuels are: conservation; renewables such as solar, wind, biomass, etc; and nuclear. Even with maximum advantage taken from conservation, there will still be a gap which has to be filled from new energy sources to maintain current standards.

The net energy available from solar, winds, tides, biomass etc, is still a matter of great controversy. While gross energy can obviously be generated, the net energy to be gained is still uncertain. There are two issues which need to be clarified.

First, what are the maximum potential yields from various natural systems? This is a matter of analysis where answers can be reasonably accurate. Many of the euphoric estimates which were based on the amount of solar energy striking the atmosphere have turned our to be far too optimistic in terms of actual available energy on earth.

The second issue is identifying the best technologies that can eventually be devised to take advantage of the energy which is available from renewable resources. Unfortunately, this type of research is only now being significantly supported. There is, therefore, little idea of the degree to which costs can be reduced. It is easy to produce energy flows once systems are set up: it is far harder to prove that significant net energy can be generated in this way if one takes full account of invention, production and maintenance costs.

The final major existing possibility is from nuclear power. Attitudes to this issue in various parts of the world are very different. The French now get a great deal of their energy from nuclear power and do not seem to be too troubled by the safety issues which have traumatised the US. The British also place greater faith in nuclear energy than America. If the developed countries want to maintain a reasonable quality of life, and if the developing world hopes to achieve it, the nuclear issue may have to be reopened. Some believe that the options will be stark: use nuclear and be able to maintain a reasonable level of comfort, abandon it and watch a rapid slide in standards as fossil fuel use is restricted to meet the needs of future generations. This fall in standards could create such high levels of social tension that the possibility of moving towards responsible freedom would cease to exist.

The extreme views on nuclear energy are clear. Opponents see in as too dangerous and environmentally damaging. Proponents paint it as the most effective, non-polluting technology. Nobody would deny that past practices in the nuclear industry, based on fission which produces large amounts of nuclear waste, have been sloppy and dangerous. There is, however, considerable evidence that standards can be dramatically improved in the future. The question is whether this will be enough to make the technology safe and cost-effective. I do not know the answer to questions of fission, but I am certain that it is only as opponents and proponents listen to each other that clarity can be achieved. Unfortunately, we seem a long way from such a desirable development.

Other analysts believe that nuclear fusion should be the goal, arguing that it will produce cheap, clean, abundant energy. Apart from the fact that fusion has not yet been proved to be feasible, critics of this answer remember that this is the same type of slogan which was initially used to justify fission. Fission was going to produce electricity which would be "too cheap to meter". Human beings like to believe that the next technology will be the one which works perfectly but the record shows that they are always problems and side-effects.

Relevant discussion of possibilities on any subject must always cover the unexpected. Is some totally new energy technology waiting in the wings? What about some of the technologies which are already being discussed, such as the potential of hydrogen power? The obvious problem with relying on new technologies is the crises that will develop if they do not arrive on time. The urgent need is for open-minded energy analysts to provide citizens with the clearest possible statement of options and choices which can then be used to determine appropriate directions in the context of already-developing environmental stress.

An overview of the recent past

There have been extraordinary changes in our general situation as we moved out of the fifties, through the sixties, seventies, eighties and nineties and are now moving into the twenty-first century.

In the fifties, we lived in a society which believed that things were just about as good as they could be. Rapid economic growth was occurring after the Second World War. People were trading up. Shortages and rationing were ending throughout the developed world.

In the sixties, President Kennedy opened a challenge. His recognition of the need for social justice led many people to struggle to advance the conditions of blacks, women and the young. The sixties were an exciting decade when it appeared that conditions were ripe for massive change. Similar visions emerged in other counties. This was a false dawn, however. Many people were prepared to talk about far-out ideas but only because they "knew" they would never be taken seriously.

The seventies were a period of withdrawal. Many people found themselves threatened by both the pace of change and by worsening economic conditions. Apart from the successes of the movements for blacks' and women's rights, there was a general feeling of withdrawing into one's shell, of hunkering down and looking inward. The visible mood of society changed from apathy to fear. Unfortunately most change agents continued to talk about the problems, rather than the solutions, thus driving people further into disillusionment.

In the eighties the mood changed again. Many went on a binge and overspent. President Reagan and Prime Minister Thatcher argued that greed was good. It seemed to many as though tomorrow would never come. We tended to admire the rich and the famous and ignore the disadvantaged. We put off the bills until later. It often appeared that the yuppies, who represented two per cent of the population, were the wave of the future.

In the nineties the bills have become due and the attitudes of the general public are changing dramatically. The sense that the world is off course is shared by a growing number of people. Perceptions regarding self-interest are altering – more rapidly than we realise. Obviously, this positive energy must be expressed in different ways if it is to be effective.

Unfortunately, the emerging patterns of thinking all too often clash with past attitudes and laws. As positive adaptations to new hopeful realities occur, some people are threatened. They then cling more and more strongly to attitudes, structures and beliefs that have been made obsolete by technological changes. The clash today is between those who are able and willing to move with the positive potentials of our times and those who would deny the desirability of profoundly new systems.

It is not difficult for those who oppose change to organise. All they have to do is claim that innovations are undesirable and unnecessary. Proposals to return to the past can be stated in clear-cut ways and require little of those who support them. For example, all of us find it difficult to cope with the implications of new biological and medical knowledge. The opposition to rethinking birth control, abortion and the right to death stem from a desire to cling to attitudes and value patterns which made sense when human beings had less knowledge.

Those who want to break out of the past face a more challenging task. For the first time in history, human beings must consciously examine all the fundamental directions they support. Nothing can remain unquestioned. There are no longer any certainties except the need for a commitment to a moral, value-based culture. We are being challenged to take a further quantum leap in our understandings of responsible freedom.

The learnings we must achieve are not, however, new. They have been taught us in the past by the great religious and spiritual traditions. We must become honest, responsible, loving and humble and understand that there will always be mysteries in life we must respect.

Traditional spiritual understandings are today supported by modern secular knowledge. There is no longer a clash between advanced theology and intelligent intellectual thinking. It is therefore time for people to come together by bridging current boundaries and challenging humanity to develop the behaviours which are vital for the twenty-first century. Forward-looking people must look for allies in new ways. The key to alignment is a willingness to listen and learn together. The new coalition will be between all the people who believe in cooperation and a value-based culture. This is the wave of the future.

It is particularly critical that we move beyond the belief that "they" won't let us do it. "They" typically means the people in power. The tragedy I have found in many situations is that the majority of people in a system may want change but still be unable to get together because of their distrust for each other. Take a typical school situation. All the players – the teachers, the school board, the management, the parents, the staff, and the children – assume that it is the other groups who are preventing forward movement. In fact, my experience shows that if these groups would only talk to each other, there would be shared interest in a profoundly different system, which would enable children to learn more effectively.

The argument about "they" and "them" sometimes gets carried to ludicrous extremes. I have been in situations where groups have argued that something cannot be achieved because "they" won't allow it. I have had to remind them that they are talking about themselves – that they are the people who have the responsibility and the power to take the steps which they claim are impossible because of outside opposition!

Given the magnitude of the problems which confront us, how can I believe that we shall seize our possibilities rather than be overwhelmed by our problems? I remain positive because I know that people have already changed their perceptions of their self-interest. They know they should save the environment, limit violence, promote justice and redesign the socioeconomy. They are looking for ways to do this cooperatively. It is our joint responsibility as leaders to provide all of us with the opportunity to be effective.

Change at the required scale will require the development of a sufficiently broad picture so that a variety of positive groups can develop common cause. There is still a great deal of unnecessary disagreement between those who understand that there must be fundamental alterations in patterns. We need to weave a coherent story and vision so that our various activities will be seen as moving humanity in the same direction rather than being competitive for scarce resources.

One way to think about the required shift is to see us as moving from fragmentation to diversity. There is already an enormous amount of positive activity in society but it is not connected effectively. We shall not be able to make the connections until we realise that there are very many conversations and actions required to create the change from the industrial era to the compassionate era. Each of us needs to do our own preferred work but also to appreciate what is being done by others.

Because there have already been so many profound changes in technology and the way we perceive reality, major future alterations in the way we think, behave and act are inevitable.

Whether the changes are positive or negative depends on our individual and group actions.

If I were still thinking as a rational analyst, who is inevitably all too well aware of the strength of inertial forces in cultures, I would necessarily be pessimistic about our future. Fortunately, I have given up this style of thinking and have become a realist. I know that fundamental change is possible and that many people are ready to support it. We do not need to begin the process of changing directions. Our task is easier. We are challenged to support the process that is already moving forward, and to do it as intelligently as possible.

Chapter 3

Mindquakes

Radicals who aimed to remake the world drove the turbulent sixties. They were uninterested in the complications posed by existing systems and believed that moving the people in charge out of power would be enough. They lacked sensitivity to the saying that "if the devil should become God, he would have to act like God". They failed to see people are constrained by their positions, and until their responsibilities are altered, the potential for different behaviour is minimal.

Successful change today requires fundamentally different processes. We need people who understand the difficulty of changing the minds of individuals and the patterns of institutions. Those who cause change in the twenty-first century will not come from one particular class or group. They are scattered throughout the society. Some of them have power and position, while some of them work "in the trenches".

Change happens most effectively when those working on the ground are informed by and inform those who communicate to the public. If society is to change fast enough to keep up with the ever-shifting realities of our time, we must discard the distrust of the creative thinker for the activist, and of the activist for the thinker. Both groups can then struggle to find out how to work with each other.

In addition, both creative thinkers and activists need to seek out those people who can provide the necessary skills to make their thinking and actions effective. While many professionals are wedded to old styles of behaviour, others are looking for ways to support the birth of the compassionate era. Wanting to do good is not enough; the approaches we use must be appropriate to the realities of today's world if we are to have the impact we so urgently need.

If the people who are committed to equity and social justice fail to move soon, there is no doubt that negative forces can seize the energy which is being created by the imbalances throughout the world. There have been all too many examples in history of positive energies turning sour when their potential has been denied. We face choice points where one branch can have highly destructive consequences and the other can move us towards the positive.

If we are to appreciate the potentials, our political systems will need to change drastically. For many years most people have based their choice of politicians on who is perceived to be the lesser of two evils. Major political parties throughout the world have come to seem irrelevant and a growing number of people have chosen not to vote. Others, while wishing they could use the Russian system which permits them to vote "against", have chosen the candidate who seemed least intolerable.

Australia's most recent federal election was an extraordinary example of the depth of frustration. As voting is compulsory most people of voting age had to make a choice, but there was a strong feeling that the election was essentially irrelevant to the real issues with which people were struggling.

Those of us who want to create a compassionate era will only be able to do so if we help people understand and support fundamentally new directions, which currently often seem threatening, but actually promise great progress. We must therefore learn how to deal with mindquakes.

I coined the word "mindquake" – the process by which our fundamental ideas change to keep up with the ever-shifting world – as a deliberate parallel to the processes involved in earthquakes. Just as a series of small earthquakes is less destructive than a large one, a process of gradual steps which changes the way we think towards the new realities of our time, is better than a massive shift. Understandings must be flexible enough so we can continuously revise them as new realities emerge.

Considerable knowledge already exists about managing mindquakes. Unfortunately it is not yet fully used. All too often we react to change by trying to restore the patterns of the past rather than keeping up with the implications of the new. For example, we ask how people can find jobs, rather than consider wider questions such as: What work will be available as computers develop further? How should tasks be structured? And what sort of financial and prestige rewards will be appropriate for various kinds of activity? Similarly, many discussions regarding population continue to assume behavioural norms which were conceived for an empty world, but which create tragic consequences in a crowded one.

Decades ago, the novelist Herbert George Wells argued that life is a race between education and disaster. His statement has more truth today than when he first wrote because the scope of potential opportunities and disasters has increased throughout the twentieth century. If we are to manage our challenges well we must learn to support mindquakes.

I first started to develop ideas that challenged existing patterns of thought in the fifties. I naïvely believed my challenges would be welcomed, and went to the Dean of the Harvard School of Public Administration and told him about my new concepts. I left stunned because he told me, in effect, that if the ideas were new, they were not significant. Conversely, he stated that if my ideas were significant, they were not new!

After long reflection, I have understood that I could not possibly have received any better introduction to the difficulties of altering thinking. Social change never comes easily. Facing the fact that people tend to maintain obsolete understandings is particularly important at the current time. For example, most economists are no more willing to rethink their fundamental goals than their predecessors who caused The Great Depression of the thirties.

Seventy years ago, the goal of economists and politicians was fiscal responsibility and a balanced budget. Because of these theories, government activities contracted as revenues fell and the economy was therefore unable to rebalance itself. The Great

Depression developed. So long as a balanced budget remained sacrosanct, the changing realities of the thirties were ignored and, in a very real sense, invisible. In the nineties, the key priority of economists and politicians has been maximum economic growth and labour force participation, whatever the human and social consequences of these directions. Challenges to current dogmas are no more acceptable than they were in the thirties.

A major political split is emerging in the world at the current time. The United States continues to argue that free markets provide the answer to all problems. More and more countries are challenging this dogma and seeking new models which provide more protection for their citizens. The US is increasingly seen by the rest of the world as unwilling to adapt to the new understandings which are necessary for the twenty-first century.

Perceived self-interest as the driver of change

Things are getting better and better and worse and worse faster and faster. This statement by Tom Atlee, a close colleague, captures the current moment perfectly.

The negative trends – the increase in poverty, high crime rates, the breakdown in medical care, the failing infrastructure – are more and more obvious and much commented upon. But as one looks around in communities one finds all sorts of building processes that are healing long-term rifts and creating new processes and structures.

The challenge today is to increase our skills so we can be more effective in supporting the often invisible, positive directions. The prime reality we must grasp is that changes in thought and action take place as people alter their patterns of understanding. Each of us does what seems good to us given all the circumstances of which we are aware at the time we take our decisions. It is therefore essential to understand what motivates various individuals and groups.

Understanding and discussing motivations is inevitably difficult. I'll illustrate this at an apparently trivial level with a story which deals with the interactions between a cat and a human being. A frustrated home-owner was trying to deal with his cat clawing at and damaging his curtains. To show his displeasure, the man threw the cat out of the house each time she did so. The cat eventually learned that the way to get out of the house was to claw the curtains! If they could have talked to each other, they might well have used the classic phrase: "What we have here is a failure to communicate."

People, and indeed all organisms, follow their perceived self-interest. The home owner wanted to deal with a problem. He wanted to convey his displeasure with the cat's behaviour and chose a route which seemed appropriate to him – expecting the cat to learn not to claw the curtains. The cat, who initially clawed the curtains because it satisfied an instinctual need, took all the data available to her, and learned that clawing the curtains resulted in getting out of the house. The cat's behaviour pattern had been reinforced rather than changed.

When a person sends a message to another person or organism, there is no certainty it will be understood correctly. Indeed, in most cases the message will be significantly distorted. This is the lesson one learns in the game 'Chinese Whispers', when people pass a sentence from one end of a line to the other. The wording of the final exchange often seems to bear little relationship to the one at the beginning. Obviously the potential for misunderstanding more complex messages and interactions is far greater.

The essential bedrock for understanding reality is that each person, even the most mentally ill and the pathological, thinks and acts in ways which make "sense" in their own world and which support their self-image. The great movie *Rainman* – in which two brothers, one of whom was severely mentally handicapped, come to love each other – made this point clear. The "healthy" brother, a manipulator and borderline crook, eventually is forced to get inside the other's mind in order to survive behaviour which originally seemed bizarre to him. Once he does this, he is able to benefit from the skills he discovers, making money from the mentally retarded brother's ability to remember cards in Las Vegas. In learning to understand why the limited brother behaves as he does, the manipulator comes to love him and wants to support and protect him. The tragedy of the movie is that this proves to be impossible.

In the 1990 Summer issue of *Noetic Sciences Review*, Elisabet Sahtouris demonstrated the significance of the differences in perception between people. She wrote:

> Perhaps the most important discovery of modern science is that there can be no single true and complete world-view. Like all species, we have only partial information about our world, and our information changes as our knowledge increases, as our inventions become more sophisticated and as we and other species actually change our world. We change the world even while we are looking at it, for we are never only observers – we continue being players.

We can therefore formulate two simple rules about human behaviour. First, organisms – both human beings and those from other species – always operate in their perceived self-interest, given all the circumstances of which they are aware at the time they make their decisions. Second, people, and indeed all organisms, change their thinking, action and behaviour when they see the possibility for more satisfying choices.

At one level, both of the statements are self-evident. People do make appropriate choices in terms of their own self-understandings even though they may seem nonsensical when evaluated by individuals with more (or less) skills, knowledge or a different cultural viewpoint. Even "destructive" behaviours make sense when the world-view behind them is understood.

To make things more complex, nobody operates from a single, consistent view of the world. The action pattern you and I choose depends on the calculus which seems most relevant to us at a particular moment. Thus it may seem important to have a good dinner on a Saturday night to relieve one's frustrations; at another time one may wish one had kept the money to reduce one's debt.

Anybody who wants to be an effective change agent must fully understand that views of their own and other people's self-interest are perceptual and not objective. Differences in perceptions emerge not only in terms of the way people view the world and their place in it; there are also deep differences about what behaviour is acceptable and valued. Thus, some consider the mugging of a stranger in the street as an acceptable way to get money, while others would recoil in horror at this destruction of self-image, preferring to starve than to abandon their values. Others see saving the victim, even at the risk of their own lives, as appropriate behaviour, while another groups would regard this sort of action as totally foolish, and indeed incomprehensible.

This inevitably means that when one talks to a group, writes a book or creates a video, the message received by each individual varies widely. Each person screens communications to a far greater extent than most of us realise. Individuals can draw extraordinarily different messages from a given presentation, a reality I have sometimes tested by asking people what they have learned from my speech, seminar or consultancy. I have been consistently amazed at the range of reactions.

Learning to listen, so we do not distort what we see and hear, is one of the critical skills for an effective change agent. Nobody can ever reach the point where they can escape their experience and conditioning patterns, but each of us can move in this direction.

Choosing directions

None of us has a complete and coherent view of our self-interest. We should aim to move up the spiral of understanding and behaviour towards a more inclusive view and a longer time-span. This is desirable because it leads to higher levels of creativity and potential. It is also a requirement for global survival because, unless more people think and work at these higher levels, massive breakdowns are inevitable. It is the responsibility of our overall educational process, acting through families, churches, schools, colleges and the media, to enable people to understand why they should care for others and the globe.

Fortunately, committing to help others, rather than benefiting solely oneself, results in profound personal gain. In an effective helping relationship, the person who is providing support receives at least as much as the person who is being supported. If this is not the case, the relationship will usually be unhealthy. We should only take on commitments to others if we believe we will benefit from the interrelationships. Otherwise, we become frustrated and expect those who are being helped to acknowledge the effort that is being made on their behalf.

It is hard enough to need help without also having to thank the donor for the effort they are making; much of the benefit of the support is lost if it is not freely given. For many years, I asked myself how some people could give so much help without burning out. I now realise that they can do so because the importance of supporting others is part of their self-perception and their goals. They therefore gain from their activities rather than being drained by them. As people learn to care for themselves, others and the globe, their view of their self-interest changes.

Understanding this reality is critical as we face the issue of fundamental change. I have been told again and again throughout my career that existing decision-makers will inevitably block positive change. I reject this conclusion on the grounds that today it is possible to show people in the establishment that many of their actions are not benefiting them. As they realise this, and see their self-interest in new ways, they will support different directions. Indeed, I find at the current time that it is often mainstream decision-makers who are most willing to look at the world in new ways. I therefore find it more and more difficult to be patient with those who argue that those in power must be treated as the enemy.

This issue is becoming a major fault line in social change activities. Some people concentrate on what people and firms are doing wrong and fight them in order to change their

70

directions. Others believe that more will be accomplished by looking for the places where positive movement is taking place and alliances can be achieved.

The challenge, then, is to help people from all groups and classes see realities in new ways rather than to assume that some types of people are going to be helpful and others will always deny the potential of fundamental shifts. There are many examples where unlikely people have led the drive for new directions. At the personal level, many of the super-rich Rockefellers have supported ideas and directions which challenge the current goals of the very well-off. Organisationally, Scandinavian Airlines, Canon, the Corps of Engineers and United Way are examples of organisations that are shifting their success criteria significantly.

From time to time, I have been able to set up activities which have catalysed significant changes in thinking. I remember a conference with a large number of people from the Young Presidents' Organisation, which brings together heads of companies. Because those of us organising the seminar had the "right" message at the "right" time, we were able to demonstrate that preserving the environment was critical to them and their children. They went away with a significantly different way of seeing, thinking and acting.

A number of people were so impressed with their learning experience that they attended a follow-up conference. We showed them the same slide-tape presentation that had sparked the change last time, but because they had now learned its message, the presentation was dismissed as superficial and boring. Indeed many refused to believe it was the same material we had showed them the previous year. The ability to bring about change is always specific to a particular moment: the possibility of an "ah-ha" depends on catching an individual or group when they are ready for new insights. Another popular way of talking about this pattern is to recognise that there are "teachable" moments when new ideas can be most easily heard.

The current challenge is to help large numbers of people through the required shifts in understanding. Today, as in the past, people perish without vision. The need to fully understand

71

this reality is one of the primary differences between the industrial era and the compassionate era. In the industrial era it was assumed that the future emerged from past trends and the clashes between them. Now we are aware that it is our visions that affect our perception and that perceptions determine what we do. Visions are "practical" – they are the primary creator of the future we inherit.

Once people look at reality clearly, they can make effective choices. They can either continue to move in the same direction or they can look for new potential. The Chinese understand this: their word for crisis contains two characters. One of them conveys the sense of the danger that will emerge if people continue to move in the same direction. The other stresses the opportunity that can develop if people use the energy from a crisis to develop new understandings. If people have a sense of their own vision, then they are far more likely to perceive, and later work towards, the potential of their situation.

Crises are times when we are challenged to face the inability of current systems of thinking and action to respond to real needs. When this moment of realisation comes, we can choose to move forward beyond the blocks of the past, or we can fail to transcend them and become more deeply mired in old models. It is in this sense that "timing is everything", and "insistence on birth at the wrong time is the source of all evil".

All too often people are unwilling to push events to the crisis point where something significant can happen. They prefer to come up with slick and easy answers to complex questions, to avoid facing the hard questions of their lives and their institutions. The only way that anything significant can be achieved is to continue to live in the question until a moment of illumination arrives which shifts the nature of perceived reality.

There is a major, systemic reason why this pattern persists. If one deals with symptoms, patterns tend to get better in the short run and worse in the long-run. On the other hand, if one deals with causes, things tend to get worse in the short run and only improve over time. In our short-run oriented world, it is not surprising that it is difficult to get institutions to look at long-run issues.

We can understand, in this context, why the most difficult people to reach and change are the ideologues. Ideologues are committed to looking at the world in a particular way: changing this pattern challenges their self-image. Economic or social entrepreneurs, on the other hand, are interested in accomplishing a task: seeing reality correctly helps them accomplish this. Today our greatest problems come from those who distort reality to maintain their comfortable illusions.

The leader's role

Society today needs leaders who can work for quiet, positive, sustainable change. We need people who can help others understand that thoughtful value-based behaviour will benefit them and their society. To achieve these shifts, leaders must understand how to help people change their self-image and how they view their self-interest.

The most resistant realities are the ones of which we are "certain", as well as those which lie below the conscious level. Part of the challenge of our lives at the current time is to become more aware of the styles and factors that control our decision-making. Some of these are personal and idiosyncratic. Others are shared by all members of organisations and cultures.

Indeed, the very language we must use to express our ideas highlights some parts of reality for us, and hides other parts. For example, the Western sense of time, which includes past, present and future, is embedded in our languages. Many other languages, such as that of the Hopi Indian, suggest that the only "real" time is the present. Modern science seems to be suggesting that the way the Hopi are forced to speak and think by their language is more realistic than Western thinking, which requires that we divide our experiences into past, present and future.

Language and culture therefore inevitably blind people to many of the more innovative possibilities around them. One way to break through this blindness is to live fully within different cultures. I have personally been fortunate because I have made my home in various places – including India, England, Scotland, France and very different parts of the US: the East Coast, Arizona, New Orleans and Spokane – for extended periods of time. I recently spent considerable time in Australia as well, and had an opportunity to see many parts of the country.

From these experiences I have developed a deep knowledge of how differently the world appears to human beings. While this is not a common pattern of experience for many people, they can nevertheless learn much by immersing themselves in the art and the films of other parts of the world. These can enhance awareness of the very different ways that various cultures view reality.

A hundred years ago each of these cultures would have seemed fixed and permanent to those living within them. Now all of them are shifting with extraordinary rapidity. One of the most exciting realities is that positive alterations have taken place in response to new developments. The belief that nothing can be done, which is all too common today, does not fit the facts. The world is changing around us: the real question is whether each of us will pay attention or pretend that nothing is happening.

Let's look at the issue of smoking, using an example from the US. I shall give away my age only too clearly when I tell you I remember the days when smokers and non-smokers sat together on planes. Later there were small non-smoking areas which were steadily enlarged over time until the smokers looked as though they would be pushed out of the back of the plane! In 1988 a ban was placed on smoking on all short flights. At the same time, Northwest Airlines decided that they could make money by advertising that they were the first airline to ban smoking on all domestic flights. In 1990, smoking was banned by federal legislation on all domestic flights except those to and from Hawaii.

This change was achieved despite the strong, continuing lobbying of the cigarette companies. An aroused public opinion – backed by the commitment of the US Surgeon General – enabled legislation to be passed which is now backed by the vast majority of people. Smokers are beleaguered and unable to smoke in most people's homes, and sometimes even in their own. The evidence shows that most smokers would like to quit but their addiction has a very strong hold on them.

There is, however, a darker side to this picture which shows the way in which positive change all too often generates negative side-effects. The movement against smoking is still largely class-based, with the poor and the working class continuing to smoke heavily, so tobacco companies increasingly focus their message on the disadvantaged groups in society. They aim to get young people smoking before they can understand the long-range costs of this decision.

The cigarette companies are also trying to make up for their loss of sales in the developed countries by promoting smoking in the Eastern bloc and the developing countries. The US even uses its clout to prevent nations from limiting the imports of cigarettes. Given what we now know about the health consequences of smoking, such behaviour is totally unacceptable and has been compared to the tactics employed during the opium wars of the nineteenth century, when Britain forced China to continue to accept opium to benefit British traders.

On a more positive note, the revolution in smoking policy is part of a broader shift. Some 25 years ago, I participated in the effort to create Hawaii Health Net, one of the very first groups to encourage people to improve their health with better diets and exercise. The general feeling at the time was that such an effort was naive and quixotic: Americans, it was claimed, were wedded to their junk foods. This has turned out to be untrue. Those who have watched the transformation of the fast-food and packaged food industries are aware that the health movement has had a powerful impact on the way adults eat. Salad bars are now advertised. More and more promotional material stresses how steps are being taken to reduce fats, particularly cholesterol. Today, the struggle is centred around a movement towards organic food and concern about the impact of insufficiently tested genetic modifications.

Along with the stronger health emphasis has been a growing acceptance of the inevitability of death. Instead of denying death, as was the case in the middle of the twentieth century, people are finding ways to help their loved ones die with dignity.

Our thinking about violence is also shifting – indeed, mindquakes are particularly necessary here – but this behaviour pattern is so ingrained in human affairs that it certainly cannot be eliminated easily or quickly. Some would say that the tendency towards violence is inevitable because it is part of our brain patterns. Each of us must surely continue to be dismayed by the degree that mental violence remains a large part of our behaviour patterns, even if we have moved beyond physical violence.

Nevertheless, I believe that our problems are largely caused by the fact that most people were brought up in ways that sapped their capacity to love. Their perceptions and interpretations are based on the belief that others intend to damage them even when this is not the case. Breaking through this type of patterning is always extraordinarily difficult because actions that are intended to have a positive set of consequences by the caring person can be interpreted totally differently by the receiver. Compassion can appear to be weakness. Love can appear to be intrusive.

Fortunately, violence can be controlled and limited in many ways. Gregory Bateson, one of the extraordinary thinkers of the twentieth century, pondered a great deal on this issue. He concentrated his attention on animal behaviour, showing that many breeds of animals have effective ways of showing their attitudes. When an animal is submissive, it will lie on its back and expose its stomach to be bitten. The dominant animal will see this surrender and turn away.

Bateson pointed out that a primary problem in human cultures is that a message of submission is all too likely to be followed by an attack, rather than accepted as an offer of peace. He also showed that our difficulties are tied to the complexities of verbal language as compared to body language. Body language is unambiguous, he argued, while verbal language permits lying to be brought to a fine art; human beings therefore have to be far more cautious than animals in their interrelationships. It is this problem which makes it attractive to keep up one's defences on all scales, from the personal to the international. It is altogether reasonable to be afraid that you may be stabbed in the back, given existing cultural attitudes.

The maintenance of violent systems also seems attractive because there appears to be fewer surprises in negative dynamics. For example, the world was more "controllable" during the Cold War than it is now. A surprising number of thrillers of the late eighties made use of this theme; the plots turned on American and/or Russian conspiracies to return to Cold War certainties, both in order to perpetuate internal power and to have an understandable context for international relations. (Reality greatly exceeded fiction however, for nobody imagined that KGB units would disobey orders, an event which actually happened in the failed 1991 coup in the Soviet Union.)

This issue of violence is one that leads to very deep levels of disagreement. There are some people who not only believe it is impossible to get rid of violence, but that it is not desirable to do so. While I know that we shall never eliminate violence totally, I am convinced that we should try to do so. It is only after this has been achieved that human beings will develop their potential fully.

All intelligent thinkers agree that there will always be a small minority of people who want to disrupt society. Those who are negative about the future believe that we shall be faced with ever-increasing guerrilla and terrorist violence. Those who are positive believe that communication and dialogue can change perceptions.

Beyond right and wrong

Moving beyond violence and dictatorships requires that people be open to new ideas. It is almost impossible to really hear others, let alone accept new ideas, so long as you know you are "right" and others are "wrong". Listening requires an open heart and mind. This is the reason why most of us reject divergent views rather than be open enough to let them challenge us.

Certainty closes down one's mind and heart. In today's changing world this is a recipe for personal and social catastrophe. Each of us needs to learn to listen to other views if we are to avoid violence. This means, in turn, that we must be prepared to move beyond holding onto our own cultural understandings to relishing those of others. Until we are willing to do this, we will be afraid of images and ideas which challenge our existing belief systems.

The patterns of violence will only be broken as we learn to see the world more positively. We can learn to be attracted to, and even fascinated by, diversity rather than being scared of it, discovering new understandings from those who have different visions of reality than we do. People will then develop their own way of seeing the world while respecting the views of others.

Movement in this direction will be more rapid when people come to understand that the quickest way of learning new ideas is to talk with somebody who reaches a different conclusion than one's own; such an individual is seeing realities one has missed. Diversity is therefore the best source of creativity. As one learns to listen to others, one discovers that there are alternative directions to those one has previously seen as necessary, and indeed inevitable. The world becomes a richer and more exciting place as the number of options in one's life expands.

A willingness to tolerate diversity, let alone to benefit fully from it, cannot develop so long as most people continue to believe that right and wrong can be easily and clearly defined. I frequently speak on radio talk shows, and when I am asked whether something is right or wrong, I respond that it is hard enough for me to make up my own mind on tough questions without forcing my views on others. Most moral dilemmas do not yield to hard and fast dogmas – people should develop their own moral code based on how honesty, responsibility, humility and love can be effectively applied in their own lives.

I believe that my ability to write and speak about controversial issues depends on the fact that I present what I say as a "belief" rather than as factual and correct. If I say that I am right then those who disagree have no choice but to challenge me directly and angrily. If I present my statements as my own way of seeing the world, then those who have a different view can state theirs and we can discover what we can learn from each other.

The classic response to my statement on right and wrong is to take an issue such as murder and to test me with a response like "surely murder is always wrong". I have learned not to fall into this trap! The taking of somebody's life without their consent should certainly be unacceptable in any circumstances, but if we believe that taking life without the consent of the other person is wrong, then isn't war also wrong? And what about the death penalty? How do we consider a social structure such as the drug trade, which creates situations where murder is a "cost of doing business"?

And what about those who choose to die – is this ever acceptable? Most cultures in the world, but not all, discourage suicide (Japan is a notable exception). Given new medical technologies, will our norms shift in the twenty-first century?

All of us should stand for "life", but how do we define life in a high-tech medical age? Are those in an irreversible coma "alive"? Should one try to save every premature child, despite our growing knowledge of the health risks? Does one use heroic measures to keep people alive, even if they are ready to die? We can only keep our tidy moral certainties by avoiding complications in our thinking and keeping our frame of reference very narrow. As soon as we look at the real world, certainties fall away and disagreements and conflict are inevitable.

Until people learn to live with complexity and uncertainty, however, non-traditional behaviours seem more and more threatening. One natural, but highly dangerous, response emerges when people grab onto a single issue and make that the core of their beliefs. Those who disagree are then totally unacceptable and any method of overwhelming or destroying them is justified. In these circumstances, civility and honest dialogue vanish from the scene – a common pattern that lies behind much of the violence in the world today.

This danger is vividly demonstrated by the following story. An abortion clinic was consistently picketed by right-to-life groups. One woman turned up all the time to deter pregnant women from entering the clinic, till the day she was found inside the clinic asking how her daughter could end a pregnancy. When questioned gently she explained that while she still thought abortion was wrong, her daughter's situation made having a baby "impossible".

Her empathy with her daughter's needs did not prevent her from being back on the picket line the next weekend, trying to prevent others from getting the help she felt she had to have for her own child.

In the United States those who want to prevent legal abortions are winning the battle. They are putting so much pressure on doctors, often using actions such as death threats and even murder, that medical personnel are becoming unwilling to provide abortions. Indeed, protesters are also forcing people out of the whole field of obstetrics and gynaecology, precipitating a crisis in the care of pregnant women in that country.

This situation calls for a rethink on the abortion issue. The real focus should not be whether people have abortions, but why there are so many unwanted pregnancies. We should stop putting pressure on women who find themselves in these circumstances.

The tragedy today is that those who care passionately about morality are arguing with each other, thus diminishing their effectiveness, while industrial-era "pragmatists" are making the choices. An alliance must be developed between those committed to values.

Some exciting progress has been made. Those who disagree about abortion are looking for ways they can work together on issues such as the care of newborns. This development shows that we can make space for different views about how to apply honesty, responsibility, humility, love and a respect for mystery.

It is reasonable for people to reach varying conclusions starting from a spiritual base. Intolerance of others' deeply held beliefs is, therefore, the real sin today. We need to listen to those who care passionately about different sides of important issues because they are the people who can move us forward toward a deeper and more complete understanding. A commitment to listening must, however, be mutual, as a vital part of any spiritual base is to know that one may be mistaken. Both sides must be willing to be flexible.

We cannot have successful dialogue with those who claim that morality and spirituality are unimportant. We need to reject the views of people who believe that any activity that makes money is "okay", regardless of its effects on people and society. We need to proclaim the importance of living on a value base.

This is a truly difficult area to understand, let alone to explain to others. One does need dialogue with those who have reached different conclusions, and who ground their personal views on a different value-base. It is impossible to work from value-bases and find common ground with those who see only the importance of material wealth and power.

Supporting positive directions

As survival requires that we learn to work with value-based people who disagree with us, conflict is inevitable. We must, however, make a clear distinction between conflict and violence. For example, President Bush often said during the Iraq crisis that he hoped to avoid conflict; it would have been far healthier to accept the inevitability of conflict and to see how divergent views could be brought into alignment. Recognising that there was a real conflict of views might have made it possible to discover fundamentally new approaches that would have satisfied the real needs of those involved.

President Bush's attitude to conflict stemmed from a belief that one's own view of reality is correct and those of others are wrong. This very Western view is prevalent in the United States, but once it is recognised that right and wrong are not so easily defined, attitudes and behaviours change radically.

One of the primary dangers today is that there is a tendency to force the weaker group to move in the direction desired by the stronger rather than taking the time to understand why people and groups see the same situation so differently. Until we are willing to work through the real reasons for conflicts, any agreements we reach are likely to collapse once stresses develop. Our unwillingness to face the stress and strain of working through different attitudes prevents us getting to a point where all involved can be comfortable with the resolution.

There will almost always be some virtue in the position of both, or all, people and groups involved in a disagreement. The leader needs to listen, and take account, of all the views and to help each side listen to the other. In addition, the leader needs to be aware that the behaviour and goals of one group will sometimes be more supportive of compassionate-era directions than that of others. When there is a clear clash between supporting past dynamics or positive new directions, the right response from a leader is not to "compromise" equally between the various views but to push towards a more desirable set of values and institutional arrangements. Leaders cannot be neutral when there is a need for change.

If you have tried to walk this leadership tightrope in your own life, you do not need to be reminded of the difficulties of maintaining your balance. You are committed to honest listening; but you also want to help people look at the long-run good of the global culture, while always remembering that perceptions are inevitably limited and partial. The moment you, as leader, become absolutely sure of what is required at a particular moment, you also become willing to use power and violence to achieve it. You take this step because you feel you have the obligation to move in that one particular direction.

At the current time, a number of leaders are choosing to use discussion and dialogue styles, rather than coercion, because there is growing evidence that they can achieve more positive changes with this style. The goal of leadership – to help people and the world move in positive directions – remains unchanged, however. This style of leadership is inspired by the saying of Lao Tzu: "When the leader leads well, the people say they did it themselves." We therefore need new tools for movement towards mutual understanding.

True leaders go even further. They recognise that continued use of coercive power and violence is the greatest danger to the human race. The primary challenge of the twenty-first century is to learn how to create a world in which disputes are settled by dialogue and creativity rather than force.

The urgent need to move beyond violence requires a profound change in our definition of positive leadership. In the past the leader was the individual who had a clear, strong vision of what was needed, and went all out to achieve it. It was accepted that those opposed to the change would be frustrated and angry – indeed these reactions were welcomed as evidence of the success of the effort.

Today's effective leaders must adopt a profoundly different role. They need to bring together the people who share a moral, value-based stance but who have different views about appropriate directions. They need to create excitement about new visions, enabling people with different views to think and act together. While there will still be opposition, the need is to seek common ground. Debate in the West tends to concentrate on disagreements rather than agreements. We should now reverse this style.

In the past, leaders were admired because of their powerful stands. In the future, leaders will be valued for their skills in bringing divergent people and groups together. This leads to a profoundly different definition of strength – ie. the ability to remain aware of one's own core while valuing the reality that other people see the world differently. This type of individual has no need for violence, being able to remain centred without impinging on the rights of others.

There is an additional difficulty that must be faced. Many of the most intractable problems in the world have deep roots in the past, and it will be impossible to resolve these conflicts without consciously abandoning past angers. The Reconciliation Commission in South Africa, flawed as it was, shows an alternative to the revenge-based systems of the West.

There is a form of magic which can resolve even the most obstinate of issues. If people can see their common humanity, then they will be willing to look at alternative points of view and find new directions that might have seemed intolerable when the "other" was defined as the enemy. Connection at the personal level is one of the essentials for such a change in behaviour.

Leadership styles

There are three primary steps leaders need to take when creating new patterns of thought and action. Deciding which one is necessary at a particular point in time depends on the nature of the interactions which are dominant in the family, institution or community to be supported. Having the ability to determine where the blocks to effectiveness are is one of the skills required of a leader at the end of the twentieth century. Organisations and communities that face new challenges will not normally be able to tell where they are blocked. This is the role of the outsider: to look at the realities and to help people concentrate on the places where they are really in need of change.

The first challenge is to help people to move beyond their cultural trance.

One task is to build trust and a sense of interdependence. Most systems today are paralysed by fear of others. This is true even of institutions – such as firms, schools, colleges and churches – which one would hope are committed to pulling together. The problems involved in creating trust are even more acute when it is necessary to bring together people from different institutions, or even nations, who have very varied images of what they want. The essential virtue which goes into this development stage is love – a willingness to look beyond the flaws in each one of us and to support our common humanity.

The requirement for success in this task is the recognition that there are goals that unite all those who are meeting together and that these are more important than existing divisions. This is the fundamental challenge when one is dealing with clashes within existing institutions or communities. It is also the challenge when trying to unite groups or nations which have previously defined their interests in competitive ways. One way to achieve this goal is to "think" through the problem. It is, however, unlikely that this intellectual process will be successful unless the emotions are also effectively engaged.

One of the most creative approaches is to find ways to remind people of their common humanity and to help them see that this is more important than differences in goals and ideologies. This was one of the first steps which was taken by citizen diplomats in the Soviet Union as they started their work in the mid-eighties. They aimed to relate to grandfathers rather than to bureaucrats. As soon as bureaucrats took off their work hats, many of the apparently insoluble differences vanished. A sense of alignment – a belief that there were overarching agreements which lay beyond the differences – began to develop.

My close colleague, Bob Stilger, has developed this process into an art form. He starts meetings with a request that people explain why they put their scarce time into the particular activity in which they are engaged. The sense of connection which normally develops provides a basis for making any tough decisions that may be required.

Today we are searching for a global "story" which can unite all the people of the world. It must be based on our common humanity – the fact that we share joys and griefs with those nearest us. Our customs may be different but our need for family and community is a constant throughout the world.

One of the fascinating insights into the Mid-East peace conferences of the early nineties came as NBC did a story on how the various countries were coping with the media. Public relations teams from the various nations found that they had been forced to cooperate to achieve a common task and that their attitudes were not very different. A sense of being colleagues, even if not friends, inevitably developed.

Trust-building requires time. There is no way to rush the process. Effective leaders have learned that they need to proceed slowly in the beginning and there must be opportunities for talk and play even though it often seems as though nothing is being learned or gained. Once people see that the others involved are human beings who share all their complexities, stereotypes will break down and rapid progress can take place. The fear that always accompanies contacts with "strangers" changes into a fascination with difference.

After trust-building, the logical next step is envisioning what should be done. However, because distrust has been so pervasive throughout the industrial era, some "new age" organisations are stuck at the trust-building stage, hoping for the development of "perfect" systems. They often fail to recognise that this goal is impossible and that the search for trust within a small group may cut them off from others who could work with them.

Building trust and interdependence is part of a complex cycle, not a goal in itself. People will be ready to talk about their visions, their dreams and what they think will make a difference, once they lose their fear. At this point, people need to think creatively together and get as many ideas as possible into the open. This requires more than "brainstorming", which all too often means that people will throw ideas off the top of their heads rather than thinking about break-the-mould directions.

When people transcend current thinking, many of their previous ideas will be useless. This creative phase enables people to begin to understand, however, that alignment towards a specific goal does not mean agreement on all matters. People can work together even though they still have differences. This period of creativity provides the raw material out of which vision emerges. The overarching challenge at this time is to be willing to be honest about one's own understandings; to bring to the surface ideas, even while believing that others will disagree. Trust is therefore a precondition; otherwise people will limit themselves to what they feel is "acceptable".

Creativity will normally stretch the boundaries of trust. Each of us necessarily thinks in terms of our experience. There will be a tendency for this stage to bring stereotypes back into focus and to cast doubt on the progress which has been made in breaking down the barriers between groups. People can only imagine out of their past experience and they will therefore come up with ideas which may seem inappropriate, or even outrageous, when seen from a different viewpoint. All of those engaged in the process must be aware of the need for mutual support.

Once the new ideas have been scrutinised and culled, the natural progression is towards action. Perceiving the possibility of enhancing their quality of life, people will want to do something.

It is possible for the overall process to be blocked at this point. Our current emphasis on participation makes it difficult for us to freeze ideas so that action can take place. We are often willing to reopen discussion again and again to accommodate newcomers. We must move beyond this pattern because the creative process has a rhythm that must be honoured. If it is lost, people will lose their energy and enthusiasm.

The action phase is the time when responsibility is at the centre of our lives. We do what we have to do because, as Martin Luther put it: "we can do no other." We have centred ourselves through our trust-building and shared creativity, now we have discovered action steps which we believe will make a difference. We therefore carry them out to the best of our ability.

But even if individuals, groups and organisations are willing to push towards action, our current culture does not possess appropriate action styles. While much has been done to help organisations learn to trust and envision, action models for the compassionate era are scarce. The old patterns, where an elite group forced changes, are being rejected. It is all too easy to fall back into them, however. What is there to take their place?

More and more people feel that total consensus should be achieved before action, but this denies the very nature of the change process. New ideas will always be controversial. Some people must be willing to step out in front – to take risks.

Action will often be divisive. Despite our best efforts, some people will see what we are doing as wrong. Rather than polarising groups however, the effort should be to minimise the differences. Inevitably action steps will also sometimes destroy patterns of trust, and it is therefore essential that the cycle of trust-building, creativity and action is a continuous one – it cannot be completed once and then forgotten.

One very useful step could be taken by pulling together information about the action models which fit the twenty-first century. The resource section at the end of the book gives suggestions for where to start looking.

Chapter 4

Ensuring Economic Freedom

As a university student I chose to concentrate on economics. I followed the advice of a career counsellor who said the subject was suitable for me because I was interested in people. It was indeed an exciting area for learning, but not for the reason he gave. I discovered that academic economists are not concerned with human beings, or even with what actually happens. Instead they make predictions based on certain assumptions, regardless of whether or not they reflect real life.

My professor at Cambridge, Richard Goodwin, helped me understand the role of assumptions in economics, and indeed all the social sciences. It is quite possible to go through a university believing you are learning about the real world. Only the exceptional professor encourages students to recognise that the basic issue is the validity of the assumptions they are studying, rather than the conclusions reached on the basis of those assumptions.

Because I learned this lesson well, my economics writing in the sixties and seventies always challenged traditional conclusions and made me seem irrelevant to those who believed in conventional economics. I therefore use the word "socio-economics" to remind people that economic issues cannot be kept separate from social impacts. In recent years, many writers have adopted similar views; an organisation to study socioeconomic issues was created a few years ago.

Richard, a truly remarkable man, would not normally have been my tutor. At Cambridge, students relate to a single college and are restricted to working with a professor from that college. Dissatisfied with the teaching I was getting, I asked for the right to work with Richard – a request that was considered unreasonable – and made a nuisance of myself until I received permission. This was the first time I grasped that behaviour which seemed normal to me – in this case seeking better teaching – could be seen as odd by people who lived by the codes of the existing culture.

Richard's teaching eventually enabled me to perceive how economics has dominated decision-making in Western cultures and, since World War II, most of the world. Raising productivity, ensuring full employment and avoiding recessions have been considered far more important than social and political issues such as poverty, health, education and crime. The human and social consequences of current socioeconomic structures have all too often been ignored; we are failing to face up to the desperate alienation throughout the world that is caused by poverty and illness. When coupled with the growing drug plague, the consequent hopelessness threatens the viability of more and more communities.

Social issues are today usually reduced to a consideration of their economic impact. As a result of our preoccupation with economics, we have accepted some extraordinary changes in the goals and organisation of society without thought. Fundamental shifts have been seen as secondary consequences of directions which seemed imperative from the economic point of view. This trend has gained force throughout the last 50 years, reaching its peak in the eighties when greed was proclaimed by many to be a virtue because it would help the economy work better.

The coming reversal of trends

The forces that drove people and the culture in one direction during the twentieth century will be reversed in the twenty-first. The pervasive emphasis on economics that has been acceptable to citizens throughout this century, largely because it succeeded in delivering increases in the standard of living, will be reduced and eventually abandoned. The willingness to be dominated by economics is already waning for many people.

I started challenging the priority when I held my first job in the European Productivity Agency in Paris in the early fifties. The task of the agency, largely driven by American influence, was to increase production in Europe. I drove my bosses crazy because I continued to ask them why increased efficiency would necessarily improve the quality of life. This questioning attitude is now the norm and an increasing number of people are putting other priorities ahead of their jobs and the creation of wealth. They are looking for ways in which the work they do, and the lifestyle they develop, serves their own desires and wishes rather than supports economic growth.

Another desire today is for closer relationships. Many people are increasingly unwilling to subordinate their time with their children and their spouses to the demands of their jobs. Throughout Western cultures, there is a sense of overload. People feel that they are being asked to do too much and cannot cope with all their obligations. There is a widespread desire to cut back on lifetime hours of work.

This shift in priorities is driven, in part, by the fact that once a certain standard of living has been achieved, people are going to look for the time to enjoy it. In addition, environmental destruction is forcing reconsideration of priorities. The natural environments where many people go to relax and "recreate" are becoming less available. This is partly because population pressure means there are more people in any given space and partly because of damage to ecological systems caused by production processes.

One key challenge of the twenty-first century will be learning to live with less. The longer we put off facing this fact, the tougher it will be to come to grips with emerging realities. Increasing costs of energy, and growing damage to ecological systems, both require that maximum growth strategies be abandoned. Each of us is therefore going to have to ask what "enough" means in our own lives.

Thrift is coming back into favour as pressures against conspicuous consumption emerge. More and more people see movement away from frenetic purchasing as being in their self-interest. They are learning to measure success in terms of their quality of life rather than the quantity of goods they possess. Reducing purchases is not seen as a sacrifice by many in the middle class, but rather as a way to maximise satisfactions.

The trend towards simplicity in lifestyles is obviously not dominant at the current time however. Indeed, it sometimes seems as though the ethic of "shop till you drop" remains central – and irreversible, so long as we maintain the current economic system where jobs depend upon consumption. Each of us must buy or others will be unemployed, and consumption is one of the few opportunities for people to express their individuality.

We need fundamental changes in economic models before we can possibly break out of our compulsive consumption habits. Perceiving what these changes should be is not difficult. The real challenge is to muster the political will and citizen resolve to face up to the realities of the moment. This will only happen after citizens recognise that economists and politicians are committed to solving the wrong set of problems. No real improvement in our overall situation can be achieved until it is understood that more energy and resources are being used in the wealthier countries than are compatible with viable global balance. For the same reason, a commitment must be taken to reduce the rate of population growth as rapidly as possible throughout the world.

The need to change direction is urgent. Unless there is significant movement, problems will become far more difficult to resolve in the near future. Before we can look ahead, however, we must recognise how the current situation evolved; proposals for new policies must fit into current dynamics. The purpose of this book is not to come up with exciting, but unfeasible, ideas. It is to suggest proposals that can be absorbed into the society effectively at this time, and thus alter the very dangerous dynamics in which the world is currently caught.

A brief historical survey

From the beginning of time, human beings have sought to decrease the effort they make and improve their conditions. Our imagination and creativity keep the world changing around us. Human beings are possessed by a discontent with things as they are. We are always looking for ways to make our lives better, although definitions of "better" continue to evolve with new thinking.

Some call this discontent divine – others see it as the curse which is destroying the planet. In either case, it is a fundamental reality society must deal with as we think about how to set up systems appropriate for twenty-first century conditions.

Until the current moment, much of human creative energy has gone towards increasing production. Since the beginning of agriculture, when humans domesticated animals and planted crops, a "surplus" above basic needs was available. Originally most of this surplus was seized by kings and priests, and people were either rich or poor, with few in the middle. This condition persisted through the Middle Ages.

Socio-economic patterns have changed completely in the last two centuries as a result of the industrial era. Approaches designed to encourage and support innovation and invention are less than two hundred years old. Even more recent is the idea that human beings could be organised into systems that would support creativity and ensure rapid and fundamental change. Some of the implications of these new styles are spelled out in a remarkable book: *The Soul of a New Machine*, by Tracy Kidder.

The most critical socioeconomic consequence of the industrial era was the rise of the middle class. When looked at in the long sweep of history, this is a truly surprising development. The idea that most of the population would have a comfortable lifestyle would have been considered ridiculous in the nineteenth century. Few people aspired to be rich – as much of the wealth was hereditary, most accepted they would be poor. The idea of upward mobility was still relatively unusual until the twentieth century. People expected, and were expected to, remain in the station to which they were born.

Early nineteenth century Britain looked down on economic upstarts. The novels of Georgette Heyer provide a delightful commentary on the Regency period when the aristocracy tried to keep itself pure and despised those in "trade" – the word for any form of business activity. By the end of the century, the pattern was profoundly different even in the United Kingdom. It was, however, the United States which led the fundamental change in social patterns. Industrialists became the centre of power and prestige.

The opportunity for upward mobility, coupled with the availability of new technology through innovation and invention, led to dramatically increased levels of economic creativity. Production rose throughout the nineteenth century but growth was uneven. The pattern of the century was booms followed by busts.

Boom times developed and continued as long as the enthusiasm of manufacturers and purchasers was high because they believed that conditions were favourable and it made sense to build up their production and stocks to take advantage of the future. Sooner or later, production exceeded orders and the boom collapsed. Slumps developed. Firms went bankrupt and unemployment rates rose to high levels, with consequent great hardship because safety nets did not exist. Over time, the excess supply was worked off and the cycle started all over again.

By the beginning of the twentieth century, people could not afford to buy what was being produced and this created major economic swings. Henry Ford was the first to grasp that rich people would not be able to purchase all the motor vehicles that would come off the newly-invented assembly line. He also realised that if more people were able to acquire goods, then more could be manufactured on a continuing basis. He therefore created a major breakthrough in economic strategy by increasing the wages of his workers to five dollars a day, so they could afford to obtain the cars they themselves produced. After initial strong opposition, other companies followed suit as they saw the benefits of this new strategy for selling goods.

Despite this extraordinary innovation, the level of demand still did not rise fast enough to keep up with supply. The 1920s saw a boom which created the belief that the good times would roll on forever. The bubble burst in 1929 followed by the Great Depression of the 1930s. During this time the priorities of government policy makers lay in balancing the budget rather than dealing with the unemployment problem. As so often happens, an abstraction carried more power than the realities of the day. Policy makers were willing to subordinate the hardship of those without jobs and incomes to the supposed requirements of economic policy.

The impact of John Maynard Keynes

John Maynard Keynes, the great British economist, created the next fundamental change in thinking. He took Henry Ford's argument and made it respectable, proving to economists that lack of demand caused slumps and unemployment. He argued that it was the responsibility of governments to act in ways that would prevent unemployment and that deficits were therefore appropriate in recessions.

By the time World War II was over, Keynes had convinced most economists that insufficient demand had been the cause of the misery in the thirties. Despite the pent-up demand for goods and services that had emerged during the war, the economics profession learned to fear a recession or slump similar to that of the thirties. Economists therefore convinced governments throughout the world that they had a responsibility to help demand rise in balance with supply so there would be enough jobs to go round.

I was at Cambridge University when this point of view was being advanced in the forties and early fifties. As somebody who had been too young in the thirties to understand what had been going on, I simply did not understand how my teachers could be afraid that supply would get ahead of demand so soon after World War II. People had money, they were having lots of children and they were more than willing to purchase. The idea that demand might fall behind supply seemed ridiculous to me – and it was. Once again, however, inappropriate parallels to the past were being drawn and irrelevant policies were being developed.

The most destructive patterns developed because government and advertisers joined together to encourage people to buy. Thrift was discouraged and credit became available for an ever-growing number of purposes. Over four decades, more and more people decided it made sense to buy before they had the required money. Individuals and families have chosen to meet their consumption needs through taking on various forms of debt in advance of receiving income. As pioneer futurist, Willis Harman puts it, most people moved from being citizens to consumers. Credit was seen by consumers as the way to gain goods they needed, even if they could not currently afford them.

Many of us fail to recognise the enormous decrease in our future real income that we incur by paying the interest costs on credit purchases. Credit is seductive, as I – like so many other people – have discovered. When you borrow money you do not pay taxes. When you try to repay the debt the difficulties begin because you have to earn enough to pay off not only the credit, but also the taxes on the money you have earned. Rising levels of personal debt have been accompanied by ever-rising levels of state and federal debt in most countries of the world.

If Keynes were alive today, he would be waging a vigorous fight against current economic policy. He aimed to show that governments were responsible for economic balance. He did not intend for them to embark on a crusade for ever-increasing wealth. Keynes clearly understood that his thinking would require citizens and governments to change the total structures of their economies and societies. He made this clear in a much quoted essay entitled 'Economic Possibilities for our Grandchildren':

> When the accumulation of wealth is no longer of high
> social importance, there will be great change in the code
> of morals. We shall be able to rid ourselves of the
> pseudo-moral principles by which we have exalted

some of the most distasteful of human qualities into the
position of the highest values.

The events of the seventies and eighties

The optimism of the fifties and sixties, and the high rates of
growth in these decades, began to alter in the early seventies.
One primary factor in this shift was the destabilisation of
Western economic systems as a result of oil shocks. More of the
income and wealth of oil-importing countries was needed to pay
for fossil fuels. Demand therefore began to move significantly
ahead of supply in countries around the world. Inflation
increased, along with interest rates.

By the end of the seventies, demand was so excessive that
inflation rates throughout most of the developed world were in
the double digits. In the United States, President Reagan broke
the back of inflation at the beginning of his first term in office
by creating a sharp recession. Increased anti-inflationary
pressures also developed in many of the other rich countries.
Higher rates of unemployment were increasingly accepted as
tolerable by most economists, because they were thought to
hold inflation down. The goal of full employment has been
abandoned in most countries as infeasible or undesirable.

One of the major results of this dramatic shift of directions
throughout the world is that the gaps between the rich and the
poor have been widening, both within and between countries.
Changes in tax structures to ensure international
competitiveness have caused increases in income to go
primarily to the top one per cent of the population rather than
being spread evenly. In addition, many jobs created in the last
decade have entailed low-paying, dead-end activities which pull
the average wage down.

The patterns which are emerging at the current time
foreshadow the massive dangers of the twenty-first century.
Future activity will require imagination and creativity.
Unfortunately far too many people do not know how to think
for themselves. People who can only do what they are told will
not have decent incomes in the future. Many of them will not be

able to find jobs at all. One reason the poor are getting poorer is that fewer and fewer tasks can be accomplished simply by taking orders. These developments have been clearly reported in Robert Reich's book: The Work of Nations.

The situation of the middle class is changing rapidly. The continuing development of the computer is steadily eroding the type of work that is done by much of the middle class. The task of middle-level management is to take ideas developed at the top level and pass them down to workers. They also synthesise the results of activities within the organisation and the feedback from workers and provide information to those at the top. Computers are continuously replacing this type of activity and will do so to a greater and greater extent in the future.

Whole levels of middle management are being eliminated and this process will continue, and even accelerate. The work of professionals is also being aided by computers. Computers, or machines guided by computers, can do any task where the exact conditions can be precisely stated in advance. The progressive replacement of human beings by machines controlled by computers is inevitable.

The good news is that more will be produced with less human effort. The bad news is that our economic system, as currently organised, turns this potential into disaster, creating unemployment rather than freeing time for creative activity. The fact that we can produce more using less time needs to be seen as the benefit it is. It can only be beneficial, however, after fundamental changes take place in socioeconomic systems which radically reduce the amount of time people need to spend on the job.

Failure to change current dynamics will worsen patterns of income distribution still further. A 1999 report of the United Nations Development Program stated: "Global inequalities of income and living standards have reached grotesque proportions." This statement is supported by the statistic that although the wealthier countries have only 20 per cent of the world's population, they have 80 per cent of its income, 91 per cent of its Internet users, and 74 per cent of the telephone lines.

Those living in the poorest countries however, have approximately one per cent of the world's income.

There are some even more startling figures. The three wealthiest officers of Microsoft had more assets than the combined gross national product of the 42 least-developed countries and their 600 million inhabitants. The 200 richest people in the world doubled their net worth between 1994 and 1998, but in nearly half the world's countries per capita incomes are lower than they were 20 or 30 years ago. In sub-Saharan Africa, income per person has fallen from $661 in 1980 to the present level of $538.

One of the most extraordinary developments of the last 50 years has been a shift in our attitude towards working hours. Until World War II, gains in productivity were used both to increase standards of living and to reduce time spent on the job. In the last half century, hours of work have actually increased in many areas and far more people are in the labour force. This pattern is only now changing with countries such as France aiming to enforce shorter working weeks.

The recent emphasis on free markets

The real-world developments of the last two decades have coincided with an enormous shift in dominant economic theories. Across the globe, the emphasis has moved away from ensuring full employment to control of inflation, and away from intervention aimed at supporting desired social goals to setting markets free.

Free markets are currently touted as the answer to all problems throughout the world – for example in the countries which used to make up the Soviet Union, Eastern Europe and the Southern nations. In effect, "cowboy capitalism", based on greed, is being proposed without thought for its social or political consequences. It is true that free markets do ensure better resource allocation than communist or socialist bureaucratic models; they are not, however, the panacea which current dogma proclaims. Indeed, the fact that free markets produce efficiency is not enough of a recommendation. Various opposition parties in Britain have it right when they propose "social markets" – unfortunately, they seem unable to describe what this statement means. They have failed to distinguish between the "how" questions which should be settled by economics and that "what" questions which should be decided by political decision-making.

They should not find this task so difficult. In the first half of the twentieth century Joan Robinson, a remarkable Cambridge teacher who recognised that economics had always advanced the interests of the ruling classes, showed what would happen if free markets were adopted in the absence of the conditions which made them appropriate. She proved that in capitalist economies, free markets would benefit the powerful and the rich against the poor and the weak.

This reality can be easily understood by taking an extreme case. A free market is often defined as one in which willing sellers and willing buyers can find a price which will "clear" the market: in other words where all available goods will be purchased. Suppose a famine develops and one merchant has grain because he has hoarded it. The food will certainly be bought at the price the merchant sets but it is ludicrous to argue that this is a free market. The possession of any sort of monopoly provides the opportunity to gain more than would be freely paid.

The same type of argument applies to free trade discussions. If the poorer countries are selling their agricultural products in a free market, they have little, if any, control of prices. Suppose, in addition, that the wealthier countries are primarily selling manufactured goods to the poor and are able to increase their prices above the level which would be set if buyers and sellers had equal clout. In this case the poor countries are obviously disadvantaged. Given that these are the current realities, a growing number of thinkers in poor countries, as well as many development experts, see free trade as being against the best interests of most developing countries.

In recent years, economists and politicians from the wealthier countries have tended to believe that the attitudes and the policies of less developed countries are obstructionist. In reality, the challenges from the developing countries to free trade doctrine are based on a more accurate understanding of economic theory than is used by most rich-country economists. Today, a growing number of developing countries are vigorously rejecting the arguments for free trade and free movement of capital and they are also gaining support in many developed nations. Other developed countries, including Australia, are more nuanced in their support of current strategies. Increasingly, the United States is isolated in its commitment to free markets, free trade and free transfer of capital without any restraints.

Neo-classical economists, who developed the arguments for free markets, stated the conditions required if they were to ensure justice. Unfortunately, the people who currently promote free markets seem to have forgotten that these pre-conditions have not been realised and that current conditions therefore benefit the rich and powerful. Free markets produce equity, if and only if:

- no large firms exist to dominate prices and wages,
- information moves perfectly,
- labour unions cannot force up wages, and
- government does not intervene in the economy.

When these conditions are not in place, as they never can be completely, then free markets and free trade will benefit the rich and powerful over the poor and the weak. A closer look at these four conditions shows that they are all related to the issue of power. Large firms often have power to set their own prices. Labour unions try to use power to increase the percentage of the resources flowing to organised workers. Information flows are often manipulated by those with power. Finally, governments use power to achieve the goals they have decided are desirable.

In the last decade, economists and politicians have recognised that fighting market forces results in inefficiencies. Unfortunately the fact that the capitalist structure distorts economic relationships has been swept under the rug. The current challenge is to dismantle the systems which benefit those with power and move towards a more level playing field.

Requirement 1: Firms should be small

Economists agree that if a single giant firm, or a small number of large firms, dominate the production or the purchasing of an item, they will inevitably have the power to control the price in ways which benefit them. They will also damage the interests of other firms and individuals. Similarly, if a country with large firms trades with a country with small firms and farmers, the country with large companies will inevitably gain an advantage. A true free market policy, therefore, would support the growth of small firms and remove incentives which support the continuance or growth of large ones.

Current trends favour the possibility of such a direction. In a world of rapid change, large, bureaucratic organisations are at a growing disadvantage compared with smaller, more flexible groups of people. Bigger organisations must move ideas through many layers of administration before they can be "heard" and then accepted or rejected. Large firms are therefore decentralising.

The amount of control held at the centre of effective large corporations continues to decline. Today decision-making frequently takes place in smaller structures, which can move far faster and more effectively. One of the dramatic examples of the decline of the "giants" has been the decrease in the power of the three major US television networks; people are watching other channels and are taking advantage of the VCR revolution.

A trend towards smaller organisations does not therefore need to be created – governments simply need to get out of the way. But this is precisely what governments have been unwilling to do. They are willing to see small firms and banks fail but they get panicky when a large enterprise threatens to collapse.

I was working in the midwestern states of America during the agricultural depression of the mid-eighties, and it was tragic to watch the effects of this bias. The collapse of a local bank in an agricultural area was inevitably devastating: the source of credit was gone, and house and land values inevitably collapsed. But federal bureaucrats who took over failed banks made matters even worse by calling in the credit the bank had extended to companies – companies which could have been viable if they had been able to maintain their loans.

The recent Asian collapse showed that large owners, investors and speculators are treated with respect while small owners go to the wall. One of the rationales for free market thinking is that those who take risks should bear the dangers. In reality, governments throughout the world have aimed to shelter those who behaved most irresponsibly rather than making them pay the price for their mistakes.

The degree to which we are caught in old thinking is shown in our admiration for trends in Japan which are actually going in an undesirable direction, given this perspective. Japan has many of the largest firms and banks in the world. Up to now this has worked for them because they have been able to keep diversity out of their country. In the future, however, their current tactics will be ineffective. A growing number of Japanese know that they are not good at managing in the chaos which is so rapidly becoming the norm throughout the world.

The essential problem with corporations today is that they concentrate on short-run profits rather than long-run development. The basic criterion is whether sales are higher than immediate costs. At the extreme, this can even mean that legality is irrelevant. Indeed, some companies clearly see fines as a cost of doing business. This leads to the development of an extremely narrow line between legal and illegal businesses. So long as both legal and illegal businesses use power to make their decisions, the border between acceptable and unacceptable practices will often be unclear. Several years ago the *New York Times* summarised a report that stated: "the qualities which lead to success in business are the same ones which lead to success in criminal behaviour."

Companies should enlarge their sense of responsible behaviour, looking at benefits and costs in a broader context. If companies do not learn to work with the overall dynamics of the culture and support it in constructive ways, they will find it more and more difficult to make a profit. In a paper written for the World Business Academy, Willis Harman asked: "What are the tasks to which enlightened business is called?" He then responded to his own question.

> If we are indeed approaching the point of "critical mass", where people suddenly realise (as in late-1989 Eastern Europe) that in some fundamental way the legitimacy of the present techno-economic system, and the values and beliefs that underlie it, has to be challenged, then the task shifts. If the transformation starts to happen with such rapidity that it generates a great deal of fear – fear of instability, of economic collapse, of mass unemployment, of an uncertain future, of the "crazies" in our midst – then the one thing people will crave most is stability. The overriding concern will be how the transition can be managed; how balance can be maintained; how we can keep the machine on the tracks. At that point the critical task changes.
>
> This is the time the really critical role of business comes in. All the rest is preparation for the truly critical time in history when somebody has to reassure the fearful that the needed transformation can be accomplished without a lot of social disruption and attendant human misery. The experience of business leaders can be critical at that point – assuming that they are sensitive and aware enough to play a constructive rather than reactionary role.

The dangers of a collapse in confidence in current systems is increasing rapidly. The tensions around the world are growing. Will business see itself as responsible for the overall health of the society or will it remain focused on immediate profitability? Failure to answer this question positively will significantly reduce the chances of a successful transition into the new world.

Requirement 2: Perfect movement of information

Economic freedom depends on the availability of good information, as does political freedom. Ideally everybody should be able to get correct information at the time they need it: differential flows of information inevitably give some people an advantage compared to others.

A lack of good information can be very costly in a very broad range of other fields. Today, almost every item is available at some sort of discount somewhere or another. This is the new version of the oriental bazaar, where we no longer bargain with individual merchants on a face-to-face basis – now we need to know where the best prices are available. Those with knowledge of and access to the World Wide Web can be rewarded with extraordinary decreases in the prices they pay. So can people who have the time and the skills to shop intelligently locally.

Obviously many people do not have the time or the skills to search out the bargains, and thus end up paying full price when they could have bought the same product for far less. Credit card issuers are now exploiting this pattern by offering guarantees but most busy people do not have the time to take advantage even of this simpler system. Knowing how to obtain good information therefore increases your standard of living, and in this area, a systemic bias against the poor and the ill-educated inevitably exists. If free markets are to be just, major efforts must be made to change this pattern. The children of the poor and the disadvantaged should be provided with opportunities to gain knowledge so they can break out of poverty. Unfortunately a systemic bias against meeting this need is developing as those with knowledge accumulate even more.

If society commits itself to eliminating the information and knowledge biases against the poor and the ill-educated, many unexpected issues will arise. For example, fibre-optics, which are replacing copper cables for moving information, provide the potential of bringing a far wider range of information into the home. Given our existing economic system, fibre-optic systems will inevitably be installed first in rich and middle-class neighbourhoods, so one of the most effective uses of government funding designed to create greater equity might be to reverse this priority and give the early opportunities from fibre-optics to poorer neighbourhoods and schools. This is, of course, a very different perspective from those that dominate efforts to help the disadvantaged at the current time.

There will never be totally accurate movement of information, of course, but if prices are to reflect real costs more accurately, we must move towards this goal. One of the most important areas where rapid progress is needed is the inclusion in costs of what economists call "externalities". A company can sell goods at a lower price if it does not have to pay for damage to the environment, and information is needed to make it possible to charge companies for the ecological damage they do. A decision to tax pollution, which is suggested in the next chapter, is a step in this direction.

There is a further problem. An enormous amount of advertising is designed to get people to see differences where none exist. Aspirin is a classic case of this issue. Branded products can sell for as much as five times the price of the generic varieties, despite the fact that the products are identical. Similarly, generic drugs can be far cheaper than the brand name versions.

Requirement 3: Labour unions cannot force up wages

Unions have lost much of their power in recent years. In part, the unions brought this situation on themselves by abusing their position and causing widespread hardship to customers. Therefore a tendency to assume that the free market system would work better if unions did not exist has developed.

While the elimination of labour power is one of the conditions for fairness of free markets, undue concentration has been placed on this condition for realising efficient free markets, while far less attention has been paid to the other three requirements. In a world where corporations are powerful, where information movement is distorted and governments often serve the rich, unions are often required to act as a counterbalance. However, if they are to play this role effectively and also to be accepted as viable in the compassionate era, they are going to have to change their directions substantially.

If we did reduce the power of governments and businesses, and the use of information distortion, then we should also need to limit union power. Until this time comes, there is a case for union power to balance power elsewhere in the system. This is particularly true in a world where corporations and governments dominate.

Indeed, this point has far wider applicability. While the thrust of my argument is the need for a radical shift away from adversarial structures, it may be necessary at the current time to find ways to level the playing field. It may sometimes be necessary to empower the powerless because this may be the only possibility of ensuring that the currently powerful do not dominate all decision-making processes.

Labour unions grew as a response to the overwhelming power of the nineteenth-century corporation. The position of workers in the nineteenth century was unattractive at best. They were hired when employers needed them, they received low wages when at work and they were let go at will. The individual worker had no opportunity to bargain on an equal basis with a far more powerful employer. Labour unions were supported because they were able to introduce some fairness into the process of setting wages. As a result of their efforts, a more reasonable share of the income of the firm went to the workers.

The strength of labour unions reached its peak in the 1950s and 1960s in the United States and many other parts of the world. During this time, labour unions and management essentially collaborated; they found it possible to raise prices and wages simultaneously, to the benefit of both management and labour. This approach worked until inflation began to increase as more players in the economic system adopted the same strategy.

In the last 20 years the unions have lost a great many members in most countries throughout the world. As a result behaviours are changing. This is true even in Britain and Australia where the unions have always been highly confrontational. It is being widely understood that unless management and labour learn to cooperate, everybody will lose.

Is there still a place for unions or are they an anachronism? It is my belief that unions remain critically important when they commit to being part of a team with a significantly different perspective, rather than spending their primary efforts in fighting management. The perceptions of workers and management will always be at odds. Union-management discussions can provide a framework where differing ideas can be shared and worked through. In this way the inevitable conflicts can be creative rather than destructive and violent.

Where will tensions remain? One obvious area is around the proper levels of rewards within the new forms of organisation which will inevitably have far less hierarchy than in the past. I like the idea of setting a maximum gap between the salary of the person at the top of an organisation and the amount received by the worker who is paid least. A number of very effective organisations have set this ratio at 3:1 and I believe that something near this level is appropriate in many cases. I would suggest that the maximum appropriate multiple might be 10:1, as this guarantees that there is no unbridgeable gap between the interests of those at the top of a corporation and those who are workers.

Unfortunately, trends have been in the opposite direction in the last decade. Benjamin Friedman, an economist at Harvard, calculated that the ratio of the average salaries of the CEOs of the 300 largest companies in the US to the average wages of their manufacturing employees was 20:1 in 1980. There is much disagreement about the current figure but some CEOs are paid at least 300 times the wage of their workers. This situation has led to much negative comment by business analysts and financial magazines in recent years, and there is also evidence that gaps of this magnitude lead to very low levels of morale.

Another unavoidable area of tension inevitably surrounds work structures and styles. People who look primarily at the overall directions of the organisation, and those actually doing the work, will have different perceptions which will need to be mediated. Disagreements will inevitably arise, and one of the most easily understood areas of tension exists in the airline industry.

Issues look very different when seen from a pilot's seat rather than a manager's desk. Management needs to keep as many flights moving as possible within their perception of safety requirements, and although pilots are interested in the same goal, the pressures to fly are stronger for management, which is committed to the bottom line. Pilots, by contrast, are primarily concerned with the safety of a particular flight. The pilot's absolute right to prevent a flight from taking off should be unassailable, and a courageous union will be required to protect this right for the forseeable future.

Requirement 4: No government intervention in the economy

The amount of government intervention required depends on two primary factors. The first is the degree to which the three conditions I have discussed above are realised. If there is a decrease in the number and influence of large companies, an improvement in information flows and a decrease in union power, then government would have less to do.

Some governmental intervention will, of course, always be needed. The relevant questions are the points at which actions should take place, the goals that should be supported and the magnitude of the appropriate effort. The most critical and difficult questions revolve around social welfare issues.

Critics have suggested that the wealthier countries are developing a welfare system for the rich and a free market system for the poor. This process has moved furthest in the United States (and is emerging in most other developed countries, including Australia) because the bills that benefit the middle-class and rich are easier to pass, while cuts in governmental activities which benefit the poor are simpler to make. Programs that benefit the underclass have less powerful constituencies than those which advance the interests of the powerful.

During the eighties and nineties, the burden on the poor greatly increased. Wealth flowed to those at the upper end of the income ladder – with the result that the safety net today is not only tattered, but torn. The tax system is far less progressive than it was in the past: the rich and poor often pay similar percentages of their income in taxes because of tax loopholes.

The challenge confronting us as we move into the nineties is complex. It is not a matter of rebuilding the liberal vision of the 1960s. The conservatives are right when they argue that the traditional welfare system encourages people to be lazy and cheat – indeed, many who are themselves on welfare share this understanding and see the system as a trap from which it is almost impossible to escape. The current arguments between Aborigines in Australia and minorities in the United States shows how complex the questions have become.

We must develop new socioeconomic systems that do provide equality of opportunity. A growing number of people are concentrating on the steps which can and must be taken to give the children of the disadvantaged a chance to escape the constraints which held their parents. The greatest positive impacts can be achieved from conception through the very young years, when patterns are often set for life. More and more programs are being devised which recognise the need to break the continuing cycles which reinforce poverty and abuse.

The potential exists for positive directions if people are willing to look at the new dynamics and move with them. On the other hand, short-term horizons promote inertia in Western societies. American anthropologist, Margaret Mead, once stated that "in America the long-run is three months"; in recent decades, the "long-run" has become even shorter! Most decision-making is today conducted with no sense either of the past which has shaped current realities nor the future to which people aspire. This failure to see the flow of events all too often means that issues are only taken up when they become crises, and drop off the agenda as soon as some other question is "hotter". To Europeans such as myself, America seems extraordinarily crisis-oriented.

Problems are increased because government agencies are all too often dominated by bureaucrats who wait out political appointees. All Presidents have learned that controlling the decision-process is very difficult. President Kennedy once said, in effect, that he had to demand that something be done, ask why it hadn't been done and finally threaten dire punishment unless it took place. Then, and only then, was there a chance that action would occur.

In summary, two conclusions on the issue of free markets must be stressed. The first is that free markets do ensure more efficient decisions than bureaucratically controlled systems – a fact proven by the collapse of controlled economic systems, such as the Soviet Union. (An estimated 40 per cent of Russian farm products, for example, never reached the consumer in the communist system.) Second, as long as there are differential levels of power, free markets and free trade will unfairly benefit some individuals, groups and countries as compared to others. One of the required commitments for the compassionate era is to move away from economic power and to permit free markets within social constraints. Fortunately, this trend is already established: all that is necessary is to release current dynamics rather than constrain them.

A new image

Herman Daly, an economist who effectively challenges the growth ethic, has claimed that our present economic system is like a jet plane that must fly at high speed, otherwise it will stall and crash. He suggested that we should start to think about a helicopter that could hover. However, a helicopter is both fuel-inefficient and noisy.

While I recognise the danger of pushing any analogy too far, I propose that we start thinking about a glider as our symbol for the future. Consider the fascinating thoughts that emerge as one considers the operation of a glider...

The glider needs some initial energy input to get it airborne, and, once aloft, the amount of time that the craft stays in the air depends on the skill of the pilot. Gliders are extraordinarily well designed to meet their purpose. Finally, gliders eventually come to earth rather than continuing to fly forever.

These are certainly useful images for thinking about economics in the compassionate era, where development and ecological balance must both be considered. First, any start-up activity will inevitably use up resources at the beginning. The appropriate questions are: what is the minimum effective amount of resources needed to accomplish the purpose? And will the gain compensate for the expenditure of energy?

Second, just as an experienced pilot can find a thermal when the less skilled may miss it, those who know how to carry through an activity have a far greater chance of succeeding than the uninformed. We can no longer justify a system that results in incredibly high failure rates for new enterprises of all types, both profit and non-profit. We need to educate and support local businesses rather than stand by and watch them fail. Communities should stop competing with each other for the limited number of firms which move each year and concentrate on supporting and developing the skills of local business and industry.

Third, just as the glider is brilliantly designed for its purpose. the post-industrial world will not have the resources to tolerate the overdesign and waste which is so common today. Overcoming problems by brute force, rather than by using imagination and knowledge, will not be acceptable in the future.

Finally, the image of the glider reminds us that nothing lasts forever, and we must face the fact that just as we are afraid of personal death, we are also unwilling to recognise that institutions can totally outlive their usefulness. Huge amounts of waste are tolerated as we prop up obsolete profit, non-profit and governmental institutions.

I am not arguing that the glider is an ideal image. But it is true that people are going to have to learn to live with limitations on their power rather than believing that anything is feasible, regardless of cost or waste. Current socioeconomic strategies stress human, computer and technological systems to the maximum. The goal is to work at 100 per cent of capacity – and possibly above. When crises come, there is little energy to cope with potentially disastrous consequences. We must put flexibility and redundancy back into human systems.

One key example of the dangers is the air controller system. Air controllers are asked to do more than is humanly feasible. The human costs to the controllers are very high, and the risk of accidents is also increased. This is a recipe for disaster.

The alternative is to design human systems with "surplus capacity" so we work within the reasonable limits of human attention. In a few areas we have recognised this need for surplus capacity, expecting systems to be down some of the time. We do not expect firefighters to fight fires continuously: our measurement of their effectiveness is in terms of response time in crises. In this case, society does recognise that efficiency and ability declines beyond a certain point.

This type of thinking can be applied throughout more and more of society. People need the opportunity to be in peak form rather than be measured by the number of hours they work. Continuing toil and overload makes little sense when computers, and machines controlled by them, can take over more and more repetitive activity. Human beings can move back to more natural rhythms. Fortunately, there is growing evidence that they want to do so.

It is often argued that the need for international competitiveness makes it impossible to permit people to work shorter hours. This statement ignores the fact that overworking people turns them from valuable creators of knowledge into far less useful purveyors of information. There is too much information in today's world – the profitable service is contexted knowledge.

During the twentieth century we have moved into a world where we have acted as though we can prevent mistakes from being made. We have developed systems which depend on everything going right. In the twenty-first century, we shall design so that people are ready to cope when the unexpected happens. This is one of the lessons which has been forced upon us by Y2K, or the millennium bug. We are learning that we cannot be sure of the future and that the core skill is to have people ready to deal with whatever develops.

Chapter 5

Economics in the Service of Society and the Planet

Most people do what they are expected to do most of the time. Organisations and cultures could not function if individuals did what seemed best to them, without consideration of the overall system. Significant change cannot, therefore, be based only on individual shifts in behaviour – institutions and societies must alter if any significant change in direction is to be possible.

Behaviours and directions will change only when we set new goals and reward different activities. This is true of all sorts of organisations: families, firms, schools, churches. It has been estimated that 85 per cent of behaviour is controlled by the organisation of a system and only 15 per cent by the choices individuals make.

We can suggest to teachers, lawyers and others that they function differently, but as long as the systems that control them remain unchanged, only a few people will alter their behaviours significantly. When those in charge of systems see the failure to make the desired changes they conclude that their initiative has failed and abandon it. They then launch a new approach without changing the system and fail again. This series of breakdowns is often called "moving deck chairs around on the Titanic".

Cultures operate in the same way. Industrial-era behaviours are based on a particular set of assumptions and goals. For example, the incentives built into traditional welfare systems are widely recognised as perverse because they encouraged people to live off the state rather than develop their own skills.

But so long as they persist, people respond to these incentives even if they are damaging to their real interests.

Real change requires putting in place a different set of reward structures that support truly different forms of behaviour. Specifically, we must abandon the goal of maximum economic growth, learn to distinguish between positive and negative uses of technology and discover ways to reduce the rate of increase in population. To do this we must rethink all the incentives built into industrial-era approaches. The approaches adopted must also help to reduce the power that people currently have to distort market forces for their own benefit.

As you read this chapter, remember that the steps necessary to achieve system shifts often sound "shocking" because they go against the conventional wisdom. They will only seem credible as long as you remember the need for fundamental change.

Taxes

One of the extraordinary shifts of the twentieth century has been the dramatic increase in the amount of money that is spent at the governmental level. Projections show the financial burdens on governments growing dramatically as the population ages. Any realistic examination of trends makes it clear that the taxation issue cannot be dealt with at the margins. There needs to a thorough rethinking of all the assumptions on which government money-raising and money-spending is based.

What goals should, therefore, be adopted for taxation systems in the wealthier countries, given the arguments I have made in previous chapters about required future directions? There are several things a tax system should be, namely:

- limited in the amount of money it collects and disburses – as the tax code in every country has become enormously costly and cumbersome, there is a need for fundamental rethinking of both revenue and expenditure
- designed to level the playing field – ie. a progressive tax system – so that the pain from taxation is distributed as equally as possible, taking more resources from the rich

than the poor (unlike our current economic system, which concentrates power and resources at the top of the ladder and unfairly discriminates against the poor)

• manageable – if tax is easy to collect and hard to escape, and contributions are fair, there is incentive for people to behave responsibly; systems break down when taxpayers feel they are paying too much either in absolute terms or because some people are cheating

• encouraging of highly desirable behaviour patterns and discouraging of dangerous ones. Although this goal may cut across the others – for example, cigarette and liquor taxation is regressive (as are higher rates of taxation on petrol) because the disadvantaged smoke and drink more than the well-off – these taxes move the culture in desirable directions and the regressive impacts can be offset by other types of taxes.

If these goals were followed conscientiously, there would be profound changes in taxation policies. Although there is a myth of progressive taxation in the wealthier countries, the rate of taxation is usually remarkably similar throughout the tax brackets, with both the poor and the rich paying a little more in percentage terms than those in the middle class.

A taxation system based on the principles described above would curtail the tax breaks of special interest groups and move us towards radical simplification of the tax code. I am, of course, aware that movements towards simplicity have been subverted repeatedly and determining the amount of taxes one owes has become more complex. However, taxpayers could demand real simplification of the tax code and impose this goal on the parliament. Movements in this direction are in fact beginning to take place as the cost of the current tax code in terms of administration becomes more visible.

No one likes paying taxes. Democracies have nevertheless been able to preserve an essentially voluntary system with tax avoidance kept to a tolerable level, although in recent years, this system has been breaking down. It can only be restored if everyone believes tax rates are reasonable and they are levied fairly.

It does need to be recognised that new problems are also emerging. The development of the Internet is cutting into the yield of sales taxes. The potential to move money makes it possible to avoid taxes in one's own country and this is damaging tax systems far more severely than is generally understood. There is a major need to rethink what is most desirable and feasible for the future.

Here are some of the primary potentials. Decision-making was moved to the federal level because people were unwilling to deal with tough issues. Now national governments are too big to deal with local issues and too small to deal with global issues. Many current government functions need to be moved to the local level at this time so cumbersome bureaucracies can be dismantled. Communities need to take more responsibility for their own directions, so that activity at the federal and state level could be largely confined to equalising the potential of rich and poor communities.

Even if societies commit to this goal, there will still be significant inequalities. But the way in which societies move forward is for some areas to do better and others to do worse: learning is then possible. The important issue is how communities are able to learn from each other, both through success and failure.

Another positive factor is that the interest cost of the debt load, which rose rapidly throughout the eighties in almost all countries, has been decreased by cutting rates of growth and inflation. Both of these help decrease interest rates and decrease the amount of money that has to be paid to service debt.

It would also be possible to cut military costs if societies would recognise that violence is not the best way to deal with conflict. Unfortunately, this lesson has not yet been learned and it is all too easy to write scenarios where more money is invested in weaponry rather than less. One of the immediate consequences of the Kosovo fighting has been to increase pressures for larger military budgets.

As we shall see in later chapters, there will be very difficult choices which must necessarily be made. The aging of populations and the increased sophistication of medical technology continues to increase medical costs. We already ration medical care, although we are unwilling to discuss this issue honestly.

The suggestions I have made above for the principles on which taxation should be based inevitably raise tough questions. Taxes impact various groups more or less harshly, depending on how they are set up. Tax systems in wealthier countries were originally set up in ways which exempted almost all the personal income required for necessities from income tax. Inflation has reduced the value of exemptions drastically. As a result a far higher percentage of the population pays income taxes than 40 years ago.

I have argued that taxes should be progressive. This statement needs some justification before I move on to look at specific tax issues. Current taxation policy is the result of a conflict between two fundamentally different ways of thinking. The first model is based on the assumption that the benefits of growth will be broadly shared and that the best way to improve the economic situation of most people is to ensure maximum rates of economic growth. A phrase that is often used to explain this set of beliefs is: "a rising tide lifts all boats".

People who think in this way argue that tax rates should be low even on large incomes because they discourage effort by the most competent and therefore damage the interests of the poor. This view has been predominant during the last few decades throughout the developed world. It is being challenged these days both on grounds of equity and the ecological need to limit rates of economic growth in the wealthier countries.

The second model of taxation proposes that the rich should pay a larger percentage of their incomes because the deprivation which results from taking a dollar in taxes away from a low-income person is more significant than the pain of taking a dollar away from the rich. The implication of this view is that taxes should be progressive with more taxes levied as people get richer.

So long as economic growth was the primary goal of economic systems there was a case for the first set of proposals. However today, when the wealthier countries need to concentrate on equity and the quality of life, the argument for adopting the second approach is overwhelming. The same logic applies in the countries that are striving for development. Large disparities of wealth get in the way of the development process rather than support it. The traditionally large gap between the rich and the poor needs to be narrowed by socioeconomic, particularly tax, policy.

Consumption taxes

A large part of the tax burden should be raised through consumption taxes rather than income taxes. Consumption taxes tend to discourage demand and encourage savings. Consumption taxes should be low or non-existent on food, knowledge and pharmaceutical drugs, higher on most other goods and highest on liquor, cigarettes and petrol. Consumption taxes should normally be included in the purchase price rather than added on at the point of sale. This is the approach that is being taken by the Australian government with its adoption of the GST.

Energy taxes are a special type of consumption tax. Almost all countries in the world have high taxes on energy products, particularly oil and petrol. There needs to be a long-run commitment to increased energy taxes throughout the world. The shift must not be too abrupt because the impact would be very disruptive. On the other hand, the decision must be irrevocable because increased prices for energy will fundamentally shift the direction of the economy and the culture. For example, assumptions about future levels of road and air travel and transport will change dramatically and necessary infrastructure costs will be significantly decreased. Given that the levels of taxes are lowest in the United States at the current time, the rate of increase must necessarily be largest there.

The case for higher energy taxes arises from the dangers of global warming and the need to preserve fossil fuels in terms of their higher value uses. The market will not serve this purpose:

indeed there has been a tendency for oil and gas prices to be dangerously low. More and more experts believe that there is a real danger of a dramatic shortage of supply of oil in the first decade of the twenty-first century.

One of the implications of high energy taxes is that it will be more attractive to produce closer to home. This will tend to revive communities as they can afford to produce for their home markets.

Pensions and social security taxes

The idea that the state has a responsibility to care for the aged is only about 130 years old. It emerged in Germany when the number of people over 65 was very small and those who had worked all their lives were likely to be in ill-health. Western societies are trying to preserve retirement as a social ideal, despite the radical change in conditions.

Today, one is typically not old at 65 and the attempt to maintain this age as a guideline will bankrupt countries – indeed, the very idea of retirement makes much less sense. More and more people do not want to be shuffled aside into communities where their options are bridge and golf; they want to remain part of the community. The intensity of their activity may change but their commitment often remains unaltered, and the question of retirement is part of a larger issue: the complete rethinking of the lifecycle, which I consider later.

There is a need for radical rethinking about funding the costs at the end of life. Today, the parent who takes care of children is typically disadvantaged compared to the person in the workforce, for they accumulate no income rights. Societies cannot tinker with these issues: they have to be rethought at the systemic level. In doing so, it will be critical that the assumption about continued maximum economic growth rates be abandoned. The rosy forecasts about the viability of social security and pension schemes are all based on a unjustified belief that it is possible to continue growth at maximum rates through the middle of the twenty-first century and beyond.

Income taxes

Consumption taxes should be the basic tax in the future. Income tax would then only be levied on incomes above the level required for basic needs and be adjusted each year to take inflation into account. This approach was used throughout the history of the income tax, until persistent inflation reduced the value of deductions in the last half of the twentieth century.

Three levels of tax might be considered. The first tier would be levied on those who earned more than the amount required for basic needs. The second tier would apply when people had more than 10 times the average income. And the final level, which would be heavy, would be paid when people received 20 times the average income. All income would be included – there would be no deductions or exemptions.

Capital gains taxes would be levied at the same rate as taxes on ordinary income. But they would be adjusted for inflation so that people do not pay for gains which occur because of rising prices. The trend towards a close relationship between state and federal income taxes would be encouraged so as to limit the amount of time individuals spend preparing their tax returns.

There are a growing number of proposals these days for a simplified tax system. Usually, however, the model suggests only one tier of taxation. It is argued that this is necessary for simplicity, but this is only a cover for an attempt to reduce the progressivity of tax structures and is totally unjustified.

Corporate taxes

Corporate taxes have dropped dramatically in recent decades. This change was based on the justification that corporate taxes are inevitably passed through to customers, workers or employees, and that this is undesirable. Corporate taxes do indeed tend to increase the cost to the consumer, and are therefore appropriate in the changed context I am proposing, because they do tend to reduce the drive towards maximum economic growth. The percentage of total taxes paid by corporations should rise again to the level paid in 1950.

Another consequence of this shift would be to decrease dividends because net profits would fall. As dividends go overwhelmingly to the rich, this would also tend to reduce the degree of income disparity.

Advertising taxes

Institutions should pay a significant tax on advertising above a minimum figure which would exclude most non-profits and small business operations – say $20,000 annually. Such a step would dramatically reduce pressures to consume. I am aware that it will be difficult to define advertising precisely, and to distinguish it from knowledge movement, but the need to reduce consumption makes the challenge worth the problems. Indeed, if the advertising tax exempts information hot-lines and other similar activities, this can shift corporate resources away from promotion and towards customer support.

Taxing advertising will have significant secondary consequences. The first would be to reduce the amount of money flowing to professional sports and popular artists who rely heavily on sponsorship and advertising revenues. The second result would be a massive shakeout in the information and entertainment industries.

Since "infoglut" is one of the most serious problems of our time, the long-run results can only be desirable, but there will be negative consequences as some information outlets are lost. It will therefore be critically important for each of us, in our personal and institutional decisions, to weigh where we are putting our information dollars. We should use them to support those publications that seem most in line with our vision of the future.

Pollution taxes

All activities inevitably create unneeded by-products, but we can make choices about how these by-products will be handled. We can either carelessly discard them, with consequent damage to air, land and water, or develop careful policies that limit negative consequences. Only recently have we recognised the danger of continuing the first pattern.

Many years ago I coined the phrase: "Nothing is ever wasted; everything is always wasted" to draw attention to the fact that a product's value is dependent on the situation. Waste occurs because something is in the wrong place at the wrong time. On the other hand, waste can often be made valuable by processing or other means. As companies and communities understand this, more and more recycling is taking place. Some companies have already seen that it is possible to move towards a zero waste policy and to make money with this type of thinking. The Natural Step's emphasis on ecological issues has been one of the drivers behind this shift in consciousness.

Any significant review of the total waste problem must recognise the relative amount of waste from households and from business and government. While cutting down on municipal waste is useful, as is already happening in a number of communities, it is also the minor part of the total problem. The real issue is to begin to reduce substantially the amount of waste in industrial, government and military activities.

Pollution and waste can be curbed in several ways. One choice is law and regulation – the route normally taken today. Fines may be levied when regulations are not followed, but as those fines are so small compared to the resources of offending firms, they are unlikely to affect the policy decisions of a company that is willing to cut corners.

The alternative choice is to "sell" licenses to pollute. This type of approach is based on making decisions about the speed at which pollution can reasonably be reduced. Once this choice has been made, pollution rights are allocated by auctions. This is only a rough measure of need but it is often preferable to bureaucratic choices. Selling pollution rights also has the benefit of raising resources that can be used to reduce the tax burden on others. In the real world, there will need to be a mix between coercion to prevent certain types of pollution and the use of the free market.

Stock and commodity transfer taxes

Stock, commodity and financial markets provide the best available way to set prices and values despite their major imperfections. For these markets to operate effectively, enough people must be involved and enough transactions made, so that all points of view about present and future realities are represented.

This valid rationale for stock and commodity markets should not be extended to a belief that society benefits from large-scale speculation, which takes advantage of very short-term market or index shifts. On the contrary, such speculation draws energy away from more useful types of activity. This type of trading could be substantially reduced by the introduction of a significant transaction tax on securities and commodities sales as well as transfers of money between countries. Such a step could bring in significant money even at a very low rate, and part of the proceeds might be used for global needs. Canada is now considering a tax system along these lines – it is often described as the Tobin tax.

Changing life cycles

Our economic system is built around a work week that typically ranges from 35 to 40 hours, five days a week. People are normally believed to work from 16, 18 or 22 until they are 65. In actual fact, patterns of work are shifting dramatically. Fewer and fewer people work the traditional work week while many people are getting out of the workforce early, while others continue into their 70s and even 80s.

Societies will only come to grips with the appropriate directions for the future after we recognise how little time people actually spend on the job in the modern world. If one relates the total number of hours in a person's life to the amount of time they spend on their jobs, it only amounts to some 15 per cent. This is down from about 35 per cent in the nineteenth century.

When I cite these figures some people look at me disbelievingly. I point out that even on a "working" day, people work only about 33 per cent of the day. They do not work on weekends, they get annual leave and public holidays. They do not start work till age 16, 18, 22 or even later. Most people are now retired by the age of 65, with many leaving or being forced out of their jobs even in their 50s; at the same time, the average lifespan continues to rise.

The figures that I have cited above do not take account of further radical decreases in hours of work, given the potential of computers. Charles Handy, a British analyst, argues that job time could decline by 50 per cent in the next generation if we were creative with the potential of technologies.

The potential for fundamental changes in the way to structure work is therefore obvious. If only one hour in seven is spent at work during one's life, the possibility of dramatic changes in life cycles is apparent: it is time we moved beyond thinking about decreasing the hours of work each week to imagining totally new patternings for life. For example, it might be beneficial for many people to take a year off every five or seven years to relearn and to recharge their psychic batteries.

This decrease in job-related activity unfortunately does not mean that people necessarily have vast amounts of spare time. Indeed, there appears to have been a decrease in leisure time for many during the last two decades. The evidence also suggests people are more stressed than in earlier periods. They are spending a great deal of time commuting, for example. The amount of paperwork required to keep track of everything from health costs to tax returns, from product guarantees to insurance, is numbing. When one adds the airline and hotel travel plans, and everything else that a consumption-conscious culture pushes on us, many middle-class people never seem able to catch up.

One of the extraordinary developments of the last 40 years has been the change in thinking about leisure. In the sixties and seventies people believed they would have more time to themselves in the future. In the eighties and nineties people find themselves increasingly overstressed and overloaded. We have created a "reverse leisure society", where those who have the most responsibility also have the least time to enjoy life.

An even more complex issue is emerging as the relationship between organisations and their workers shifts dramatically. People no longer expect to stay with a single institution all their working life. Nor do they believe that their basic loyalty belongs to the organisation for which they work: they place importance on their family, their community, their church and other relationships that impinge on their lives.

In reality of course, only a small number of people were willing to give up their whole existence to their organisations, even in the past. But enough people chose this lifestyle that it became the norm for those who wanted to get ahead rapidly. Today, however, institutions are being forced to develop a wide range of options if they are to hold onto their best workers. They are finding that this does not raise nearly as many problems as they originally thought.

There is no longer a single track from the bottom of an organisation to the top. You will no longer automatically be sidelined if you are not totally committed to the success of the firm, but have priorities of your own. A growing number of firms are actively encouraging part-time, flexi-time, shared jobs and other creative options. They recognise people are more creative when they are happy, and that overloading employees is a recipe for failure. Recent data shows that people who choose to work part-time are able to be as successful as those who work full time.

Christine A Scordato, director of research for Catalyst, an organisation which fosters leadership development for women, recently conducted a study on flexible work programs. She found that:

> The vast majority of the companies in our study were
> overwhelmingly pleased, sometimes much to their
> surprise. They've become advocates. It's a good way to
> retain qualified, experienced employees. One manager
> said: "I'd rather have half of that person than none."

Charles Handy has coined the term "portfolio career" to describe his vision of individuals consciously creating a pattern which makes their lives exciting and their skills useful, rather than working in a single job. As one talks to young people, one discovers how many people are moving along this track and find it far more enjoyable than the narrow boundaries that existed in the industrial era.

In the future, people will change their activities continuously, even if they remain in a single profession all their lives. The skills needed by plumbers and doctors, electricians and astronomers alter as new technologies are learned. Life is becoming a mix of work and education. Those who do not keep up are going to lose their chance at a fulfilling life. Life cycles therefore need to be restructured so that learning can be more effectively integrated into them.

We can anticipate great changes in the way life is structured in the future. The current division into three periods – education to prepare for a job, doing the job and being retired – is a uniquely industrial-era pattern. Retirement did not exist in hunting and gathering or agricultural societies; people were expected to do their part until they died. The idea that there needed to be a long preparation for usefulness in the work world also first emerged in the industrial society. These patterns will not persist into the compassionate era.

It is therefore critically important that we consider how life-cycles are likely to change. First, the idea that education should be concentrated in the first 15 to 25 years of life must be abandoned. This will be a pragmatic decision driven by the speed of change and the absolute necessity for people to continue learning throughout their lives. In addition, work will start earlier. It will be recognised that adolescence should not be spent in the classroom because people in their teen years are full of energy and need to use it. Much of the discipline required for life can be learned in these years. Activities enabling people to meet others from all classes and races has much to recommend it at this time of life. Cultures are developing various programs which permit people to "earn" credits towards academic degrees by doing work in their teen years.

At the other end of the life-span, the current concept of retirement will be abandoned. This too will be a pragmatic necessity, because of far longer lifetimes than in the past; personally-challenging and societally-supportive activity will need to continue into the 70s and even the 80s. Although people will want to decrease the intensity of their activities as they grow older, most will stay involved. While many individuals are today fleeing their jobs as soon as they can afford to do so, there is also a growing search to find activities which contribute to the society and provide personal satisfaction.

A third major shift will take place in family life. As is well known, the number of women in the labour force has increased steadily during the second half of the twentieth century. Too many of them have so far been confronted with an effective ultimatum: give your full life to the company or be relegated to the "mummy track", where there is little chance of developing your skills to the full.

The Western commitment to maximum labour force participation has produced a growing number of families where both parents hold jobs. The pressure for single parents to find paid employment is increasing: the requirement to do so is strongest in Britain and the US. This has created enormous challenges for schools, which have to carry out tasks which were previously the responsibility of parents. It has also produced an ever-growing demand for child care.

In the future, new structures must be set up which permit both males and females to take time off for parenting. Time spent in this way should be seen by both parents and employers as an opportunity for self-development. The skills required for successful parenting are high-level ones; taking time out to raise children should therefore not be seen as disqualifying people from a successful career.

Two profound shifts are required in parenting strategies. First, people should not choose to have children unless this is truly important to them. At present, many couples decide to have children when they realise their fertile years are almost over; they are traumatised by the ticking of the biological clock. This is no longer an adequate reason for child-bearing unless it is accompanied by a passionate commitment to raising the next generation of children so they can develop their potential to the fullest.

The second need is to break out of the belief that all families should be small. Some people who find their satisfaction in raising kids may well choose to have several children, and those concerned with population growth should not denigrate them. Parents who can raise competent and compassionate children are highly valuable. The increase they cause in the population can be offset by others choosing to remain childless, putting their energy into being actual or surrogate aunts and uncles. Each of us needs to commit to raising the next generation in ways that gives them the maximum chance.

Rethinking income distribution

Our attitudes towards income distribution are distorted by a high level of misinformation. At the end of the nineteenth century, economists developed a remarkable theory which "proved" that the amount each person was paid was equal to the value of their contribution. Unfortunately this theory only applies in a simple agricultural world and has little relevance in today's complex societies, where we are all dependent on the efforts of others for our success.

In today's conditions, income distribution depends largely on social norms. The amount teachers get paid relative to plumbers is not primarily a result of supply and demand but of accepted patterns of thinking. The wealth paid to people who manage the society does not result from hard data that proves a CEO is worth a given amount – it often arises from a cosy relationship between those who set salaries and those who receive them.

One of the more shocking examples of our current models is the low incomes paid to executive secretaries to CEOs, who enable them to function efficiently.

The relationship between the payment to a nation's leader and that paid to sports stars is evidence of warped priorities, not of relative worth. Similarly the fact that Bill Gates, of Microsoft, has been able to accumulate $US90 billion is not evidence of his value but of deep inequities in the way that we have set up our socioeconomic systems.

Given that income levels are largely set by social norms and not by economic imperatives, we must begin to ask ourselves what is the appropriate gap between the rich and the poor in a society. I have already argued that the amount of power in the society should be reduced, and that the progressiveness of taxes should be increased. This will result in a decrease in the size and number of high incomes.

I want to examine at this point how we should deal with the problem of the underclass. Almost everybody agrees that this issue is becoming increasingly intractable. People who do not have the ability to learn throughout their lives are doomed to exclusion from any chance of an effective life. We must therefore deal with two factors. One, which is taken up in the next part of the book, is the need to design a society where learning is at the centre of life.

The other is to determine whether a society can afford a permanent underclass or whether the costs are too high. The evidence about the dangers of a permanent underclass is increasing every day. Cities are disintegrating as the number of poor increases. Crime rates are rising. The percentage of the population that is not being educated continues to grow. Something different obviously has to be done. The answer I developed to this problem in the sixties was Basic Economic Security (BES). This was later called a "guaranteed income" or a "negative income tax". BES would provide all citizens with a basic standard of living because they are living in a rich country. There were two primary rationales for this proposal. One was that we were already guaranteeing incomes; nobody was permitted to starve but the approaches used were messy, untidy and costly. Second, the idea of income as a right would help to destroy both the psychic and practical aspects of the current welfare trap.

President Nixon adopted this idea when be proposed the Family Assistance Plan in 1969. Many other countries have looked at this possibility over the years. If the idea had been developed at the time when it was initially proposed, I have no doubt it would have had highly positive consequences. It would have given everybody a basic income. This would have provided a sense of self-respect and an opportunity for self-development. At the end of the sixties most people hoped for better things and believed that the government was benign. It would also have stopped the development of many middle-class support programs whose rationale would have been undercut if appropriate mechanisms to deal with poverty had been available.

Today, the balance is harder to draw. There are many potential negatives which could sabotage a guaranteed income plan in today's world. One of the greatest dangers is the one expressed in Kurt Vonnegut's *Player Piano*, and echoed by many other science-fiction writers. They fear that if people – particularly those in the underclass – are provided with an income as a right, they would then be ignored and deprived of any possibility of purposeful activity. As a result, this group would be marginalised to an even greater extent. Given the increasing possibility of replacing workers with machines, it is easy to imagine a world in which it is more attractive to just pay people off and forget them than to find ways to ensure a meaningful life for everybody.

The second problem with a BES system today is that more people feel justified in abusing government systems than in the past. The degree of disaffection with centralised systems has grown. A properly developed plan could have provided many people with a sense of pride if it had been introduced 30 years ago. Now a larger percentage would simply waste the funds rather than use them effectively.

Even so, I am convinced that the benefits of BES exceed the costs. BES provides resources to everybody without being dependent on bureaucratic regulations and whim. It signals that a relatively wealthy society can afford an income for all citizens based on the wealth accumulated over time. It simplifies the maze of regulations that have sprung up and will help to eliminate many middle-class support measures that should not exist. It encourages society to remember that the justification for providing resources from government is primarily financial need. It could radically reduce the amount of people required to administer welfare systems. It would place the responsibility for decisions back on the individual and the family.

Nevertheless, BES proposals are still a stopgap. We need to move forward to a time when support to individuals is primarily carried out at the community level. We shall do better when there are fewer federal taxes and services. More money should be left in the community so that it can make its own decisions about how help should be organised and the amount of help that should be given.

One desirable step in this direction would provide communities with waivers that permit them to organise economic support systems in ways that seem good to them. As communities take more responsibility, the amount of money their inhabitants send to state and federal governments would then be decreased.

Social service agencies are already being challenged to rethink the way they operate. The present welfare model demands a set of clear rules for allocating benefits. The employee working with the client is responsible for understanding the rules and applying them exactly. When an employee fails, that person is called to account for the employee's errors. The federal government requires the error rate to be kept as low as possible and has penalties for states and organisations that cannot get the error rate down below the required minimum.

People are unique, however, and no set of rules covers all the possibilities. The greater the number of rules and regulations, and the larger the number of possible loopholes, the harder fairness becomes. If, on the other hand, there is a very tight framework, many people will not fit within the rules.

What is the alternative to current models? Society ought to help people in terms of their individual requirements. It should enable them to find the type of help they require when they need it. One first step towards developing this model would be the availability of an information line to inform people where to apply for help through a single phone call. Such a system should be staffed by individuals who are competent enough to discover real needs in a complex human situation. This sort of system exists everywhere in Britain and Australia. It is also developing in a growing number of communities across the United States.

If helping systems are set up for this purpose, workers cannot be supervised in the traditional way. They cannot be evaluated on the basis of whether rules and regulations were correctly applied. Instead, judgments must be in terms of whether the available resources were used as effectively as possible to help those in need. We must therefore learn to distinguish between those who are deserving of help from the community and those who are not. Some people who have had a run of bad luck genuinely need support, while others are willing to take advantage of any available programs.

I have come to believe that the ability to make this type of judgment about commitment and effort is central to life itself. All our relationships are in a very real sense governed by the need to make this choice. When do you push children harder? When do you give them love and care? When do you push for creativity? When do you help a co-worker over a rough patch and when do you demand performance? When do you help a family and when do you demand they help themselves?

If we were all fully adult, this problem would not arise but many of us are not mature now and are unlikely to be at any time in the foreseeable future. Choosing between those who need support and those who are abusing systems is always a judgment call. It depends on hunch and instinct and guts. It is one of society's primary responsibilities.

Is there a way to dramatically lessen the number of people who cannot care for themselves? I believe that there is. If society were willing to make a massive commitment to making sure that everybody had a maximum opportunity from conception to age five, many dynamics would alter dramatically. There would be a chance to break the cycle of poverty and neglect.

There is plenty of evidence that such a strategy would not only improve the quality of life for many people but would be cost effective. It would lessen the number of premature births. It would cut down on the number of people who are difficult to educate. It would reduce the number of child abusers in the next generation and lessen the amount of crime.

This might well be the single most critical step a society could take towards change, and hopefully it will be adopted in the near future. More and more government jurisdictions and non-profit groups are working towards this goal.

CHAPTER 6

Positive Actions as Consumers and Workers

You and I can directly affect our lives through consumption, work style and workplace decisions. The individual choices we make alter the perceptions of producers and decision-makers. Choices in these areas often have far more impact than our votes, where there is, all too often, little difference between the candidates of the various major parties.

Why do so many of us fail to recognise the impact of our personal choices? Part of the reason is the current belief that only those in power can create changes in a culture, when in reality, the impact of a shared change in tastes and styles is far more pervasive than that of orders given by those at the top. Each of us needs to think about the things we buy, the ways we spend our time, our use of resources and the possibilities we have for influencing patterns in our place of work.

Our consumption decisions are "votes" about the future of ourselves and our society. If we perceived our purchases in this way, we would be far more careful about our choices. One dramatic shift in consumption patterns is the movement towards healthier prepared foods. More and more packaged foods have low fat and sodium. The people's demand for better nutrition has led manufacturers to invent new lines. These have increasingly taken over the available display space from less healthy dishes. Similarly, some takeaway food outlets and restaurants have reduced the amount of fat in their dishes.

There is, of course, further to go. Because of the amount of packaging involved in prepared foods, their environmental costs

136

are high. It would be better if people were willing and able to buy in bulk and prepare more foods for themselves. A significant shift is taking place as more and more people are moving to organic production and consumption and often buying in bulk.

Another area of significant change has concerned alcoholic drinks. More companies are reformulating some products so they are less alcoholic. Non-alcoholic wine and beer are also more widely available. This direction has been supported by the growing public anger against drunk driving and the toll it has taken. Similarly, decaffeinated coffee and tea are now easy to find on supermarket shelves.

Huge changes have already taken place in the way we live. We often fail to recognise them because we concentrate on the alterations that are not yet complete rather than on the gains we have already accomplished. As a result, we sometimes conclude that our situation is hopeless instead of recognising significant progress. Certainly the shifts are slower than would be desirable but a better awareness of our accomplishments would encourage each of us to go further. Feeling that nothing is happening hampers our ability to be creative and take risks.

Another indicator of our positive directions is the growing availability of recycled products. Recycling aluminium cans was one of the first significant efforts. This happened because the economics were easy. Recycling aluminium is much cheaper than getting it from bauxite. More recently, great progress has been made in the field of paper. Recycled paper damages the environment less than cutting down additional trees, but the economic benefits are smaller, and recycled paper may still cost more than virgin.

The block to greater levels of recycling often results from a failure to develop the demand for the recycled product. In all too many cases, the commitment to recycling has grown faster than the creation of uses for the recycled product. Each time this happens it slows the development of a viable system because the amount of money a recycling process can then earn is inadequate to support businesses. Becoming an ardent recycler is not enough – we must also support those who create and sell recycled goods, buying them whenever we can.

As we begin to think about what we should buy, all sorts of complexities emerge. For example, there has been a considerable controversy around whether cloth or throw-away nappies are more damaging to the environment. At first sight, the resources used to produce disposable diapers, and the environmental costs when they are thrown away, seem clearly higher than for those made of cloth. However once all the costs associated with the transportation and washing of cloth nappies have been taken into account, the equation is not nearly as obvious.

We have to increase our judgment skills. We must be careful about accepting all the claims of companies adopting environmental themes. We need to ask whether their ads are a public relations ploy or whether they have actually shifted to styles of production less damaging to the environment.

In addition to changing our shopping habits, we can be proactive by asking the managers of stores to stock more desirable products. They pay an amazing amount of attention to the few people who speak up. For each person who makes requests, a dozen or a hundred keep silent. By changing the purchasing patterns of stores, we break through another of the problems innovators face. While they can commit to better products, they will only stay in business if they can sell them.

How we spend our entertainment and information dollars also has strong impacts. If we support violence in the movies, there will be more violent movies. If we support pornography, there will be more pornography. If we support family values, they will appear more often in our entertainment. If we are willing to support local drama and the arts, our community is more likely to have a vibrant cultural life. Each of our choices have remarkably direct consequences on the directions of our culture.

Another critical question is our choices about where we spend our knowledge dollars. Many groups are trying to share ideas about the compassionate era, but most of them are struggling. Their problems result not only from competing groups, but from the fact that too many of us are spending our money on industrial-era information systems rather than supporting those who support us in discovering new directions. The transformational media that gives us a better grasp of where our culture is moving and thus enables each of us to make better decisions.

Another way we can make a major difference is to move away from consumption and towards saving, deciding we don't need many of the things we are buying. Many impulse purchases languish on our shelves and stuff our closets: how often have you heard people lament, when they are moving, the amount of junk they have accumulated over the years? One of the best ways to shift our priorities is to think in terms of the amount of time it will take us to make a purchase rather than to calculate in money terms.

Buying less decreases the damage we do to the earth. Fortunately, thrift is becoming a "growth industry" as people are starting to wonder how they got caught up in the desire for possessions and forgot about having time for themselves and their citizenship obligations. They also see thrift as a way to live more lightly on the earth. Being thrifty and savings-oriented is a challenge in a culture that bombards us with consumption opportunities, but thrift must become a priority, with savings a first step.

Savings impact our own lives, of course. But a significant move towards additional saving would also dramatically change the functioning of the economic system. Demand would drop below supply and a recession or slump would develop. At this point, unemployment becomes a problem.

Given today's thinking the only response that seems appropriate to most people is increasing demand again. In effect, then, economists and politicians will try to neutralise and reverse decisions being made by citizens. So long as industrial-era thinking persists, this is indeed the only option: there are no real choices so long as this style of thinking is perpetuated.

An obvious alternative does exist. We could reduce supply. One of the most viable ways to achieve this goal would be to reduce the number of hours that people spend working during their lives. People could be released from job structures they find unattractive and freed to do more of the things they enjoy. Stress is one of the central problems of the late twentieth century. This move would be popular because recent polls have shown that people would like more time for themselves even if this reduced their income. This opens up the whole question of the work we each do, and should do, in the future.

Right livelihood

As we think about the work we want, we need a sense of historical perspective. Slavery, bond service and serfdom were once the most common forms of master-worker relationships. The American Civil War was the watershed that changed these patterns forever. The dominant mode after this time was the wage-contract, although slavery still persisted into the twentieth century and will still exist in the twenty-first.

The employer became responsible for paying a wage whenever the worker was present on the job. The new pattern had very different consequences from the old. People had increased freedom to move upwards in the society. But conditions for most wage-earners in the late-nineteenth century remained poor. They could be laid off whenever the employer wished and no security existed for the unemployed. The stories about the sweat shops of the late nineteenth and early twentieth century make this point vividly. Today, the same patterns exist in the poorer countries where prestigious companies make goods for the wealthy, employing workers at very low wages and all too often, in intolerable conditions.

Only at the end of the nineteenth century did social safety nets begin to prevent the starvation and early death of those who were unable to find work and had no kin to look after them. The twentieth century saw an ever-growing commitment to support those who were unfortunate; the way to best meet this responsibility is one of the most debated issues as we enter the twenty-first century.

One of the results of our changing structures is that the commitment to a day's work for a day's pay is a declining ethic.

More people see their jobs as a necessary evil which enables them to do what they really want. Work is not seen as worthy of commitment but as a way of getting money. High quality standards and good decision-making are, of course, impossible so long as these patterns continue. In addition, those who are willing to be creative often find themselves blocked by rules and regulations. Most people are now so busy doing their "jobs" that they don't have any time to do their work.

The proposals now being made for "right livelihood" must be understood in the light of this historical evolution. Right livelihood is one common term used to express the desire people have to make a living in ways which satisfy themselves and support the planet. It expresses the desire to find work for which individuals are competent and where their skills contribute to something worthwhile. We therefore need to reform our educational systems so they will help people discover their strengths and weaknesses and enable them to choose where they can be most effective.

Another aspect of the necessary evolution of work structures at the end of the twentieth century, is helping people re-evaluate whether they want to continue to hold a job. The trend in the last 30 years has been for more and more people to enter the labour force. The first major wave was made up of women who wanted careers. The second wave has primarily consisted of people, largely female, who feel they must work in order to make ends meet.

Many people, however, earn less from their job than they pay in additional expenses. After deducting taxes, childcare, increased costs of food, clothing and transportation, as well as money spent on weekends to make up for the frustration of the excessively busy work weeks, net income is often negative. This point was made clear to me in an Iowan community where I lectured, when a person I talked to afterwards told me that his secretary was quitting because a debt-counsellor had shown her and her husband that they would have a better chance of balancing their income and expenditure if they abandoned one salary than if both of them continued to hold their jobs.

People can earn a living while spending less of their lifetimes working for financial compensation than in the past. This goal can be achieved in several ways. One of them is for one income-earner in a multiple job-holding family to quit. A second is to decide how many hours to work; this may involve part-time work or job-sharing. These are personal choices.

The third alternative would involve social change. Fundamental lifecycle changes would be made and the rights of people to income and services would then be structured in very different ways. Here are some examples of possibilities.

Imagine a society where the right to go to college at reduced fees, or none at all, could be secured by community service work in the teenage years. Those who chose not to take this option would be required to pay for their education. Another option would be for retraining and re-education credits to be part of workplace benefit packages. If people took advantage of them, they would accumulate credits over several years which would enable them to spend significant time catching up with changes in their own career area – or to move to a new one if they wanted to do so. Both of these options already exist in limited forms and could be widened.

The philosophy of right livelihood does not imply that all of life will be enjoyable. No form of work is pure pleasure; all activities are boring and frustrating at times. The goal, however, should be to ensure that round pegs are placed in round holes and that people learn, as they are growing up, not to expect Utopia. This goal also implies that no group or class should be freed from doing the toil of the culture. One of our current problems is that there are too many people who simply have no idea how much unpleasant, tedious and repetitive work is required to support their "high-level" activities.

I realise that the goal of right livelihood will appear unrealistic to many. Sceptics will doubt that people could manage this much responsibility for themselves. They will refuse to recognise how many decisions people already make in order to manage their lives in today's complex societies. This cynicism about the capacity of individuals emerges from the same set of beliefs that has denied the validity of all the past movements towards greater freedom in human cultures – from the abolition of slavery to giving women the vote. The current economic crisis will, however, only be solved if we move beyond the control models which prevent imagination and enthusiasm.

Human beings will continue to be economic and social entrepreneurs. Their goals, and motivations, will have to change so that they are concerned not only with financial wealth but also with ecological integrity and social cohesion. One of the more fascinating arguments of our day is whether the most creative people would work so hard if huge monetary rewards were not available. What really motivates people today and will encourage them to be creative in the future?

The relationship between work, income and prestige has already changed dramatically and will continue to alter as we move into the twenty-first century. Industrial-era systems wrapped these three aspects of life into a single package. People's jobs determined not only their income but also their status, while work either provided the ability to grow or forced people into dead-end job – and life – situations.

In the compassionate era, lifestyles and lifecycles are going to be radically different. More and more wealth is going to be created by machines, continuing a trend which started at the beginning of the twentieth century. It has been possible to manage this trend up to the current time by raising wages, shortening hours and extending social safety nets.

The ability of past solutions to manage the impact of computers is weakening fast. The problems of poverty are becoming more severe in the United States and most of the developed countries, while welfare systems are increasingly recognised to be counterproductive. We now know that the rich-poor split is creating increasingly dangerous conditions for all of society. Only a radical shift in the way we manage the problem of poverty and class will make a difference to current dynamics.

Creating change in organisations

I have dealt so far with the ways in which people can affect their own lives. I now want to take up a more complex issue: how can individuals be effective in changing the nature and direction of the organisations in which they work? A growing number of approaches are being used. I set out below one set of guidelines you can choose to start the process of change.

We now know that each organisation has its own unique culture and that change must grow out of the success criteria already in place. Each organisation defines certain types of activity as acceptable and denies validity to others. Most people tend to go along with what has been defined as the norm and to reject those patterns which are perceived as undesirable. Those who choose to challenge the institution often find themselves shunned or even fired.

When conditions were stable, perpetuating past patterns made sense. Today, when all of us live in the rapids of change, stasis is fatal. How can each of us be involved in helping organisations discover their success criteria for the future? People must learn to recognise that their existing organisational culture really does dominate thought and action.

So long as people remain blind to the ways current structures control behaviour, suggesting alternatives is ineffective because they will be essentially "invisible". The first step, then, is to get people to think about how the organisational systems within which they work and live constrains the way they look at the world. One person who works to shift perceptions has gone so far as to organise "funerals" for the old organisational culture in an attempt to free up space for new ways of looking at the world.

The second step is to help people see the difference between the stated and the actual culture. Even if a shared understanding exists about how an organisation operates, it will almost certainly be inaccurate. Beliefs about the ways things are done within an organisation, and what actually occurs, are always

144

widely divergent. This is not only true for organisations. Long ago, anthropologists discovered that there is always a significant difference in societies between the "stated" culture and the "actual" culture. People assume that life is carried on in a particular way, but the real-life patterns are often very different.

Changing dominant patterns of thought is far more difficult than might be expected. People can hold remarkably divergent views without being aware that their positions differ from those of others. In addition, there are usually major latent clashes within organisations which emerge from varying perceptions of past history. These are typically hidden from view because nobody wants to deal with them. A process of dialogue must move through many levels of mistrust and miscommunication before new, shared understandings start to emerge. This effort is normally slow, painful, and time-consuming, regardless of the skills and sophistication of the group.

Shortcuts develop as people learn to trust in each other. One primary problem in change work is the sense that the "other" person or institution is "the enemy". We are finding that the way to move beyond mistrust and fear is to share personal stories which create a sense of our shared humanity. Once this has been established, problems which seemed insoluble often become unimportant or even irrelevant. Those who work in this way are aware of the possibility of this form of "magic". Unfortunately, those who live in a violently competitive world often have no sense of the possibilities created by dialogue.

Guidelines on institutional renewal

Following my work on institutional renewal at Eastfield Community College, where I spent considerable time in the 1970s, I developed a set of guidelines which seem appropriate for effective institutional change work.

*   All existing and emerging leaders should have the opportunity to be involved. This attitude has two primary consequences. On the one hand, everybody who is

willing to lead needs to be given the chance to do so. On the other, expecting everybody to be involved is neither possible nor desirable. Starting with one to five per cent of an institution is enough; any more may overwhelm the initial energies. Once the process gets moving, others will join. (At the end of the first year of our Eastfield effort, many of those thought to oppose change adamantly were helping the process along.)

• The changes of success are vastly increased if those at the top of the institution are "on board" and willing to be highly supportive. Heads of an organisation cannot, however, renew an institution by themselves. Indeed, too much involvement by top management can be counterproductive. Those who are actually doing the work must believe they are supported by those at the top, otherwise they will feel they are going out on a limb which may be sawn off at any time.

• The people at the top of the organisation must be sophisticated in managing "boundary conditions". Many programs fall apart because what goes on in one institution challenges others. There can also be failures because those who govern or fund institutions fear the loss of control inherent in a participatory mode and therefore want to maintain their power. It is essential that boards and funding bodies be kept aware of what is going on in ways that prevent them from feeling threatened.

• Coordination must be by "people persons" and not "program people". Dozens, even hundreds, of models are available which would improve systems if people were willing to adopt them. The basic problem is not a lack of programs but rather the unwillingness to be involved that persists because people feel they cannot make a difference. Those involved in facilitating change need to motivate and inspire people to alter their self-images, and encourage those who are dubious about their capacity to make a difference. This type of process will develop the next generation of leadership. More and more people are

key to success. This is a partial view and therefore highly dangerous.

We shall need all our skills to prevent breakdowns resulting from the effects on morale that will inevitably follow from the rapid decline in the numbers of middle managers and the firing of production workers. There is now strong evidence that downsizing produces immediate positive results on the financial bottom line but has considerable negative impacts at a later date. Keeping organisations operating effectively during the shift from a hierarchical to a communications-based structure is critical, and also difficult to achieve.

Those who still have roles to perform in an institution that is changing rapidly may become less productive because they worry about being fired. The process of downsizing middle management is costly, not only in terms of paying for early retirement but also because of the inevitable damage to morale. Every time that a RIF (reduction in force) takes place, people are less willing to place their trust in the organisation and do their best work.

Constant reorganisations also take their toll. Compassionate-era structures only work effectively when people come to know each other and are able to anticipate what behaviour will be acceptable and what is not. Individuals need to know each other's styles so they can play to strengths and avoid weaknesses. If turnover is constant, relationship building does not occur and effectiveness declines.

The difficulties increase with each reorganisation. People begin to realise that the time spent on rebuilding trust after each organisational shift is wasted, because as soon as relationships begin to develop they are torn apart once again. The problems are increased when organisations commit to a "lean and mean" philosophy. The rhetoric is meant to apply to the outside world but all too often it also impacts on internal behaviour.

There is increasing understanding that firms have two choices. They can concentrate on immediate profits, but there is increasing evidence that while this strategy does increase financial rewards in the short-term, it damages potentials over the longer haul. The alternative is to create strong levels of commitment to the institution, a move that increasingly seems to be the only possible way to keep up with the rate of change. Profit in the conventional sense may be lower but the potential for the future is higher.

The trend towards reductions in the number of middle managers has been most dramatic where whole levels in many corporations have already been wiped out. Governmental systems, on the other hand, have been less impacted by the new understandings and normally still have the same number of management levels. One of the trends in schools and colleges has been an actual increase in the numbers of managers as compared to those actually doing the work. Significant reform will not start to develop in government and education until many of the structural layers are removed.

There is currently a clash between three types of authority system which may co-exist within a single organisation and lead to dangerous confusions and a loss of morale. One is the top-down power model, which persists despite many institutions pretending that it has been abandoned. The second suggests that everybody has equal authority, while the third proposes the use of teams led by the most competent people.

It is the latter approach which holds promise for the future. It requires, however, a level of maturity to which people must be educated. Unfortunately our current schooling system does not usually support the learning of the needed skills for teaming. The emphasis is on individual accomplishment rather than shared learning and action.

Using diversity

It would be difficult enough to make the required changes in organisational structures if everything else were stable. The task is made much more difficult because the labour force of most organisations is increasingly diverse. The percentage of minorities in the labour force is growing fast and it will continue to rise in the future. Some estimates suggest that, in the United States, as much as 80 to 90 per cent of the increase in the labour force will comprise minority groups. This same issue is critically important in Australia and other developed countries. The percentage of women has also been increasing although it may be reaching a plateau and some forces may lead to a reversal of the past growth.

This movement towards increased diversity is irreversible. The issue is not whether we want diversity or not, but whether we understand how it serves societies – ie. how it provides a source of strength for those organisations and cultures that are willing to work with it. Given the pace of change, it is essential for organisations to have as good a grasp as possible of what is going on in the world. The more different viewpoints they can access, the better off they will be.

There are today, for example, very strong feelings about a number of marketing techniques which are being employed to exploit women and other minority groups. This is particularly true for cigarette marketing: the heavily male, white management of tobacco companies clearly underestimates the long-run dangers of the approaches they are taking. They assume that the decline in smoking by the middle class can be made up by attracting the disadvantaged, women, the young, and those in Third World countries. They would do well to heed the backlash that is already developing.

Fortunately a growing number of firms are realising how much they can gain from listening, and many approaches are being developed to learn more about internal and external attitudes. They are not only used to ensure more commitment to existing goals but also to permit discussion about directions which will benefit all the stakeholders in organisations.

An effectively pluralistic society will challenge all the current prejudices about the relative competence of women, members of minority groups, youth and older people. These prejudices continue to affect judgments to a far greater extent than most people are willing to admit, and one can discover how little has been achieved by observing group dynamics. Men will interrupt women more than each other, and those in power tend to ignore young people (of either sex) and well as the aged. Stereotypes about minorities are still very strong, despite 40 years of attempted integration.

Few institutions really use the strengths which people from these groups can bring to a system. If women and non-white people want to advance professionally, they are usually required to adopt the styles which are predominantly used by white males, rather than bringing their own strengths into the organisational system. Most institutions are willing to promote women who adopt male styles and minorities who adopt white styles. Those who persist in acting "differently" will typically find it far harder to be successful.

Even those organisations which recognise how difficult this issue of diversity really is, and make major efforts to accommodate different styles within the organisation, typically do not manage all the problems well. I know of one non-profit group which is strongly committed to compassionate-era style activities; interestingly, most of the staff are females who seem more comfortable with process and cooperation than men. This organisation makes efforts to honour people whose style falls outside the mainstream. Despite their very real commitment to diversity, they sometimes find that the differences are too large to bridge, and the person chooses to leave or is let go.

In addition, there are many institutions that are still largely unaware of the need for sensitivity and continue to perpetuate the patterns which lead to continued frustration from women and minorities. As recently as the beginning of the nineties, I heard about a board meeting where the vast majority of those present were male. At one point the chairman announced he was going to the men's room, and invited everybody to come with him so the meeting could continue – effectively isolating female board members. While this example is particularly outrageous, it does reflect the attitude which still exists in all too many organisations.

The changes which are needed to support and benefit from diversity will disadvantage those who only know power approaches. There will be two levels of struggle. One will be more or less out in the open, with people consciously challenging any diminution in their ability to use coercive power. An encouraging trend in the last twenty years has been the number of people who have learned, in the course of discussions about power, that more effective styles can be adopted.

More serious problems occur at the subconscious and unconscious levels. It is difficult enough to get people to change even when they have the skills and the willingness to discuss effective decision-making rationally. It is far harder to break through the blinders which prevent some people from recognising that current management and organisational styles advantage the white male and make it difficult for women and non-whites to make real progress. One cannot discuss an issue of which an individual or a group remains unaware. The process of chipping away at blindness is always slow and painful and often seems impossible.

I have been learning skills to make this process easier throughout my work life. The key reality, of course, is that there are no slick formulas. There is a need for much patience and empathy with others. Above all, we must have a major commitment to staying open personally and recognising that our own blindness to certain issues, of which we are unaware, is as irritating to others as their blindness on other issues is to us. Mutual tolerance of the inevitable frustration which exists when people of different views get together permits continued struggle and keeps the learning process moving forward. So long as nobody believes they have the whole truth and others do not, there is a possibility of mutual growth.

One of the hardest lessons I have had to learn is that any possibility of positive movement vanishes as soon as I, or anyone else, is convinced of their own personal superiority. All those involved in discussions must agree to the search for new understandings. When this commitment does not exist, the dialogue efforts of one group will be lost in the self-righteousness of the other. Real progress towards more effective styles depends on discussion among the people at all levels of organisations.

The leadership styles required for compassionate-era institutions are profoundly different from those which were effective in the industrial era. The question is how we can learn the new skills which will work in the future. All sectors of the community have much to learn about this transition. All of us need to be as open to each other as we possibly can, recognising that we are exploring extremely new territory.

This is a good place for me to explore the apparent contradiction in my work. I argue that we "must" make certain changes but also claim there is no absolute truth. There is a way to resolve this paradox. Our traditional patterns of thought assumed that it was possible to make absolute statements. I believe that we "must" abandon this belief because the new knowledge patterns that have already developed make it clear that it is incorrect.

Once we have abandoned a belief in absolute truth then we necessarily must learn to listen to each other, for otherwise we are condemned to live in a Tower of Babel with no ability to find shared beliefs or to act together. Some variations of post-modernism, one school of philosophy, assume that there is no way to settle disagreements about values. It is my contention that listening provides the necessary cohesion. The trick is to spend enough time in dialogue until only the truth remains. And the truth will then be relevant for a specific time and place and will need to change as realities change.

Maintaining positive relationships

More and more organisations are recognising that it makes sense to satisfy those people with whom one is already in relationship than to have to "buy" new ones through advertising. An ever-wider range of techniques is being adopted to satisfy people, and once again, businesses are in the vanguard.

In the early 1990s the *Wall Street Journal* ran a story on the ways in which companies react to complaints. It found that most responded rapidly and were willing not only to make amends for poor products and services but also to provide extra coupons (store credits) and even monetary repayments for frustration. More and more hotlines have been created to inform callers how to use, assemble and repair products. Guarantees are typically longer lasting than in the past and have fewer exclusions.

When I was the keynote speaker at the Interactive Industry Video Conference in December 1989, I spoke with an executive of one of the major computer companies who told me that starting from the Spring of 1990, their salesmen would be told to pitch the products of rival companies for specific purposes, if this would keep their customers happy. More and more effort is being made to maintain relationships because these provide the marketing opportunities for the future.

In a growing number of areas even the price of the product has become minimal or is given away free because it is the service stream rather than the product cost which is critically important. Mobile phones are an example of this trend, and the price of computers is moving in this direction. The tendency to concentrate on market share rather than profit is another way in which this pattern of behaviour shows itself.

In this new context, it is also going to make increasing sense to ensure that products have optimum lives. Even if people are able to keep an item longer without repurchasing, thus decreasing sales, satisfied customers are likely to inform their friends and this will increase the overall market for the product.

The advantages of keeping customers happy may seem obvious. But until recently there was little interest in the customer after a sale. Once the product had been purchased, it was often felt that the transaction had been completed. Those stores or businesses which took a different attitude were the exception rather than the rule.

Businesses often have an easier time seeing the importance of a shift towards service than government and non-profits. The consequences of changes are visible both in terms of the bottom line and because customer satisfaction is an effective marketing and public relations tool. The advantages for non-profit organisations and government agencies are often more at the interpersonal level, and have been more difficult to perceive without a profound change in patterns of thinking.

The attitudes that still dominate many non-profit organisations, church groups and government agencies may make it difficult to achieve the necessary changes in directions. Non-profits often assume that people ought to be "grateful" for the services they are receiving. So long as this remains true, there will be little perceived need to serve clients well – rather, the primary effort will be to satisfy the employees and the volunteers who are seen as doing unpleasant jobs. When employees and volunteers do believe their work is worthwhile, they will have the psychic energy, enthusiasm and joy which makes serving others a pleasure.

Most government agencies are so caught up in making sure that they don't get into trouble that they have little time, or space, to worry about the personal needs of human beings. Indeed, meeting real needs is not really the defined goal of bureaucratic systems. They are set up to carry out a task defined by others and the fact that the task may not mesh well with the needs of the population being "served" may well be seen as irrelevant. In addition, the feedback loop from the government worker to the politician who sets tasks, or even the political appointee who determines how the task will be carried out, is in almost all cases weak and sometimes essentially non-existent.

"Success" is therefore often still measured in terms of whether the rules and regulations are observed, not whether actions help people. I once spent time with people from the Arizona State Department of Economic Security, discussing how workers could be given the freedom to address real needs rather than those defined by state or federal authorities. In the end we decided that there were few areas where significant progress could be made so long as current systems and expectations remained intact.

Minimising waste

A final area where each of us can have impact is in finding ways to limit waste. There have been two major sources of waste in the production process up to the current time. First, a large number of companies have had ineffective quality controls and have had to reject a significant amount of their production. The drive to satisfy customers will reduce the amount of waste from this source. The costs of having to scrap or recall products, or redo services, are increasingly recognised as intolerable because of the impact they have on costs and marketing. More and more organisations are therefore putting their emphasis on creating conditions so things can be done right the first time.

The second source of difficulties is even more pervasive. There has been a tendency to assume that it is cheaper to discard wastes than to recycle them. There is today a growing recognition that "waste" can be a profit-centre rather than a cost. More and more companies are seeing that it does not make sense to junk products which can either be useful to them or can be sold to others. This movement towards cost-effectiveness will usually be more feasible than legal prohibition.

I recently received a newsletter from the manager of a printing company which showed the potential from recycling. "I had no idea that the economics of recycling could be so dramatic for a company our size" it read, and went on to detail the initiatives.

> Thomson-Shore recycles film, plates and paper (we actually sort waste paper into seven separate categories) to the extent that we recover over $1500 per week from these recycling efforts. Now, following an employee suggestion, we have added significantly to that savings.
>
> For years, we have used a rubbish hauler to pick up the material we could not recycle. This was office waste, trimmings with glue in them, cardboard, etc. We filled up six dumpsters per week and paid roughly $2700 per month to have it hauled away.
>
> Now, with adding the recycling of about two-thirds of our office waste and all our cardboard, we switched from using dumpsters to renting two trash compactors, which we have emptied once each in six weeks versus six times in six weeks for our dumpsters. This has cut back our waste disposal cost to about $850 a month. In addition, our income from recycling is going up a bit.

Firms are now moving on to taking the position that zero waste can be both a feasible and a profitable goal. Governments are

159

also pushing the argument that companies are responsible for the scrapping of their products after their life-cycle has been completed. This increases the pressure to make the various components more easily distinguished and recycled but also to lengthen the lives of products.

The overall message of this chapter is that all of us, regardless of our role or our position, can participate in the movement towards more sustainable patterns. Some of the activities can be personal. More of them require us to work with our peers and colleagues to change the way we think and work together. In this area of life, as in many others, change does happen when a lot of people do a lot of things in slightly different ways.

Chapter 7

The Learning Society

The development of learning societies is one key challenge of the twenty-first century. This new goal should replace the drive for economic growth that has dominated Western society during the last hundred years. We shall therefore need totally different yardsticks to measure the success of human cultures in the future.

Learning societies will not emerge automatically from our so-called Age Of Information. Information itself is not useful because when it doubles, knowledge halves and wisdom quarters. We are therefore living in an age of misinformation. This is, indeed, one of the primary causes of dissatisfaction. The gap between what we are told is going on and our personal observations of reality is now too wide to be bridged without trauma.

The underlying requirement for a learning society is that we develop high levels of communication skills. This will permit us to filter out misinformation and also to create our own more accurate knowledge sources. Sir Geoffrey Vickers, a remarkable Englishman, made this point clearly in a highly provocative speech at a seminar in Spokane in 1974.

> The world we live in demands and depends on skill in communication and in knowledge relevant to communication to an extent far beyond anything previously known...
>
> Communication also depends on trust... and imposes on communicators a duty to sustain the level of communication, not only by their skill and knowledge but by being trustworthy communicators.

This is the more important because there is a "law" of communication similar to Gresham's Law in economics. Bad communication drives out good communication. A small minority with a few bombs and a lot of self-righteousness can soon reduce the level of communication in a whole society to the basic level of mutual threat.

Thus the duty I have described assumes an importance, as well as a difficulty, which can hardly be exaggerated. It seems to me a trans-cultural human duty to sustain the level of communication, to resist its debasement and to cooperate in raising it.

The direction in which this duty points seems to me the direction of the more human, rather than the less human; a vector which we can recognize as transcultural and which claims the allegiance of the whole species. It may be the only dimension in which any kind of progress is possible. It is surely a precondition for progress of any other kind.

The challenge is, of course, immense. In today's society there are a great many people who make their living by saying anything, however ridiculously false. Indeed, gossip of the worst kind has been raised to an art form in the daytime expose talk-show which is popular because it is salacious, while still sounding familiar. Communication within cultures is therefore being degraded.

Communication across cultural barriers is far more difficult. The Japanese film *Rashomon* was perhaps the first to enable us to see the same story from very different points of view. A story of violence by a Samurai warrior towards a woman was shown in several ways. The viewer was left to decide where the truth lay.

This movie showed body language and styles to help us understand what was really going on. It introduced us to the difficulties of discovering when people are telling the truth and when are they shading it or deliberately lying.

The quality of messages also changes with the medium used to send them. Text, art, games, video, audio, computers and telephones all have their own quirks and implications. Some people learn best from one medium and some from another. Meshing the message to be sent with the best way to send it is one of the biggest challenges in communication.

Another way to gain additional insights about how communication really takes place is to learn various languages. Perfect translations from one language to another are impossible because a language carries a world-view with it. I speak French well: it therefore compels me to be a different person than when I think and conceptualise in English. Unfortunately, languages are taught in school at the wrong time in children's lives. There is clear evidence that learning a language is fun before the age of 10. In teenage years and at college it is a chore, if not worse. As a result, far fewer people benefit from knowing other languages than should be the case.

There are many other "languages" besides those we normally consider – for example, physics is a language which provides a unique way of looking at the world. I first fully understood this when I was being driven back from a speaking date. A high-school physicist explained to me that, when working with students who were only taking a single course in his subject, he did not primarily require them to perform experiments. Instead he concentrated on why he personally found it interesting to look at the world as a physicist.

Similarly, astronomers and engineers, artists and physicians, plumbers and golfers all have unique views which are worth understanding. This is the reason why I find it easy to talk with other people and to learn from them. The world they have chosen to live in is fascinating even if I do not have the time to enter it for myself – and in some cases would not want to have anything to do with it.

Beyond nineteenth-century schooling

The need for effective communication, as Vickers presents it, goes well beyond current understandings. Indeed, we all too often act as though information, communication, learning and schooling are the same concepts. We seem to believe that if we improve the schools, we shall ensure communication and guarantee learning. This simplistic thinking conceals the urgent issues which face us today.

We all too often forget that existing patterns of schooling only go back as far as the middle of the nineteenth century and that they were bitterly fought when they were introduced. John Taylor Gatto, New York City Teacher of the Year in 1990, made the point this way in his acceptance speech before the New York State Senate.

> Our form of compulsory schooling is an invention of the State of Massachusetts, around 1850. It was resisted, sometimes with guns, by an estimated 80 per cent of the Massachusetts population, the last outpost in Barnstable not surrendering its children until the 1880s, when the area was seized by the militia, and children marched to school under guard.
>
> Now here is a curious idea to ponder. Senator Ted Kennedy's office released a paper not too long ago claiming that prior to compulsory education the state literacy rate was 98 per cent, and after it the figure never again reached above 91 per cent, where it stands in 1990. I hope that interests you.
>
> Here is another curiosity to think about. The home-schooling movement has quietly grown to a size where one-and-one-half million people are being entirely educated by their own parents; last month the education press reported the amazing news that children schooled at home seem to be five or even 10 years ahead of their formally trained peers in the ability to think.

Traditional schooling patterns work against the imagination and relationships we shall increasingly need as we enter the twenty-first century. The underlying messages of traditional schools are to:

- obey those in charge without question,
- put excessive emphasis on specialisation,
- erect rigid boundaries between courses, particularly those in the arts, sciences and humanities and between academic and practical subjects,
- expect certainty and stability,
- understand that the world is divided into superiors and inferiors and therefore learn to struggle to be on top.

How are these lessons taught? The teacher and the principal are authority figures with the right to reward and punish. Children and young adults are expected to obey rules, largely without question. Margaret Mead made a wry comment on this pattern. She pointed out that children who left school for the real world at the age of 16 or 18 were expected to make decisions for themselves while the high-school and university student continues to be protected within an artificial world.

Traditional teachers also lead their students to believe that there are answers to all questions. Most students still see no necessity, or even possibility, to be creative because they are brought up to believe that the teacher knows the proper response. This pattern also leads them to expect certainty and stability. One of the most difficult steps in my own career came when I discovered that there was nobody who would, or could, do my thinking for me and that I had to work through realities for myself.

The acceptance of traditional educational patterns is ingrained in students over time. In the sixties I managed, after great effort, to convince a college teacher that he ought to consider working with students in a dialogue mode. I didn't know whether to laugh or cry when he came back after one hour in the classroom saying: "Well, I tried to get the students involved but they weren't interested. I always knew you were wrong when you talked about the potential of kids." Reversing 12 or more years of using one style is not achieved in a single hour!

Industrial-era patterns of grading impose a model of superiority and inferiority. They force people to see themselves as "good" or "bad" students. Good students are usually defined as those who feed back to teachers what they have previously been taught. Bad students are often people who rebel against the system; some of them are very bright while others find the whole process of schooling irrelevant to their needs and potentials. The ideas of "bad" students are frequently the most novel, but they tend to be silent because they have been suppressed in the past.

The imposition of a single method of evaluating people also prevents us from recognising various types of skills. Current patterns of grading reinforce the failures of existing educational systems. Passing and failing grades are based in large part on the relationship of the teacher to the student. Good students are nurtured and therefore do better; weak students are often ignored and do worse. Grades are therefore, in large part, a self-fulfilling prophecy. There is a classic story about this pattern. On one occasion, a teacher was provided with a list that reversed the grades of students. At the end of the year most of the young people had met the expectations which were thus generated. Weak students blossomed under the increased attention they received. Those who had previously done well withered, because they were ignored.

Another example of the power of expectations developed when a teacher went into a classroom at the beginning of the school year and gave all her students As. She also made it clear that she expected them to learn to live up to this standard. By the end of the year, parents were besieging her to find out what she had done for their child because grades had improved so greatly. The change was not so much in the teaching – it was the context that had been altered to demand excellence.

Our grading patterns introduce an even more serious problem. So long as the only options a student knows are being on the top or at the bottom, most people will find it more attractive to be among the successful with power and money than to be without. Indeed, once people have experienced superiority, even equality with others begins to sour. This is the viewpoint which Gilbert announced in one of his comic operas, claiming: "when everybody's somebody, then no one's anybody."

On the other hand, current patterns of schooling are providing many people with such a poor self-image that an increasing proportion of the population are resigning themselves to being on the bottom. They downgrade their very real skills and come to feel that they have no significant contribution to make. The waste of human potential which occurs in this way is huge and chilling. We have all met many people who could have done far more with their lives if they had been challenged.

Perhaps the worst consequence of traditional schooling is the way it isolates students from reality. The better the school, and the teaching, the more complete the isolation. When working with Oakland Community College, I had an opportunity to meet with students from one of the "worst" schools and one of the "best". The drop-out rates in the bad school were horrendous but those who remained were aware of dynamics in the real world and able to resonate with the real issues I raised. They knew the way human beings interrelate and the dynamics of the culture; they had "street-smarts".

Those in the wealthier school had the academic learning but no ability to understand reality. They were informed about the Amazon Rainforest but had no idea why people in Brazil acted the way they did. They assumed that all behaviour could be changed by laws. They lived in a narrow context with a single set of patterns and had no idea that others saw the world in profoundly different ways.

New educational directions

The amount of ink spilled around issues of educational reform shows no signs of abating. Regrettably, the real questions remain illusive, and we can only understand the debate if we recognise that the educational world is locked in a major struggle at the current time. Some want to maintain current schooling patterns while improving their efficiency.

People who advance this view argue that there is nothing seriously wrong with what is currently taught by industrial-era schools and colleges. They want to recommit to their traditional goals of providing the best current answers to questions and testing people on their ability to regurgitate them.

While testing approaches are becoming more complex (one current buzzword is "authentic assessment", using portfolios, essays, and sometimes even critical thinking) the emphasis is still on learning a core body of information which is the same for all students and can be measured by national tests. Unfortunately, the greater the emphasis on tests, the more teachers concentrate on helping students pass them to the exclusion of other needs.

Those on the other side of the argument believe that students need to learn to learn if they are to enjoy, and be competent in, the compassionate era. They propose that people should be evaluated on their ability to continually develop themselves. They recognise that each student has unique potentials and that it is the purpose of education to unlock the drive to develop, believing that great teachers connect with the unfolding child. This group recognises that once students have been challenged, they can be given their heads for they will find their own way.

It was Richard Goodwin, my British economics professor, who started my commitment to learning. He forced me to look at theories in more imaginative ways. He kept after me when I accepted, at face value, ideas developed by earlier economists. He expected me to use my brains, not to adopt arguments made by others. He was one of the primary people, besides my wife, who started me on my learning-to-learn journey.

Understanding the nature of the educational debate and its direction is increasingly difficult today. Despite their very different goals, people who support fundamental change, and those who deny its necessity, use the same rhetoric to support very different proposals. There are, however, major surprises as one evaluates the arguments used to support various positions. Many of those who reject the need for radical reform support their case by quoting the "success" of the Japanese educational system. They fail to recognise that Japanese educators are dubious about the long-run consequences of the rigid Japanese system which emphasises data and logic.

There are at least five major areas of disagreement between those who believe that fundamental change is necessary and those who are convinced that limited reform of current systems will be enough.

- The current system concentrates on what happens in schools and colleges while those who want change argue that education must be broadened to include parents, churches, the media and indeed all the forces that can help people see the world in a new way.
- The current system concentrates on the period from five to 16, 18, 22 or 30, while those who want change look at the whole of life from conception to death.
- The current system uses a very limited number of styles of learning, while those who want change believe that people learn in a wide variety of ways.
- Those who want to preserve the current system opt for a broadened core curriculum while those who want change believe learning can only be achieved by treating everybody as an individual.
- Traditionalists opt for teaching answers while those who want change believe that the best learning comes as one struggles with questions.

Widening the learning process

There are many forms of competence. Bruce Campbell described the issues involved for *In Context* magazine.

> In recent years, new definitions of intelligence have gained acceptance and have dramatically enhanced the appraisal of human competence. Howard Gardner of Harvard University, in his book: *Frames of Mind, the Theory of Multiple Intelligences,* suggests that there at least seven human intelligences, two of which, verbal/linguistic intelligence and logical/mathematical

intelligence, have dominated the traditional pedagogy of western societies.

The five non-traditional intelligences: spatial, musical, kinaesthetic, interpersonal and intrapersonal, have generally been overlooked in education. However, if we can develop ways to teach and learn by engaging all seven intelligences, we will increase the opportunities for student success and create the opportunity to, in Margaret Mead's words: "weave a social fabric in which each diverse human gift will find a fitting place."

Gardner has since added an eighth area: that of spirituality. I would personally add a ninth: the ability to discern patterns and contexts.

The traditional norm has been that every student should learn a core curriculum; if they are failing at one subject in this curriculum they should spend more time on it. This approach is designed to assure that there are no major gaps in an individual's knowledge. A basic problem with this approach is that it forces students and teachers to concentrate on palliating weakness rather than developing strengths.

The second flaw in the core curriculum model is that there is too much "central" material today for anybody to learn all of it. The validity of the concept of "core" can only be preserved by assuming that the political, social and cultural history of one's own group and area is critically important and that of all other cultural groups is marginal. This pattern of thinking is one of the primary causes of current violence because individuals do not develop the ability to empathise with different visions.

Human survival now requires the development of a planetary consciousness, and a sense of the cultural contributions made by people around the world. This must be woven into a recognition of the need to live within a value-based culture which recognises the ecological limitations of the world. This is the "story" which can permit us to live in peace and to ensure the well-being of our descendants.

Students need to grasp this understanding at the same time as they are encouraged to do well in their best subjects. One primary advantage with this new approach is that students find out where their commitments are and can move with them. Future learning systems should provide people with opportunities that fit their developing skills; they should also measure abilities in terms of how close people are to fulfilling their personal capacities rather than against an average for the culture. There will be continued opportunities to learn later in life if something important has been missed.

One of the primary problems at the current time is that learning is normally defined in academic terms. As a result we fail to recognise how much people know about their chosen subject – whether it be automobiles, gardening, the raising of children or computers. Indeed, there is a particular block around computers. Because the younger generation is so much better with computers than those who are older, adults still tend to grossly underestimate both the skills of students and the importance of competence in this area for the future. A few schools let teenagers teach computers because they have the best skills – I wish more would do so for this makes it clear that competence, rather than a degree, determines whether one teaches.

One critical lesson we must grasp is that people learn remarkably rapidly when they have a reason to do so – they seem "dumb" when the subject does not interest them. The consequence of teaching to peoples' strengths will therefore be most dramatic for those whose competencies lie outside the academic arena. Learning occurs most rapidly when people are passionate about the topic.

At the current time, the dominant pattern is that students in most developed countries are typically taught using the same basic track until they get into high school. Then those who are not "good" enough to go on to university suddenly get shunted onto a vocational or general education track which can seem like failure to them and to their parents.

Alternatives should be provided for students who do not fit the verbal/linguistic and logical/mathematical styles starting from their early years. Societies must recognise the need for many different types of skills. Indeed, there is more danger that the world will come apart because of a lack of plumbers than from a shortage of thinkers! I am also more worried about the limited number of people who have empathy as compared to the huge number who concentrate on logical analysis.

Many educators fear any system which excludes some students from academic success and the opportunity to attend university. Once we accept that academic studies are not the only valuable type of learning, this criticism obviously becomes invalid. Society today sacrifices much of the potential of those who have non-academic skills. In the future, it will be essential to give everybody their best chance to develop in ways which will advance their competencies and skills. Errors will inevitably be made but if the system is open enough, nobody will be forced to continue along the wrong lines.

A growing number of tests have been developed which enable parents and children to learn what activities are most appropriate for each young person. These tests are not foolproof, of course, and they should not be used to force a child to take a route which does not seem desirable to him or her. But there will be fewer problems in education if we teach people using the styles which come naturally to them and support them in achieving their desired directions than if we set societal goals and force everybody to meet them.

A full commitment to providing relevant education for each individual will require society to face a further very difficult issue. Children who are cut off from positive experiences in their first five years are unlikely to become learners when they enter school. There is also clear-cut evidence that abused children very often turn into abusing parents, or resort to other criminal behaviour.

To break the cycle of poverty and abuse, disadvantaged young children will need far more support than they currently receive from conception to their entry into school. Because bureaucracies are unable to work with the required sensitivity, tactics and strategy to achieve this goal will have to be developed at the community level, using skills created by community and family education. One of the largest breakthrough potentials would emerge if we would commit to providing every child with maximum opportunities from conception to age five.

The benefits are obvious. We know that people who cannot learn are likely to be aggressive or delinquent. We also know that the transmission of negative traits can be broken by love and care. This is the way to alter long-run dynamics. Not only are they desirable but they are cheaper than allowing current dynamics to continue.

Learning results from challenge. There will be few positive changes so long as schooling remains homogeneous, bland and boring. Education, like life, should be exciting, surprising and fun. Positive development occurs as people have experiences with the unexpected. The vital skill is to stretch students and to challenge them to do a little more than they feel capable of managing, not only intellectually, but in many other ways.

John Dewey argued this point in *The School and Society*, published almost 100 years ago, highlighting the importance of close and intimate acquaintance.

> ...with nature at first hand, with real things and materials, with the actual processes of their manipulation... The School has been so set apart, so isolated from the ordinary conditions and motives of life that the place where people are sent for discipline is the one place in the world where it is most difficult to get experience – the mother of all discipline worth the name.

Learning societies will be designed to prepare people to live in a radically changing world. They will encourage students to understand that change can be exciting rather than threatening, and provide each of us with the skills to manage our lives. Teachers will enable people to grasp the thrill of living for personal growth and development rather than dull security.

Some critics argue that most people cannot understand broader horizons. I am personally certain that the essential reason for so many of our failures with young people, and indeed older ones, is that we underestimate their competence. They are far more capable than we give them credit for being. If we treated students, and citizens, as if they were twice as bright as we think they are, I know that half of our educational problems would vanish.

We need to help people to dream large dreams about a better world. It is only as we do so that we may be able to break out of the current cultural trance.

Readiness for change

There is a general assumption today that educators want to continue current patterns and would reject a move towards a person-centred lifelong learning curriculum. My experience is exactly the opposite. In meeting after meeting, the hunger to support children and learners is present. Administrators, teachers, board members and parents are looking for ways to move but feel hog-tied by current rules and regulations.

In the early nineties I worked with a group drawn from all parts of Lewis and Clark Community College in the River Bend area of Illinois, just north of St. Louis. After a good deal of struggle, we managed to reach conclusions which stressed very different educational challenges from those of the past. We produced the following statement.

> We believe that education empowers individuals by giving them choices. Education enables them to develop their personal potential by eliminating or bridging obstacles. Education allows citizens to participate in the political, economic, scientific, technological and aesthetic progress of their culture to the greatest possible extent. Formal education is not an end in itself: it supports a learning process which continues throughout life.
>
> Lewis and Clark Community College is a community of learners, mutually committed to the pursuit of excellence in the learning process and to providing open access to education. This is the vision which has inspired the community college movement from the beginning and it has resulted in a system of education which is significantly different from the traditional one.

We are committed to creating an environment in which creativity can flourish. We believe that progress is the result of purposeful, systemic, rational and compassionate decision-making. The most effective learning occurs when conscious and consistent efforts are made to integrate theory and practice.

Members of this learning community are characterised by:

- a sense of the responsibilities of global citizenship and environmental stewardship
- an ability to work with others and to share skills to achieve goals
- a flexible mind, able to adapt quickly to change
- a wide range of communication skills, including reading, writing, listening and speaking
- an ability to make ethical and moral decisions
- an ability to analyse problems and think critically
- a mastery of independent learning
- a mastery of appropriate content.

This statement was adopted as the credo of the college and was placed in the office of teachers, staff and almost every member of the college administration.

Education should be based on a belief that every healthy human being, and indeed every organism, has a desire to develop. If this commitment did not exist, life would never have emerged and would not continue. People do not need to be forced to learn. Rather they need to be provided with a context in which their natural drive to learn is set free.

Positive education starts from a belief that children are whole. This conviction is echoed by Marillee Masters, founder of Childlight.

Children are connected to their inner self in a rather magical way which allows for delightful creativity, spontaneity, and freedom to be who they are. As adults, we seem to be searching out paths to this very end – this sense of ourselves as whole and wonderful, capable and lovable, creative and healthy. Is it possible to continue to nurture this innate way that children begin life here as human beings, so that they stay connected to their inner self – whole, healthy and positive about the individual they are? Could this be the missing link in education today? Many educators and professional childcare givers are answering "yes" to these questions.

Current schooling destroys spontaneity and creativity. This is often done physically as well as mentally. Fortunately, the compassionate era we are entering requires the enthusiasm and drive of all human beings and education must therefore be restructured so it will support these skills. A New Orleans ghetto school has proved that this is possible. Based on the vision of a nun, students were taught in ways which supported a positive self-image and world-view. At the end of one year of this type of schooling, existing students were telling new ones that "fighting" was not acceptable behaviour.

New knowledge structures

We are all continuously knocked off centre by events but we need to come back quickly. You may have seen the dolls which rest on a circular base but have weights which cause them to recover their upright balance when they are pushed to one side or the other; this is the balance model towards which we must strive throughout our lives. Balance permits us to live in the question, to face the issues with which we are struggling rather than endlessly trying to escape them. In order to be able to live in this way, knowledge will have to be structured in new styles. It must be available to everybody so they can learn what they need to know at the time they want to learn.

It is often stated that information doubles every three or five or seven years. The figure used depends on the method of calculation employed by the individual making the announcement. When I hear this type of statement, I reply that while information may be doubling, there is ample evidence that knowledge is halving and wisdom is being even further reduced. People maintain power by monopolising and distorting information. If they know something that other individuals and groups do not, they can run rings around them. If they can get their preferred statistics used, rather than those of another group, they are far ahead of the game.

The level and standard of discussion has declined drastically in the second half of the twentieth century. Statistics developed on different bases are used as clubs to convince rather than as sources of illumination. The support of ideologies is more important than respect for others. Elections are fought using distorting images: positive for one's own side and negative for the "enemy". Truth, and the search for truth, have been primary casualties of the last four decades. While truth has always been the first casualty of war, the damage was particularly severe in Kosovo. We live in an Orwellian world of massive information manipulation.

Even those who want to handle information honestly have major difficulties in doing so. One central problem with current information techniques is that they are still largely geared to the time when the world was more or less stable. Students are therefore taught using textbooks which were written as much as five, or even 10 years ago. This is disastrous because, in today's conditions, the speed of change makes material written as little as a year ago obsolete. Any world affairs textbook written before the break-up of the communist empire and the invasion of Kuwait is wildly misleading. Indeed, it sometimes seems as though even magazines are out-of-date by the time they are published.

There is a fascinating parallel here to the problem that those preparing people for technical careers have already had to master. Teaching people how to work with a particular machine or technique was proving counterproductive. New approaches have had to be developed which encourage students to learn to learn so they can keep up with new developments. Automobile mechanics, for example, cannot only understand a particular model; they have to develop the skills to keep up with constant change.

It is deeply depressing that academic fields have lagged behind in making this shift: students are still taught the conclusions derived from assumptions which were valid in the past rather than being challenged to develop the skills to change

177

their assumption patterns with events. Given the progressive breakdown of current information systems, there is an urgent need to develop a process which will provide an continuously updated overview of primary issues.

My proposal is that teams be established to do this work. They would have the responsibility of stating the various credible views on a particular topic. In an approach I have described as a possibility/problem focuser, the group addressing an issue would listen to those on all sides, then push and probe in order to discover the extent to which the positions advanced were coherent and consistent.

They would then state the arguments made by the proponents of the various positions stressing, in particular, the areas of agreement and disagreement as well as the causes and consequences of different positions when these could be understood. The viewpoints would then be presented to decision-makers and the public so that the clash between various attitudes and proposals could be worked out in an intelligent and creative dialogue. These groups would not search for a single, objectively correct statement but rather for a way to bring together divergent perceptual views.

For these documents to be useful, the debate cannot be defined simplistically or academically. Most people are not "tidy" thinkers. The wide range of opinions that exist around each issue must be stated so that people will feel comfortable about surfacing their own ideas. A colleague of mine, Eugene Martin, has developed this technique to the level of an art form, using audio tapes.

Why is it necessary to create a balanced picture of various debates which are currently occurring within our culture? If our views are not supported by reality, then it is important we change our positions rather than continue to push them. Commitment should be to the truth and not to one's own current views. I am personally delighted when I find somebody who can show me why my views are incorrect and thus enable me to gain a more accurate picture of reality. Anybody who takes this stance will inevitably support a p/p focuser approach.

On the other hand, those who are primarily interested in manipulating people, will disapprove of broadening the debate to look at all relevant viewpoints. I went to Washington DC soon after I had developed this approach, expecting to find support because it seemed to me that the p/p focuser approach would improve policy. An individual, who was far more realistic than I, pointed out how this approach would make it far harder to exercise power and would therefore be unacceptable to most politicians and special interest groups.

My hope is that p/p focusers will become available on every critical topic at a number of levels of difficulty and in various media. P/p focusers will, of course, be available on line through computers and also in print, video, audio and interactive formats. Another critical requirement is that the arguments by p/p focusers be kept constantly up to date. These documents cannot be written and forgotten. They must reflect the current state of ideas in the light of changing realities.

The teams responsible for these documents must therefore stay together and revise as frequently as is necessary. P/p focusers also need to be written for people at various decision-making scales. For example, individuals need to consider different issues when thinking about how to continue their own education as compared to those which should be examined by those who have the opportunity to change educational systems.

Two primary questions have to be considered before we can be sure that the p/p focuser system of ordering knowledge will move us forward. First, how will it be decided what are the most important questions which need to be considered? Fortunately this question does not have to be decided centrally. If this form of knowledge structuring becomes accepted, competing p/p focusers on the most important topics will be issued by various groups. Colleges and universities will come to concentrate their efforts on subject areas rather than disciplines.

The second question which has to be examined is how to determine what viewpoints are "credible" and therefore deserve to be included in a p/p focuser. Fortunately, this issue will also be resolved idiosyncratically by the many groups which are engaged in the production of p/p focusers. The logic of the p/p focuser approach, however, is to push forward to an ever-more inclusive vision.

The p/p focuser approach will help recreate the centre in politics. Political decision-makers will gain the knowledge and support which will make it easier for them to support positive directions rather than going along with the special interest groups which so often harass them. Once a p/p focuser which covers all the issues is available, it will be easier to place the ideas of a fringe group in perspective because their place in the total debate about a topic will seem less compelling. The p/p focuser, and other similar techniques, are the best we have for breaking through the patterns of the past and discussing the potentials of the future.

This brings us full circle. Geoffrey Vickers demanded that society commit itself to ensuring that accurate information be available. This requires profound change in our social and educational systems so that institutions no longer have the right to distort information to achieve their goals.

The breakdown in our ability to make effective decisions is increasingly obvious. It is time that we looked at new ways to bring people together in collaborative ways. The p/p focuser is one potential tool that will move us in this direction.

Chapter 8

Redesigning Social Policy

People will develop positive directions for themselves if they can find challenging images, understandings and models in storytelling, art, their families and real life. Today these necessary supports are in scarce supply, particularly for minority communities. Our culture concentrates on the depressing and the negative rather than seeking out the developments which will create a higher quality of life.

Facts and data do not usually help people to see a new world. Rather, the challenge is to help people find a different perspective from which to view reality. More and more people are realising that it is the images we use to look at conditions which determine what we see and what we ignore. As our images change, so do our understandings and our behaviour patterns. Today, a new way of viewing the world – a new story – is developing rapidly around us.

We need to learn a lesson from businesses. They are beginning to understand that concentrating on their possibilities, rather than their problems, leads to far more dynamic results. They are therefore moving towards approaches that support positive directions and creative individuals, rather than spending most of their time concentrating on what is wrong. Families and communities will become more effective when they adopt similar strategies.

Supporting people in change processes, rather than being negative about them, will be one of the key elements in moving us from the industrial era to the compassionate era. Learning to see individuals as having potential rather than being weak, shiftless and negative is a key need of our current time. Most people respond positively when they are given the chance to develop themselves – on the other hand, they behave ineffectively, or even destructively, when the culture makes it clear that it expects nothing from them.

Matthew Fox, the theologian who was excommunicated by the Vatican, talks about this shift as the move from thinking about "original sin" to "original blessing". Riane Eisler, author of *The Chalice and the Blade*, sees is as a shift from a dominator model to one of partnership. There are many terminologies being used at the current time. At the heart of all of them is a recognition that civility, courtesy, grace and love enable a society to work well by highlighting changes in realities that may be disguised if we operate out of fear.

There are many reasons for failures to change behaviour as outside conditions alter. As the pace of change gets faster, many people get frightened and tend to cling to the past to avoid being overwhelmed by the future, maintaining moral and social codes even after they have obviously become irrelevant. In addition, it is easier to live with certainty than uncertainty: if one is absolutely sure what is moral and what is not, thinking becomes unnecessary.

People can also find it difficult to distinguish between the continuing need for moral values and the specific codes which are appropriate for particular moments of history. Honesty, responsibility, humility and love are as important today as in the past, but the way these values can be realised in present conditions is inevitably very different from what was appropriate in previous centuries. The challenge today is to develop policies and directions that will encourage as many people as possible to achieve their hopes and their goals, within the context of a viable, long-run ecological system.

In the remainder of this chapter I shall look at a number of issues where directions must be dramatically changed. I have aimed to discuss those issues where the most fundamental changes are required, and are feasible, at the current time.

Health

The health issue has been forced into the forefront of political activity by the frustration of citizens. In the United States, over 30 million Americans have no health care insurance; those who are not poor enough to qualify for government support and not well off enough to purchase insurance have the most serious problems. Costs for those who do have insurance protection continue to spiral upwards. In other countries that theoretically provide medical care for all on the basis of tax revenues, delays in getting needed treatments are steadily lengthening. This can lead those who have adequate resources to take out private insurance. Australia is one of the countries caught in this dilemma.

Unfortunately, most of the responses to the current crisis are based on a simpler, long-vanished world. They do not face up to the increasingly esoteric, and painful, questions that have developed along with advanced medical technologies.

We must develop new health systems. Market approaches are clashing with personal and social taboos around life and death issues. The growing ability of doctors to diagnose and treat patients forces us to reconsider our economic limits and our moral beliefs. We ration access to medicine but we are unwilling to have an open debate on the choices we are currently making.

I can only deal with a few of the core questions. What sorts of interventions in reproductive technology are appropriate and which should be prevented? Does it make a difference if the mother paying for surrogate pregnancies is unable to have a child or simply wants to avoid the frustrations of pregnancy or the pain of giving birth? What happens if a child born to a surrogate mother is disabled? Should people go overseas and buy organs which increase the risk of ill-health, or even death, of the organ donor?

These are no longer esoteric questions – they are becoming mainstream issues. We are no longer sure who should make the most critical decisions. Much of the discussion of health issues

183

is currently being dominated by finances: we need to bring it back to the central question of who will make the tough decisions and what will they be.

In addition, the rights of patients and parents to make choices is denied in a surprisingly large number of cases. Doctors, and law courts, are claiming that they should make decisions for patients. Many hard choices have been pushed into the law courts in recent years. It is all too obvious, however, that judges have no more skills in making these hard choices than anybody else. Indeed, the law's commitment to objectivity is not helpful here. Tragedy cannot always be avoided. We need systems which support those who have to make tough decisions and to honour them with compassion and dignity.

The most difficult issue is around the right to die. The number and percentage of people throughout the world who are being kept alive solely by modern medicine is rising. The cost of delaying death creates a high percentage of medical care costs, as a very large proportion of the medical bill comes at the very end of life. Many of us have faced the challenge of how to support a loved one at the final stages of their life, with all too little guidance from either our doctors or our religious advisers.

When should people be allowed to die? The early nineties interest in the book *Final Exit*, which provided information on painless ways to commit suicide, shows the growing concern about this topic. Votes around the world on the right to die show the issue will not go away. People are already finding ways around the commitment of most people in the medical profession to keep them alive. Society must now develop new approaches which prevent people from choosing suicide when they have the potential of a good life ahead – while supporting them, and their loved ones, when death makes sense. Hospices are wonderful institutions that have found ways to support patients, their relatives and friends in these transitions.

Behind these medical issues is a far broader question. Should the ability to obtain health care be determined by command of resources or based on some other set of criteria? We are learning so much about how to keep people alive that hard choices are going to have to be made about who gets the health care which will preserve their health and maximise their lifespans. Once we look honestly at the current directions of the medical system, it is clear that fundamental choices are already being made without really facing up to their implications. The state of Oregon has made an honest attempt to prioritise the care that can be afforded, and has often been vilified for its efforts.

One of the most obvious questions revolves about when heroic efforts should be made to save premature babies. Technically, it is now sometimes possible to keep a child alive when its birth weight is around 250 grams. Should society pay the costs of the procedures necessary to accomplish this, which are often in the hundreds of thousands of dollars? Given that the amount of money available for health care is limited, is this the appropriate way to use resources or do higher priorities exist, such as routine care for the disadvantaged? Should the rapidly growing evidence that severely premature babies will be far less healthy and more at risk than children born close to term make any difference to our decisions?

This question has further ramifications. It is now broadly agreed that providing pre-natal support for all is far more cost-effective than intensive care for premature babies because mothers who do not get pre-natal care are most likely to have early, and small, babies. Why don't we provide money so that everybody gets the help they need to bear babies near – or at – full term, rather than have to provide major funding for dealing with premature births? Should our priorities be rearranged so as to support pre-natal care? The potential to be creative is shown by one county in Oregon which has committed to supporting all pregnant mothers and has decided that "no one will be refused service based on inability to pay".

We need to spend far more money on promotion of health than we do at the current time. This can save resources and limit total spending. We are increasingly aware of the factors that cause disease. Just as much of the improvement in health came from clean water and better disposal of sewage in the nineteenth century, the greatest potential will now come from providing people with more control over their lives and reducing the gap between the rich and the poor.

These steps will not, however, avoid the need for rationing medical care. Most of the current discussion about the future of health care repeats the pious hope that the goal should be to provide all the quality care required for all citizens throughout their lives. This goal is infeasible because of continuing advances in medical knowledge; society cannot afford to deliver all possible care to everybody.

Medical care is already being rationed – the amount of knowledge now available makes this pattern inevitable. The real question is what principles, and processes, should underlie this rationing. Should it be by age, money, skills, or contacts? There are elements of all of these approaches in the current mix: what is the right pattern for the future?

The medical issue is difficult enough when we look only at the wealthier countries. Once we consider the gross disparities between the rich and the poor, the issues become far more difficult. For example, AIDS is treatable in the wealthier countries, although it is hardly ever survivable. In the poorer countries, it is an early death sentence because the money is not available to access existing medical knowledge. Life expectancies are declining in many African countries as this disease continues to take a terrible toll: over 50 per cent of people in some of these countries are infected. One very recent breakthrough does provide hope, making it possible to break the transmission of AIDS from mothers to child at a very modest cost.

In the poorer countries, gains in primary health indicators such as length of life and infant mortality are more effectively achieved by improving water supplies and sanitation rather than by better individual access to medical care. Limited funds must therefore be concentrated on public health for many decades into the future.

Equality of opportunity

The sixties saw two major developments which aimed to help the disadvantaged. I was active in the United States at this time so I am most aware of the patterns in that country; very similar developments took place in other developed countries.

A variety of programs were pulled together in what was known as The War On Poverty. The programs were designed to produce a social safety net so nobody would starve, and most people could avoid severe hardship. President Kennedy's policies, which were expanded by President Johnson, revolutionised our perception of the problem of poverty.

Parallelling The War On Poverty, the US government recognised its obligations to African-Americans. It broke through the segregation barriers in the South and began to develop programs to compensate for the continuous pattern of neglect which had kept blacks, and other minorities, from being able to compete fairly for available opportunities. Women also forced the recognition that they too had been unfairly disadvantaged; they were therefore included as beneficiaries of several government programs which aimed to level the playing field.

These developments are under challenge today. Anecdotal stories of gross abuse of government programs have led to a growing backlash in countries throughout the world. It is increasingly agreed that everybody should hold a job, or if no job is available, should work in some other way. The emerging strategies are often given the name "workfare", and this view has become so widespread that those challenging it are often seen as outside the mainstream.

There is no doubt that welfare strategies have often been destructive. The availability of automatic support has led to laziness and a downward spiral in many cases. Some Aboriginal leaders in Australia have been attacked because they have admitted this obvious fact; so have African-Americans for speaking of the same reality.

The fact that old forms of welfare caused problems does not mean that the current drive to abolish it is without major dangers. Is it desirable for everybody to hold a job? For example, is it more valuable for a person to work at a minimum wage rather than to stay home and look after their children? The growing costs of absent parents and broken homes are increasingly obvious. We shall inevitably gather extremely bitter fruit from the violence which has become endemic in so many slum areas. Raising children well is, in my opinion, more important than forcing people into meaningless, dead-end jobs.

Governments are too often oblivious of the need for people to regain a sense of self-esteem. A job is certainly better than the deadening sense of despair which welfare fosters, but supportive parents are critically important in today's culture and if people are willing to play this role they should be honoured, rather than denigrated.

Current strategies are often sold to the public on the grounds that they will reduce taxes substantially, but even if every able-bodied person on welfare is found a job, it will only eliminate a small proportion of the total bill. Even the most optimistic estimates of savings promise little relief from taxation. Welfare abuse and cheating is not the cause of the great bulk of payments: it is the growing number of people who are aged, sick, disabled and ill-educated which is forcing up costs.

The drive to promote workfare has become, in many parts of the United States, an opportunity to promote racial prejudice with an acceptable face. Despite the evidence that the poor of all races are caught in the welfare trap, white people find it convenient to blame minorities, particularly blacks, for excessive welfare rolls. Similarly, drug problems are usually presented in ways which emphasise black and minority offenders and exclude whites.

The increasingly bitter clash around affirmative action to support certain groups of people as opposed to others emerges from this clash of perceptions. Whites believe they are excluded from jobs because blacks get preferential treatment. Blacks, on the other hand, feel that little progress has been made in equalising opportunities. Those who continue to demand affirmative action programs point out that the average wage for minorities and women is still well below the national average, even when corrected for educational levels. They also stress the abundant evidence which proves the existence of a "glass ceiling".

While there is still clear evidence of needed support for minorities and women, it is also obvious that massive opposition to affirmative action programs has developed. These programs will almost certainly be withdrawn, or gutted, unless they can be restructured in a way which will be seen as fair by the majority of the population. Can strategies be developed which will maintain our commitment to those who need help?

I believe we can, and must, find ways to care for the underprivileged. The critical step is to decide to help all the disadvantaged, regardless of sex or colour. It is time we moved beyond helping all minorities and all women, regardless of their current skills and income – rather, we need to support people who have few resources and whose children will be even worse off unless we develop new policies.

How can we define the disadvantaged effectively? Several approaches might work. One would be to ensure that all individuals and families who fall below a certain level of income and resources would receive help: this would be an extension of the Basic Economic Security approach described in Chapter 5. It would use the income statistics which are already available. Several countries have proposed variants of this approach which could most probably be achieved through a negative income tax.

An alternative would be to provide support for all people who live within geographical areas which are significantly poorer than the average. This approach has already been used for certain educational and economic development programs. The US court cases that have led to greater equalisation of school costs per pupil across states are an example of an approach which targets poorer geographical areas. Providing resources to everybody within a given area can have positive consequences

– better-off people may be prepared to stay in the area so as to receive benefits, and if they do so, this may break one of today's primary problems, where poorer areas remain disadvantaged because those who succeed move out of them as soon as they can afford to do so.

Once selection criteria have been defined, the most effective styles of programs would have to be determined. At one level, it is easy to see what is needed. Most of us now recognise that it is more effective to "teach people to fish, rather than to give them a fish" – in other words, to move people towards self-esteem and self-support rather than developing programs which provide resources which are immediately used up and generate no significant improvements. Indeed, satisfying short-term needs may even further reduce the level of commitment in the community.

Up to now, self-support and a job have normally been seen as synonymous. Given the revolution in production technologies, the range of activities which communities support must inevitably widen. Raising children, caring for parents, enhancing neighbourhood solidarity, solving societal problems, supporting fundamental change ... these are all roles which will be needed and should be supported in the future.

There is another level of activity that might have more impact than anything else. We now know that the critical period to break the cycle of poverty is from conception to age five. Children who have not gained a sense of the excitement of learning and life by this age have little chance of being successful adults. A massive commitment to support those who are disadvantaged during these early years could have extraordinary results in terms of increased happiness – and in reduced social costs. Statistical data is readily available to prove this point.

If we were to commit to this route we would need to recognise that some parents will welcome help which gives young children a better chance than they had themselves. Others will resist. One of the hardest choices in the future is when we should force opportunities on poverty-stricken families. The rights of the individual and the community can clash dramatically at this point.

Justice systems

Western justice systems are out of balance. Our current patterns emerged from centuries where power was all on the side of the prosecutors. An accused person had little chance of going free even if they were innocent – a truth that pervades the folk-songs of the seventeenth and eighteenth century. This reality lies at the heart of some of the most basic understandings of the founding of Australia. As a consequence, until recently, one primary commitment has been to prevent the excessive power of the state from overwhelming criminal defendants. Today however, the emphasis is shifting. In many parts of the world, and particularly the United States, long jail terms are seen as the way to resolve criminal problems.

The pendulum has swung; the rich and the powerful have found ways to manage the current legal system so as to avoid punishment while the poor are far more likely to go to prison. And when the wealthy do go to prison they spend their time in far less unpleasant surroundings. I find it shocking that we excuse the privileged with the statement that "they have suffered enough" while the poor, who may steal because of the needs of their children, are attacked with the full weight of the law.

There is growing evidence that the criminal classes are learning how to operate in our rapidly changing world faster than our legal systems can adapt. Our clogged courts are unable to deal rapidly and successfully with new forms of crime; dangers which are emerging through the Internet and World Wide Web are particularly difficult to prosecute using current legal tools. We have to be far more imaginative if society is not to be overwhelmed.

American and British legal systems are based on adversarial strategies. The idea that the truth might be discovered in any other way seems incredible in countries where this model is prevalent. The law courts can be compared to a medieval jousting ring where the strongest prevail: all too often it is the person with the best lawyer who gains the favourable verdict rather than the person with right on their side.

Alternative forms of dispute resolution are gathering more and more support. One of the reasons for this move is the clogging of the courts which makes it impossible to schedule timely trials. But there is also a growing sense that a more advantageous settlement to both sides can be found through dialogue than by using the court system. This change is happening for both the largest and the smallest cases – for example, some Australian states have developed an approach which permits neighbours to settle boundary disputes in many cases without going to law.

It is long past time that we faced up to the fact that we have a class-based system of justice where the rich can afford to hire those who know how to work the system while the poor use court-appointed lawyers. The resulting mess is only kept from collapsing by inequitable plea-bargaining where the powerful cut good deals and the poor often go to prison. The search for a just society must therefore inevitably precede any hope for a fair legal system.

Some positive steps could, however, be taken even without systemic change. The law could learn to distinguish between the one-time offender and the repeat criminal. The object of the justice system should be to keep people out of jails unless they are hardened offenders. Everybody can make a single slip; it is the repetitive pattern which must be avoided. People who go to jail all too often emerge as committed criminals, and it has sometimes been argued that jails are the only really successful educational system, producing criminals with an 80 per cent success rate! Fortunately, significant efforts are being made to encourage new approaches to justice for the young – without sending them to juvenile centres or prisons. These approaches reduce the chances that they will continue to offend.

There is also a continuing clash between those who want to use the justice system to rehabilitate and those who want to use it to punish. We must recognise that the goal should be to improve the future of the individual, if possible, and to protect the society, when necessary. Criminals who can be redeemed should be, so they can benefit themselves and their society.

This does not mean that there will be no jails; some individuals are apparently incorrigible. They need to be locked away, if necessary for life. The fact that their fate may be a result of their parents' behaviour, or their experience in the society in which they were raised, does not change the reality that they are too dangerous to be free. The cost of incarceration should not, however, exceed the amount charged for attending Harvard. (This is a prime example of misplaced priorities.)

One of the real problems in moving forward to a more intelligent system is that criminology cannot be an exact science. Some people will inevitably be released and then commit further crimes, while some will reform and renounce the criminal mind-set. Parole systems are run by fallible human beings, and expecting zero errors is an unreasonable assumption.

We need to develop a broad and deep recognition of the violence which current social patterns inflict on the lives of the poor and minorities. Violence goes both ways in societies: there is the individual violence of the criminal, and the systemic violence against certain classes and races. Denial of the feedback loop between these two patterns is naive. England's Archbishop of Canterbury received a negative reaction when he dared state this inconvenient truth.

Underlying all these issues is the loss of our moral codes, which must be regained. Religion, spirituality and system theory all confirm that societies will not work without honesty, responsibility, humility and love.

The drugs issue

Justice questions are today closely related to drug strategies. Well over 50 per cent of the current crime problem in many countries results from the purchase, sale and use of illegal drugs. Despite this agreed reality, the official rhetoric is that we must continue the same policies. Decriminalisation is often dismissed as totally unacceptable, and those who raise the subject accused of being addicts themselves. (As I am one who supports this alternative, I should therefore state that I have never used illegal drugs and, indeed, aim to avoid any form of medication where possible.)

The parallel with prohibition also goes largely unrecognised in the so-called War on Drugs discussion, but this was a relevant lesson. America's attempt to ban drinking via a constitutional amendment failed, and when prohibition was repealed – with liquor sales heavily regulated and taxed – over time there was a sharp decrease in the sales of hard liquor, and a movement towards less alcoholic drinks. Given the success of this strategy, why are we unwilling even to consider the same approach for currently illegal drugs? Both alcohol and illegal drugs alter human consciousness, with the costs of alcohol abuse estimated to be 10 times as high as those of drugs.

Indeed, if one broadens the picture and also looks at the issue of cigarette smoking, it becomes even more clouded. While damage figures are obviously dubious, smoking has been estimated to do 10 times as much damage as alcohol and 100 times as much as that of drugs, yet smoking is not only legal but tobacco growing is subsidised. As we look even further, we are forced to recognise that prescribed drugs are also routinely overused and abused – there is plenty of evidence of "respectable" people using both uppers and downers to control their moods – though this aspect of the drug issue is officially side-stepped.

There is no rational reason to treat various harmful but addictive substances so differently. It is time we faced the fact that they are all dangerous and damaging. I can understand why people try to prevent their children using drugs, but I remain shocked by the fact that some parents are willing to encourage their children to drink alcohol in order to keep them off illegal drugs. This was an accepted practice in many parts of Arizona when we were living there.

What would be the benefits of decriminalising drugs? One primary gain would be to eliminate the obscene profits which are the direct result of drug prohibition. Limiting supply through police control keeps prices and profits high and makes the drug business financially attractive. If drugs were decriminalised, fewer people would find it worthwhile to sell them, law enforcement would not be corrupted to the same extent, and whole countries would not be at risk of being governed by drug cartels. The profitability of attracting addicts would decrease.

Another gain would be the reduction of crime and the overload in the criminal system. The number of drug-related murders which is a significant proportion of the total in many areas, would fall dramatically because drug profits would be far lower. Decriminalising drugs would also reduce one of the primary dangers to civil liberties at the current time, as the fear of drugs encourages visible, and invisible, attacks on civil rights.

One of the most serious of these dangers comes from mandatory sentencing guidelines which leave no opportunity for judges to consider individual situations or circumstances. Judges should be able to consider all the circumstances of a case when sentencing – though relying on individual judgment is, of course, also inequitable, with some judges being "too strict" and others "too lenient". But the injustices which come from differing sentencing patterns by various judges are less serious than decisions made without looking at all the realities in a case, particularly when the penalties are excessively severe.

What would be the primary dangers of decriminalisation? It is usually argued that young people would be at still greater risk – a claim I consider nonsense. Just as alcohol and cigarette sales to minors are controlled, drug sales could be far more easily limited if decriminalised. Minors would actually be safer because the number of pushers would be significantly decreased by the lessening of profits. Some young people would, of course, continue to use drugs – but then tobacco and alcohol also continue to be used and abused among the young, despite our best efforts. Total control of harmful products is therefore obviously infeasible.

Would drug use among adults increase or decrease? There is no way of forecasting. The future would depend on whether a major societal effort was made to reduce the use of all drugs, including those currently illegal, as well as prescription drugs. The current campaign against illegal drug use loses much of its effectiveness because it does not seem logical. Why are drugs illegal and alcohol legal? Why is it acceptable for people to damage their functioning with prescription drugs, while marijuana is illegal? Why do we make a joke of Dad coming home drunk? Only a coherent message will help people, especially children, avoid addiction.

Decriminalising drugs will not be enough by itself, of course. The whole issue of drugs is bound up with the growth of the underclass in Western societies. A fundamental change is required in the way we support children from conception through their schooling years if the cycle of dependency and abuse is to be broken. You may believe that people would never stand for decriminalisation, but my (admittedly unscientific) polls have shown that there is already substantial support for this step, even if many "respectable" academic and political voices have not had the courage to speak out for it. I am convinced that if the public were officially polled on this issue, the results would be very surprising.

If you couple the stance that drug decriminalisation is wrong with a belief that you should prohibit smoking and the use of alcoholic beverages and control the abuse of prescription drugs, I have to admire your logic. I also have to dispute the practicality of your ideas. If you want to confine the ban to illegal drugs only, then it will be obvious by now that I do not understand your position.

If drugs were decriminalised, then we could apply the same sorts of controls to the sale of illegal drugs as we do to alcohol and to prescription drugs. Some people would get around the rules, as is always the case, but most people would work within the system that had been developed. Truly dangerous drugs could be placed on prescription, which is also the case for legal drugs. While there will still be abuse, it can be more easily limited once the high profit factor is removed.

During the nineties, there has been a significant shift in rhetorics and understandings around the drug issue. An open debate has been started in Australia about how to minimise the damage. It accepts that there are no ideal answers, and recognises that the problem will become even more difficult to handle as more powerful drugs develop. But it does face the fact that the current model has to change.

The drive to self-destruction has deeper roots than can be tapped by the criminal code. The need is for a more loving and caring society where children are given the chance to develop their potential. We need better parents, not more laws. We need more caring helpers, not more regulation. This is the real choice in the twenty-first century. Shall we commit to rebuilding a loving and caring society? Shall we recognise the rage that our current systems are creating in people at all levels of society? Shall we face what happens when middle-class children are given all the consumption goodies they want but are deprived of loving support to discover who they really are?

Addictions develop because we are not happy in our skins. The real cure to the drug problem can only come from a deep level of change that provides most people with a positive sense of themselves.

Birth control on request

I have so far dealt primarily with issues affecting the wealthier countries. The next two sections discuss global and Third World questions. The basic long-run threat to personal freedom throughout the world results from overpopulation; in a growing number of geographical areas, serious shortages of land, water and breathable air are inevitable. This is not a long-run extrapolation where unexpected developments may change the final outcome – it is a short-run certainty.

Before I start discussing this issue in any depth, I need to mention an issue which is all too often ignored when population statistics are developed. There are serious thinkers who believe that radical lengthening of lives is possible – some people even talk about immortality. Strangely, this is largely ignored by those who develop long-run population statistics despite the extraordinary potential implications.

There are two primary requirements for economic and political stability in the twenty-first century. One is that people in the wealthier countries stabilise, and eventually reduce, the amount of resources each of them considers as basic to a decent standard of living. Some population experts have come to see this reduction in consumption in the developed countries as the only critical issue. They argue that the degree of population pressure can be best determined by multiplying the number of people by the standard of living. It is indeed important to recognise the validity of this approach. All too often, people from the wealthier countries prefer to concentrate on the rapid increase in numbers as this appears to lessen their responsibility.

This approach nevertheless oversimplifies the population question. It is possible for the absolute numbers of people to be so large that they stress natural systems even if there is only a very low standard of living. This danger is already emerging in many of the poorer countries. There must therefore be a very rapid and substantial decline in birth rates. Fortunately there is plenty of evidence that there is an unsatisfied demand for effective birth control technologies in most of the developing countries. The need is not to create it but to satisfy it.

Reproductive rights are still perceived by many people as the most personal of all the freedoms, despite the fact that individual choices have enormous impact on societal issues. It is inevitable that once the state begins to control this aspect of life, it will intervene in many others. China has already been forced to restrict births dramatically as there is simply not enough land for the population to continue to expand. The country has therefore developed, and fairly successfully enforced, a policy of only permitting a family to have one child.

It is tempting to spend considerable time looking at the implications of such a policy for the long haul. What happens if there are only single children to support and nourish? There has been much talk of the "little princess syndrome", where young people are spoiled. What does this imply for, for example, China in the twenty-first century? How does one prevent infanticide of female children so that a male child, who is much more valued within the Chinese culture, can be born? What would be the implications of combining a single child policy with a growing capacity to determine the sex of children? Regardless of such fascinating issues and byways, we need to recognise that maintaining the policing structure required for the compulsory limitation of births will prevent the Chinese government from moving in the directions required for more responsible freedom. The level of coercion required to control births almost inevitably requires the maintenance of a police state.

If compulsory birth control is to be avoided in the future, then voluntary contraception must be encouraged now. A total and immediate global cultural commitment should be made to ensure that anybody who wants to prevent conception has the information, the means and, if necessary, the financial support to do so. The mechanisms chosen for this purpose should be appropriate to the culture, and the value judgments of other societies and religions should not be permitted to impinge on such choices. If birth rates are not reduced soon, death rates will rise again dramatically through famine, plague, infanticide and warfare. Indeed, this pattern has already started to develop: the latest United Nations population projections reflect the rise in death rates which is developing in Africa, as well as in the countries which were part of the Soviet Union.

Why has the subject of high birth rates failed to be placed at the top of the world agenda? Many have hoped that birth-rates in the poor countries will fall without government intervention. They have based their beliefs on a parallel with the experiences of First World countries. As standards of living rose in the Western world, many families chose to have less children; the belief was that a similar pattern would develop in the poorer countries. In many nations this pattern has indeed occurred but it is not developing rapidly enough to resolve the problems that are already emerging.

What are the fundamental causes of high birth rates? They are in part traditional: children are evidence of male potency and female fertility, both of which are highly valued in traditional cultures. These attitudes change slowly, of course. While many women would be delighted to decrease their number of births, men are often unwilling to accept such a change in values.

Another critical factor is that children in traditional societies are the primary method of providing social security to the old; young people are the (presumed) guarantee that parents will not be in want. The United Nations, particularly UNICEF, now hopes that parents will come to believe that the first two or three children will live long enough to support them in their old age, therefore leading to a willingness to cut back on the desired size of families. While this approach could be effective if people do believe the argument, the AIDS epidemic will inevitably make it far more difficult to convince parents that their children will survive.

There is a final issue that still confuses discussions. Power was based on numbers in the past, for people provided "cannon fodder". In today's world, numbers still translate into clout at the ballot box, and these factors still lead some leaders of minority and ethnic groups, as well as countries, to fear a low birth rate and to support pro-natal policies. A 1980's book by Ben Wattenburg, deploring the "birth dearth" in the United States, received an enormous amount of attention for these reasons. Similarly, several European countries have developed pro-natalist policies. The desirable long-run figure for Australia is also highly controversial.

The danger in the future is overcrowding. In almost all areas of the world today, increases in population implies a decrease in the quality of life.

The need to limit births as effectively as possible raises several critical issues. First, experience shows that female birth-control risks significant side-effects for many women, whether the intervention is chemical or invasive. In light of this reality, it is highly unfortunate that modern birth control technology has been biased towards controlling the female capacity to conceive rather than limiting male capacity to inseminate. I am convinced that the primary reason for this bias is that most birth control researchers have been male and that most men are still terrified of any form of intervention that might negatively affect their potency.

This pattern is fortunately already changing. The number of vasectomies that have taken place shows that men are willing to take risks with their own reproductive systems to enable secure, effective birth-control. It would, however, be highly desirable to develop long-run chemical inhibitors of the fertility of sperm which had no impact on sexual desire or potency, and without the largely irreversible character of vasectomies. There has already been progress along this line and it is highly probable it could be accelerated.

Rapid progress in any birth control technology is however unlikely at the current time because of a second central problem. As there can never be totally safe interventions in the human body, many pharmaceutical companies, particularly in the United States, are not willing to risk being sued in the inevitable cases where something goes wrong. Even where effective research is going on, such as in France (where a substance has been developed which acts immediately after conception to prevent the development of a viable foetus), United States companies have been slow to take the risk of making it available in America. The legal system has to be changed if the necessary rapid development of birth control technologies is to take place.

Current legal liability patterns raise an extraordinary issue. Cigarette and alcohol companies can sell a product, which is agreed to be dangerous, and the law courts have so far usually held that they are not liable for damages. (As this book is written, there are signs that juries are changing their stance.) Similarly, suits are now being brought against gun companies for selling unsafe products. It is still, however, easier to win suits when birth control technologies, which are designed to meet a major need, fail. The argument appears to be that because cigarette companies label their products as dangerous, they are exempt from legal liability. Does this mean that it is enough to label prominently all the possible dangers from a product? For example, if packets of birth-control pills were covered with similar large-print warnings from the relevant health authority, would such a move exempt birth control technologies from legal liability?

The third problem is even trickier: What can be done to shift the official views of many religious groups – eg. Catholic and Muslim – on birth control? What will it take to get the hierarchy of churches to understand that their concern for the preservation of the foetus in under-developed, over-crowded countries increases levels of suffering and death? How can caring people encourage births in countries where the death rates of infants and children are already so high?

I see policies which prevent birth control as a classic case of developing rules for a particular time and forcing their continuance long after they have become totally inappropriate. In a world where life was short and infant mortality was high, it made sense for families to be large, even at great risk to the mother's life. This goal started as a secular imperative which eventually, and perhaps inevitably, came to be stated in religious terms. To buttress this view in today's radically new circumstances, and even to reinforce it, is tragic and unacceptable.

Support for the Catholic position is the belief that the soul comes into existence at the moment of conception. It is argued that from the moment that the sperm and the egg join, a different quality of life exists. It is difficult for most outsiders to understand this stance – indeed, many Catholics in the United States have already rejected church doctrine in the area of sexuality. Unfortunately, most of them seem content to restrict their thinking to local situations without accepting their responsibility to support people in other parts of the world where old doctrines continue to be enforced.

In an American context, the resistance of the Catholic Church to changes in sexual mores and patterns cannot be discussed without also challenging the policies of the government. Many attempts to limit births in the poorer countries have been sabotaged by the United States insistence that no support be provided for abortions. It is surely the height of arrogance to force nations to base their policies on the biases of some Americans. The unwillingness to accord validity to the behaviour patterns of other cultures is one of the primary factors which leads to such cynicism about the openness of the United States to a pluralistic world order.

People have been struggling to draw public attention to the problems caused by rapid population growth ever since World War II, but this issue has never managed to get the attention it so urgently deserves. Continued rapid population growth will certainly destroy any potential for resolving the crises of our time. This issue has to be moved off the back burner and made central. The population bomb may not be as immediately dramatic as environmental concerns – there are certainly deeper and higher emotional barriers to facing its dangers. Nevertheless, the long-run consequences of population growth at current levels will inevitably be disastrous, both to human freedom and ecological balance.

Urban-rural balance

What settlement patterns will be most appropriate to provide a high quality of life to current and foreseeable populations? The answers to this question are complex. Relatively few people realise that the largest cities in the world are no longer in the developed world but in the poorer countries. Migration to cities occurs for a number of reasons – many of them essentially uncontrollable. The first was well expressed in an old popular song from the World War I: "How are you going to keep them down on the farm after they've seen Paree?"

The bright lights are attractive to young and ambitious people and they can seem far more exciting than rural life. Knowledge of the bright lights is of course far more pervasive than it used to be: it is spread by television, where satellite broadcasts bring glitz and glitter into the slums of the Third World. The flickering light of a television set is now one of the constants wherever electricity is available.

The realities of the big cities have, of course, often been a disappointment to those who go there with exaggerated hopes. (The streets of New York are not paved with gold, and the unhappy aspiring film star who moves to Los Angeles is still a staple literary and movie plot.) Conditions in the large cities of the poorer countries today are infinitely worse than most people who live in the developed world can imagine: polluted water, food scavenged from garbage dumps, disease, high infant mortality, violence and living as squatters are all part of the basic conditions for many urban dwellers in these countries. The recent Asian meltdown has greatly increased the numbers of people living in extreme poverty: the World Bank estimates the growth at 100 million.

Why then does migration to urban areas continue? There is a well-known tendency among migrants to exaggerate the benefits and to minimise the costs of any move they make; they are thought to do this partly to bolster their own self-image and partly to look good to those they left behind. The consequence, however, is that people in the rural areas gain a far more positive picture of the benefits of moving to cities than is warranted by the facts. Migration is also supported because relatives who have already moved into the city are expected to give support to others who come later.

How can the balance of advantage be shifted? It would help if a fairer picture of the advantages and disadvantages of city life was available and there has, in fact, been a little progress in this direction since the glitter days of the eighties faded. Most communicators nevertheless see the city as exciting and the rural areas as lacking amenities. This attitude inevitably affects habitation patterns and will continue to encourage movement to the cities until it changes.

So long as areas outside the cities concentrate on their deficits, people will continue to leave smaller communities. There is today a growing emphasis on the positive advantages of living in small towns and villages. When this happens, people start to look at the balance of advantages and disadvantages of the two lifestyles, rather than seeing only what is missing in rural situations. A recent trip to Bridgetown in Western Australia confirmed that this type of positive thinking was developing rapidly.

It is important to recognise, however, that part of the perception which causes people to move to the city is based on a bedrock of reality. Duncan Goheen, who has done a great deal of work in the Philippines, made this point well in a letter to me.

> I interviewed migrants who moved from the countryside into Manila. I asked them why they traded fresh air and open space for the squalor and seemingly unbearable conditions of street living in Manila. Their answer was that when the rice bowl is empty, it's empty. Starvation is at the door. In the city, there is always a way to earn a few pesos. A few pesos a day will put enough rice on the table to ward off starvation.

There are several very substantial steps which could be taken to cut down on migration from rural areas. First, governmental policies still tend to advantage city-dwellers over those in rural areas, often by providing cheap food and petrol to reduce the prospect of riots. Mexico City, despite its overwhelming problems, still provides incentives for people to move there. There needs to be a rigorous re-examination of all current policies to equalise conditions, or maybe even to advantage the rural areas.

The second step is to look at how rural life can be made more attractive and more exciting. The potential of video and computers to change the balance is very great. Far more attention should be paid to wiring rural areas with telecommunications and electricity than to improving transportation, which demands non-replaceable oil products. There should also be a major effort to teach people via audio and video, rather than by insisting that information be primarily gained through reading. The Yavapai Apache describe their library as primarily designed to support "paper-reading"; they recognise that there are other forms of communication such as sand paintings, rugs, dances and conversation.

One primary challenge of the twenty-first century is to make rural life more attractive throughout the world. This will be achieved in part as people come to see the costs as well as the advantages of city living. More importantly, with the true coming of telecommunications, people will be just as much in touch when they live in a rural area as in the cities. To realise this potential, however, the current gap between the number of computers in the United States, as compared to the rest of the world, will have to be closed.

The recovery of rural life also depends on a profound shift in economic thinking. The economies of the poorer countries will be damaged so long as food aid is sent to them on a continuing basis. (Famine relief in times of natural disaster is, of course, a totally different matter.) The availability of cheap food from other countries destroys the viability of the rural areas, making it impossible for communities in the countryside to sell their goods at reasonable prices or maintain social cohesion. The agricultural areas of the poorer countries need to be strengthened rather than undermined.

Raising the economic issue leads, of course, into some of the trickiest questions of all. There is a need for land reform to support peasant farming in many countries, and the future seems to lie with locally controlled development initiatives that are labour intensive, Aid should be given out in small amounts that support small-scale activity. A number of approaches have already been created to hand out micro-loans: the default rate is unbelievably low. The current "ideal" model which provides all types of food all over the world regardless of the seasons, is being challenged as people recognise the costs of global transportation.

Twentieth-century development models have failed. There has been a significant decline in living standards in many poorer countries over the last two decades. There are several reasons for current trends. One is that the poorer countries are facing heavy interest costs on their past borrowings – in many cases, they are actually paying out more in interest than they are receiving in new loans. In effect, the wealthier countries are today receiving money from the poorer countries rather than sending it to them. The wealthier countries have agreed to forgive some debts in some of the poorest countries, but unless patterns are changed, this will only provide a short-run benefit.

A second reason for the worsening conditions in the poorer countries is that they are often paying more for their imports and getting less for their exports. A growing number of specialists in Third-World issues believe that the continuing integration of the poorer countries into the world production and trade net is worsening their situation rather than improving it. They are challenging the belief that freer trade will benefit the developing world.

We can no longer base our planning on the belief that people around the world can reach developed-country standards of living. Until now, world development theory has been driven by the belief that every area could eventually come to enjoy the wealth currently available in Europe, Japan, North America and Australia. The fact that very few of the poorer countries were actually moving in this direction was largely ignored. Similarly, disadvantaged people within the wealthier countries assumed that their children, or at least their grandchildren, could eventually be rich. We have to recognise at this time the ecological limitations which will prevent rapid worldwide economic growth.

So long as we could hope for an endless increase in income and wealth, gaps between the rich and the poor seemed acceptable, whether within or between countries. There was always the hope that you, or somebody you knew, would get to the top. Today the recognition of limits makes great differentials in wealth increasingly unacceptable. Energy and ecological restraints have transformed the debate around income distribution. In the future, we shall have to accept "enoughness" rather than struggle for an ever-rising standard of living.

Choices

What then are the options for the future? The first is to hope that the gap between rich and poor can persist for an unlimited amount of time into the future without causing unbearable tensions and violence. The second is to assume that the violence between the rich and poor will become increasingly dangerous because the gap between rich and poor persists and the deprived are no longer willing to tolerate it. The third is to develop directions so that the gap between rich and poor begins to close.

The first scenario may initially seem the most probable. The tragedy of poverty has continued, and even deepened, in the second half of the twentieth century. Despite many efforts and much frustration, the poorer nations have failed to develop effective mechanisms to challenge the socioeconomic structures which tend to advantage the wealthy.

The harsh fact, however, is that the steady increase in population in most parts of the world is bringing more and more areas to the brink of crisis. There is great anger in those countries where standards of living are not rising, particularly among those who have suffered because of the Asian meltdown. In the wealthier countries, there is increasing rage and violence among the poor. This is still largely directed at people who also live within poorer communities, with those outside them being relatively safe. The failure of the educational system to provide real opportunities to the underclass, however, could see a rapid worsening of the situation. Violence may then move outside the poverty areas and affect the middle-class and the wealthy to such an extent that their quality of life declines precipitously.

People might have put up with misery if they were still isolated and unaware of alternatives. But today the gap between the standards of living of the richer and poorer countries, and the rich and the poor citizens within countries, is broadly known. Indeed, people living in slums in many countries of Latin America can receive Western television programs which inevitably create envy. Frustration is increased because those who watch in the poorer countries think that the standards shown in these programs represent the norm in the richer nations. The viewers do not know that they reflect the patterns of a tiny group of people engaged in conspicuous consumption.

Each of us has a choice. We can support the process of creating a just society and increase our own chances of having a reasonable quality of life. Or we can watch current trends continue and condemn ourselves and our children to patterns of breakdown which we cannot even imagine.

Chapter 9

Rebuilding Communities

Communities are healthy when leaders grasp opportunities as they become available and tackle problems before they become crises. Each of us need to be a leader in this sense, sharing the responsibility to help shape the future.

Effective community is dynamic and even, at times, chaotic. Much disagreement and conflict take place in functioning communities while order exists below the surface. People are willing to make decisions based on the overall interests of those involved, understanding that although their perceptions will necessarily differ from those of others, this does not prevent them from seeking common ground. They work to achieve their perceived self-interest, but define it in very broad terms.

The conventional image of the way to manage cultural affairs in the United States has been a melting pot. It was believed that all differences between cultures should be submerged and a single pattern developed, as this was the only way to bring together the immense range of traditions of America's overwhelming flood of immigrants.

While melting pot models have been a major theme of American thinkers, they were always more image than reality. Today, ethnic groups are increasingly unwilling to submerge their past histories and cultures into a dull uniformity. Each group wants to draw on its traditions for sustenance in the rapids of change, and if they do not already have their own traditions, they create patterns which distinguish them.

Throughout the world multi-racial and multi-ethnic cultures are emerging, and we therefore need to move beyond the melting pot image. My favourite replacement is a tapestry: the

210

colours of each of the wools is unique, and together they produce a picture. Suggesting that the colours of the wools be toned down is neither wise nor desirable. The various strands should be used where they will add rather than subtract from the overall design. An effective community will honour and enjoy the many traditions of the individuals and families within it, and in return, will ask everybody to support the larger whole.

The compassionate era is based on the belief that security comes from mutual understanding, support and partnerships. The basic step we must all take is to learn to enjoy diversity and to live within pluralistic systems. Strong people are fascinated by differences and realise that they can learn from others who do not share the same world-view. Only as we change our images of leaders can communities flourish.

People need to find differences fascinating rather than frightening. Many of us are still afraid of others who are different because of their cultures or the colour of their skins, and as we move towards learning societies we shall recognise that we can benefit most from people who see the world in significantly different ways.

In the future, we must not only cope with different sexes, ages and races, but we must also cease to marginalise the disabled by seeing them as totally different. All of us are handicapped in that we have areas where we are incompetent. I have, for example, no spatial sense. We need to recognise that those we single out as handicapped have specific areas where they do not function well, such as their hearing or sight, but they can more than compensate for these limitations by their other strengths.

What tasks will vibrant, resilient communities undertake? They must support and guide children as they grow, provide educational opportunities throughout life, and honour their ageing members. Communities must provide economic opportunities, help people to maintain their health and ensure protection for their members. Communities must prevent violence and provide social justice – and communities must be fun.

Communities have many faces and each member will see his or her community somewhat differently. They are also complex

211

and ever-changing, and – because their members inevitably have their own unique quirks and patterns – can never be utopian.

This chapter is primarily centred on communities in a geographical context, but the word also has a broader meaning and many of the ideas presented here can be extended to cover other patterns. Work and professional groups, social service organisations, churches, bioregions and people with the same hobbies can all be called communities; the concept is, in many ways, a state of mind. It can be found on the Internet as well as in person. It exists whenever people are committed to each other and willing to work to achieve desirable goals. Effective communities require people to be open and honest with each other rather than hiding their motives and commitments.

We must not confuse family and community. Most families are small enough that people feel a profound and immediate sense of commitment to each other and have deep empathy for the joys and sorrows of those within their family. While community can also be built on personal relationships, the larger number of people involved makes having the same depth of feeling impossible. We will not feel the same about friends as we do about our spouses, partners, parents or children, because our lives would be an unmanageable roller coaster.

Deciding whether a group of people should aim to relate as a family or a community is one of the crucial decisions in human relationships. Some firms and organisations call themselves "families"; determining whether this is an appropriate image for them is very important to their eventual success or failure. I challenged one organisation in this area recently. A number of its members found it freeing to be permitted to break out of the family metaphor because they felt the required "togetherness" was phoney.

Community cannot be achieved once and for all – it requires continuing effort. Like all human patterns, community tends to break down over time unless it is nurtured. The sense of community has been weak in the second half of the twentieth century because of the consumption emphasis of the culture and general overload.

I have devoted a great deal of time and energy to this issue in the last couple of years. Using the phrase "resilient communities", several colleagues and I have worked in a number of ways to help people understand how brittle our systems have become and how dangerous this conditions is as we move through the rapids of change. We have recognised that our lack of time and space, due to our severe overloads, is one of our primary problems at the current time.

The pressure to cooperate

The most visible challenge today is maintaining and restructuring relationships between the diverse groups of communities. The need to keep up with the pace of change makes this continuing task more difficult. Old assumptions and ties are being shattered, and all too often new ones are not replacing them because of the lack of trust between groups and organisations. People and groups feel abandoned; they believe their contributions are being ignored or dishonoured. Walls of mistrust increasingly divide communities.

Mistrust between groups is dangerous at any time. It is particularly destructive at the current time because communities are facing ever-growing pressures to economise resources. They will only be able to provide even basic services if they deliver them in the most cost-effective way. Fortunately, potentials for major savings do exist, one approach being to eliminate duplication between programs. In most larger communities, several organisations deliver similar services with little or no coordination (this is particularly true with addiction-related services). As our commitment to boundaries between communities and organisations decays, the wastefulness of this pattern becomes more obvious but we still do not have many skills in creating the collaborations which will lead to higher levels of effectiveness.

Too many municipalities and overlapping service districts hamper the effective delivery of services. Rearranging boundaries is not enough, however, because they themselves are becoming "fuzzy". The industrial-era belief that each area and activity was separate is being subverted by the growing knowledge that everything is related. There is growing recognition that this poses an acute challenge because all our current institutions grew within a world-view which emphasised difference rather than similarities.

I have been talking to state and federal agencies which recognise that the "silo" approach to decision-making is no longer effective. I have been working with universities which recognise that disciplinary boundaries are obsolete. But while there is a growing recognition of the importance and severity of the problem, little progress has so far been made in taking effective practical steps.

Another reason for high costs and waste is that many facilities are idle much of the time. For example, churches intensively use a large proportion of their buildings only once a week, and most office buildings are empty on the weekends. Greater collaboration would make it possible to use existing buildings more effectively, so additional structures would be unnecessary.

We shall also change the way we organise our calendars. Major shifts are already taking place in the US as children move to year-round schooling and the summer vacation ceases to control scheduling. Education is being provided at the times when people can take advantage of it and when they find they learn best.

Even the weekend may be abandoned in the twenty-first century. Work facilities would then no longer be used intensively for five days while recreation facilities have light loads with the opposite pattern holding true at the weekend. We will still need times of rest, but they would be staggered – indeed, as one looks at the reality of our societies, rather than their formal structures, far more moves have taken place in this direction than we normally recognise. Retailing is already a seven-day-a-week operation and a growing number of meetings happen on weekends to take advantage of the cheap fares airlines provide if the passenger stays over a Saturday.

Given the overloads that people feel at the current time, many wish that we could go back to the time when the culture dictated the need to stop and rest, for example on Sunday or the Sabbath. I do not think that such a reversal of trends is likely, or desirable. Each of us is being challenged to find ways to make sense of our own lives in our own ways. Each of us will need to make decisions about how to find rest and leisure in our lives rather than having our patterns dictated by the culture.

Even when the potentials for reducing resource use are highly visible, individuals and groups are often still unwilling to collaborate. Many people prefer to control their own organisation rather than work with others. Human survival requires that each of us learns to move towards collaboration, recognising the barriers our attitudes and organisational structures create. Even with the best of good will, collaboration is difficult, and particularly so among private, public and non-profit organisations.

A first step to break through the barriers is to help individuals and groups communicate openly. The typical community is divided into cliques that distrust, and even fear, others. Few "safe and open spaces" exist where people can say what they believe without fear that it will affect them personally or damage their careers. I continue to be amazed in my consulting work as I watch people argue with each other although they are really agreeing. I have taken to responding to many critical comments about something I have said by asking whether we are actually making the same point.

We can use many models to encourage communication. I have worked as a consultant for a year in the River Bend area of Illinois, which contains 10 industrial communities just north of the Mississippi River from St Louis. People were challenged to work together to create a better future, and an intelligently developed program broke down barriers and led to more creative decision making. One of the most exciting aspects of the project was watching an evolution in relationships: people started off "knowing" that their own position was right and those of all others were wrong, but as the year progressed, there emerged far greater respect for, and understanding of, the views and positions of others.

People began to recognise they were seeing different realities and, for this reason, supporting different goals. This sense of diversity evolved from two strategies. First, we encouraged everybody to listen to the views of others. Second, we placed the clash between visions in the context of the nineties and the twenty-first century, making the distinction between dying and emerging systems as clear as possible. Over time, people came to see that continuing to support past success criteria was impossible. All those involved came to see new directions as essential.

Supporting greater openness was not, of course, easy. Two steps were taken. One was to bring new ideas in from the outside, and creative and dynamic speakers were invited, while the most exciting and forward-looking materials in book, audio and video form were recommended and made available in libraries. The effect of this approach was limited, however, as most people do not integrate new ideas rapidly – they continue to work with their existing models despite challenging input.

We therefore encouraged local people to surface thoughts and ideas normally considered too controversial or too far-out for discussion. Other participants then began to broaden the scope of discussions and to transform the nature of possible solutions. We used a number of techniques to encourage movement in this direction. One of the most useful was to help people see that ideas they hesitated to talk about because they considered them "far-out" were, in fact, credible. As people realised they were not alone in their views, they were more willing to talk honestly about what they really wanted.

One of the more interesting River Bend groups brought together several of the business people in the community with those in charge of school systems. Initially, the business people were sure that easy ways to economise must exist, and were shaken when they discovered that the educators had already taken the most obvious steps and that few easy options remained. At the end of the first year, the members of the group had made significant progress in setting up a continuing dialogue. Many other River Bend groups developed similar patterns.

Lately I have worked with a large number of Australian groups. The models which we introduced slowly and painstakingly into the River Bend context were already broadly understood in many of the communities in which I have been involved. People are aware that the success criteria of the twentieth century cannot be continued into the twenty-first. There is a recognition of the need for profound, systemic change.

Paradoxically, an increase in cooperation within and between communities can also lead to problems. Too many "coordinating" groups may spring up, each feeling it has the right, and possibly the power, to make decisions. I first saw this problem clearly when I was working in Spokane. A relatively small number of people met in a large number of different organisational settings, with each group developing ideas without considering the impact on others. To illuminate the reality of this situation for them, I created the image of a number of trains in a station, with people moving from one stationary train to another, yet never managing to get any of the trains moving out of the station.

My first instinct to resolve this problem was that an effort should be made to create a single coordinating group to make decisions. As I thought further, it became clear that this approach was not going to work. Each organising group saw itself as critically important and was therefore unwilling to subordinate itself to others. Indeed, a significant number of groups felt they should have primary control.

The political system was naturally led by the city council and believed that it should make the basic decisions. The business community looked to a new organisation called Momentum. Other groups in the non-profit sector also tried to influence directions, particularly through the Community Foundation. I therefore decided that the only way to achieve progress would be to develop far higher levels of communication between the various groups.

This type of activity requires a new type of networking which has an "empty centre". People in this empty centre aim to connect those who they feel are working in similar areas. They then encourage deep connections to be made between these people so they can gain the ability to see potential synergies. The essential challenge is to bridge different styles and images so as to see the core agreements.

Teilard de Chardin, the great Christian theologian, wrote about the potential of this sort of work. He saw it as connecting those people and groups who were ready to cooperate creatively; he called the result the "noosphere". The increasingly dense communication patterns which are emerging around the world among non-profit organisations are a part of what he envisioned.

New decision-making structures

Communities will only be effective if they accept the responsibility for dealing with tough issues. A primary reason why so much power moved to the national level in the twentieth century was that many critical questions were allowed to fester. Only central governments had the courage to make tough choices in the forties, fifties and sixties. Today this pattern is being reversed. Imagination is most visible at the local, and sometimes at the state, level.

The power which has been progressively concentrated at the nation-state level during the twentieth century must now be diffused. I am well aware that moving in this direction requires a reversal of trends. The risk in providing communities with freedom to make their own decisions is, however, less than that which exists when a centralised system is asked to come up with answers to cover a wide range of different realities.

The mark of the well-informed citizen in the past has been an understanding of world affairs. Today we need to spend more time learning about our own communities because this is the level at which we can make a difference. Positive movement in communities depends on the willingness of government, business and non-profit leaders to commit their energies to their local situations. The way that the global imperatives of social cohesion, ecological integrity and effective decision making can be achieved will vary throughout the world.

There has been a downward spiral in relationships between leader and led in recent years. The reciprocal obligation between the person in office and the citizen has been broken, with fewer and fewer good people running for office because they find the political process demeaning. Citizens see no reason to support their elected officials because they detect no signs of courage or commitment. My favourite story, which may not be true but certainly makes the point, concerns a mayor who had been begged to run for office. She eventually succumbed to pressure, was elected, and the day after she won, was asked why she was on the take!

In most communities, the vicious circle is still worsening. But there are places where significant efforts are being made to bring people back to a sense of responsibility for their own future. The common factor behind the successful efforts is a commitment to discussion and dialogue. A friend of mine recently told me that he was going to vote for an "honest" political candidate with whom he disagreed but where there was the potential for conversation. He decided at the same time to oppose a person who was grandstanding on an issue in which he believed. He was completely convinced that progress could only be made if dialogue developed.

Our most basic challenge is to recognise the common humanity of each person. We must learn to judge not by age or sex or race but to listen to what people really say and think. We must commit to supporting those who are willing to stand for office because they desire the good of the community rather than because they want power or position for themselves.

My vision of the future is that more and more worthy candidates will agree to accept office despite the strains it creates for them. I am convinced that most people at the local level should serve for only one term, or at a maximum, two. Fresh blood is of enormous benefit. But I do not want to make this a rule, because the greater the number of rules, the lower the flexibility in the culture. Rather I would hope that both candidates and voters would be aware of the advantages of turnover.

Leadership does not, of course, only come from government. The patterns of the United Way, the Chamber of Commerce, the churches and other key non-profit organisations do as much to determine the style of a community as its formal political structure. The commitment of top management in business is also critically important. There are severe problems at many of these levels, and one of the trends which has been discussed far too little is the breakdown of locally-based leadership.

As firms and banks are bought by out-of-town organisations and conglomerates, their management becomes part of a revolving door. It is increasingly rare that anybody stays in a community long enough to develop strong local ties. Corporate leadership, which was one of the primary resources of communities, is therefore increasingly denied to them; similarly, leadership of key non-profit organisations is often also recruited from out-of-town. It seems unlikely that there will be any short-run reversal of these patterns. The only hope is that organisations will begin to inform managers that a significant part of their evaluation will be based on involvement in their local situations.

The tendency for corporate control to be located outside local communities makes it increasingly difficult to raise money. A colleague who works in Edmonton in Canada exemplified this reality with a tale about a local grocery executive, who was very willing to give $50 towards a children's picnic being organised by a local charity – while a very large chain with major sales in the area, but with its head office in Calgary, sent only $20. Even when firms outside the community do give generously, bureaucratic requirements are almost inevitably more extensive and time-consuming.

One of the extraordinary trends of the last few years has been the growing ability of Internet communities to affect political dynamics. Those who can find a resonant issue, and have the skills to link the players creatively, can create a far larger impact than the numbers of people involved would warrant. There have been two extraordinary examples of this trend recently. One of them was the effective opposition to the Multilateral Agreement on Investment. The other is the ongoing opposition to genetic manipulation.

Internal self-sufficiency

The industrial era developed a very strong bias towards central control of economic decision-making, with control of directions exercised by the power to tax. About 35 per cent of income, or more, is taxed in one way or another, and this heavy tax load makes it far more difficult for people to find the resources to support their local communities. Reducing the central tax bite, as proposed in Chapter 5, would make it possible for people to give more and also permit local taxation to be heavier so local needs could be met.

Communities have very limited powers to stop an unwanted industry or business from moving into their area. For example, even if the building of a large chainstore in a small town will probably result in the bankruptcy of many local merchants, these disadvantages cannot be used as a justification for refusing entry. Some control can be exercised through planning and zoning but this is a blunt tool for those interested in the long-run viability of a community.

Certain steps can nevertheless be taken to promote local enterprise. The first is to support existing merchants by providing better information to citizens and businesses about the types of goods and services which are available locally. People will then be more likely to buy within the community rather than from outside, keeping resources within the community, supporting its autonomy and helping to reduce the costs of transportation. In addition, a strong, supportive local community may also make a major difference when a firm considers moving to a location with cheaper labour or other apparent advantages.

In addition, resources could be saved if the failure rate of new businesses could be reduced. The general estimate is that four out of five new businesses fail in the first five years, with consequent loss to the owners and to the local economy. There is an urgent need to set up effective advice systems which would discourage people from going into business when they do not have the necessary skills and capital. Marginal entrepreneurs can be provided with the information and knowledge they need to have a better chance. Incubators, which provide more intensive support for new businesses, are also an effective tool in increasing viability.

If communities are to make more decisions for themselves, they must be able to insulate themselves to some degree from national and world dynamics. Unfortunately, the tendency in recent decades has been to integrate communities more and more closely. This is another of the trends which needs to be reversed as Western society emerges from the eye of the hurricane.

The dangers which emerge from the collapse of large interlinked systems, as has been seen in the Asian economic meltdown, are much greater than those which result from small local breakdowns. The real issue is whether we should aim to produce structures which "cannot fail" or systems which are resilient when they do "inevitably" fail. Industrial-era structures have been based on the belief that human beings are bright enough to prevent breakdowns. Today everybody is aware that this is all too often untrue. Much of the debate on Y2K has been around the dangers of our ever more complex technological web, which very few understand.

Local currencies

Banks and banking are usually seen as purely economic concerns. In fact, the decisions made in this area at the time of the American Revolution are one of the primary factors which have led to centralisation of US society. Any attempt to get back to community-based decision-making is impossible until there is a change in the structure of banking. In a speech entitled "The Need for National Currencies", Robert Swann made the argument for a return to a decentralised system. He stated:

One of the major arguments against "free banking" in the 18th century, indeed the one that persists today, is that the many small local banks which issued their own money sometimes failed and this hurt many of their small depositors. Some of these banks truly were run by scoundrels who created money for non-productive purposes such as helping their friends buy land for speculation. The feeling was that such abuses could be controlled if money were issued centrally.

But decentralisation and diversity have the benefit of preventing large-scale failure. This is as true in banking as it is in the natural world... Today we are facing the failure of the entire system. When third world countries default on their debts which, in fact, they are already doing – even if it's not called default – billions more will be added to the national debt in order to bail out big banks.

There is a way out of the centralised control imposed by current banking systems. Community financial autonomy can be increased by creating a supplementary local currency. When communities are depressed, and there is open or hidden unemployment, people would be willing to produce additional goods and services which others would buy if the money were there to facilitate exchange.

If banks cannot lend enough, what about the possibility of developing a type of money which could only be used for local interchanges? People might then be willing to sell their goods and services for a mix of monies, part of which would be national currency and part only good in the immediate area.

Let's consider some simple examples. Assume a shop sells shoes. Some of the costs come from buying the shoes and this will usually have to be paid to merchants outside the community. Some of the costs will, on the other hand, result from local activities. Rent and electricity may be paid to nearby companies. Wages will certainly be due to local employees. The shoe seller might therefore put a price on the shoes which would be 75 per cent in national currency and 25 per cent in local "money". At the other extreme, one might imagine somebody who produces crafts which almost all the costs are incurred locally. Seventy-five per cent might then be accepted in local currency and only 25 per cent in national.

Once a local currency became established and had a wide range of uses, people might be willing to increase their percentages of local currency if they knew it was widely accepted within the community. It is also obvious that the larger the size of the community in which the currency circulates, the greater the percentage of local exchanges and the higher the percentage of local money which might circulate. On the other hand, the trust required to support a local currency requires a relatively small community.

It is easy to see the implications of this model for shopping patterns. At the current time, people tend to shop in the larger towns because the price is lower. If, however, the actual federal dollar cost were lower in the small community, the pattern of advantage is changed. People might then shop within their community rather than elsewhere.

Local currencies have functioned successfully in recent years. Sophisticated computer-based bartering systems, often called LETS (Local Employment and Trade System) systems, have also been developed. There is significant evidence that they can enhance the amount of interchange in a community permitting people to use their time productively instead of being forced into idleness. Many Australian communities are using variants of this approach.

Money is, however, extremely tricky stuff. Long ago, Gresham discovered that bad money drives out good. Watching the "exchange rates" between local and national currencies would be a constant struggle. It would be all too easy to set up local systems in ways which caused demand to exceed supply and thus devalue the local currency.

Models

Many of today's community problems stem from the fact that there are not enough leaders for all the tasks that need to be done. When older leaders get tired, younger leaders do not necessarily emerge to take their place. While there are fortunately a growing number of leadership programs, all too often they teach the skills of the current generation of leaders rather than inspiring servant leadership styles which are necessary for periods of fundamental change.

I have been encouraged by the shift I have seen in leadership programs in recent years. There is a growing recognition that there has to be a change in directions and that leaders must be part of this change. One of the more interesting programs has been set up by the Sydney Benevolent Society. It brings together people who have the ability to affect dynamics and helps them to see the underlying questions.

How can communities learn to work together more effectively? There are three basic requirements which must be met under all circumstances. The way they are actually developed will depend upon the pattern of support available in each community.

The first is to ensure that people become more aware of the changes which are taking place in the world so they will be ready to move in new directions rather than trying to solve problems using old information and techniques. There is a need to go further and to move from a problem orientation to concentrating on emerging opportunities.

The second requirement is to get existing and emerging leaders from various groups to talk and work together. This statement has two implications: all the existing and emerging leadership must be encouraged to be involved, and it should be recognised that not everybody will be ready to be leaders. It is essential to start with those who are most committed rather than try to move a whole community or organisation at once.

The third normally required element is to have a neutral player in the system. A great deal of distrust exists in most communities and breaking through it requires high levels of skills. It is always challenging and exciting to play this role because there are no rules: one must always look for the specific steps which are appropriate at a particular time.

One of the most exciting community projects I ever observed developed in Pasadena, California. Husband and wife, Denise and John Wood, decided that they could improve conditions if they were willing to serve as neutral observers in the sense I have described above. Their commitment to this style over a period of about a decade changed the climate in the city. A large amount of the decision-making in the community came to use this approach. The Woods have now left the city but the process has been institutionalised within the Episcopal church, concentrating particularly on health care for young at-risk kids and drug issues.

The Woods suggest 10 points which they describe as a mindset to help anybody come to grips with the needs of a city.

- Hold to the expectancy and the determination that you and others can make a difference in your community.
- Study the city by listening to its people one-by-one to gain a living picture of the city's needs, strengths and possibilities.
- Reveal the city to itself – the pain, the facts, the hopes, the moral imperatives you have learned – not in name-calling and blaming but neither in watering down the truth.
- Think and speak for the whole city.
- Bring people together, not in confrontation but in trust, to tackle the city's most urgent needs.
- Build on the agencies and the people who are already at grips with a given issue and, where need be, encourage new initiatives and conditions.
- Take care of the care-givers of your community so they know they are not alone and can receive the citizens' support they need.
- Aim to build lasting relationships.
- Know there is more power in appealing to the very best in people rather than the worst.

•   Persist when everything seems to fall apart, be conscious that it takes patience, perseverance, and passion to move a city.

In some communities, it may be necessary to rebuild trust before moving on to envisioning and decision-making. As a result of one of my visits to Anchorage, Alaska, the city redeveloped an old community model on a slightly more formal basis. In many towns there used to be a table reserved in a local restaurant where the leaders talked once a week or more. Knowledge was shared and ideas were advanced – indeed, decisions were often made.

The Alaska model revived this approach. It was called the Wednesday Roundtable (it met on Wednesdays) and anybody was welcome to come to an early morning continental breakfast and talk about what their ideas were and what they thought might be important for the community. The group met for several years and specific ideas spun off from it, which gathered their own support. Similar models, with different names, are springing up across America.

In some ways the Wednesday Roundtable is a twenty-first century service club. It is often forgotten that most of the service clubs were created in the late nineteenth and early twentieth centuries to provide specific support to their communities. These groups inevitably adopted both the agendas and the social styles of the societies of their time. They typically invited people from one sex or the other and they also tended to include people from only one class.

Wednesday Roundtables are different. Anybody who wants to be a leader, using influence rather than power, is invited. People do not have to make a long-term commitment: they can miss meetings without penalty. A wide variety of topics are covered and participants can be honest because they know that this is not a decision-making body; their statements will not be used to undermine them. Specific ideas are spun off from the group so that the freewheeling discussion can be continued.

There is in a sense only one rule: that there are no rules. But this does not mean that there is no commitment. The commitment is to listen to others and to learn to trust. The

227

Wednesday Roundtable is based on a belief that a value-based culture is a necessity and that the seeds of such a value-based culture need to be planted on a small scale and at a local level. Communication between leaders in various parts of the community has been significantly improved as a result of the Wednesday Roundtable.

This development may move in two obvious directions. One is to encourage other communities in Alaska and elsewhere to adopt the Roundtable model. Ideally, small-scale Roundtables would develop in neighbourhoods and interest-groups throughout communities. The overall effect would be to change the dominant style so that people would learn to collaborate rather than fight in order to change their goals.

The other is to imagine what the next stage of such a process might look like. My personal vision is that a meeting place would develop which would become the networking centre of the community. The basic approaches of the Roundtable would be preserved but in a broader context. This would be the place where all the information about events, dynamics, trends etc. would be gathered. It would be a place where people could propose projects, find colleagues, discuss directions. It would above all be a place where people could discover what it would be like to work with others in tough, compassionate harmony. Conflict would be recognised and worked through. The commitment would be to manage it so that interpersonal violence was avoided. A local list-serve and web-site would be a critical part of such a process.

Such a "place" could, of course, be developed by members of a Roundtable. It could also develop from the coffee shops which exist in many cities and combine food and discussion. It could be a project of a church which would see the importance of bringing together leaders and information so that the community became more self-aware. It could be developed by one of the social service agencies which understood its mission as supporting interaction between existing and emerging leaders. It could be created by a city council that really wants to serve its constituents. It would be a natural mission for a community college.

It could also be a free-standing club which would be formed for this specific purpose. Such a club would invite all those who wanted to lead and were willing to commit to living on a value-base. It would be sensitive to issues of race, class and gender and would put into place specific policies which showed this commitment. For example, dues might well be based on a percentage of income rather than on an absolute figure.

These places would support the development of the type of activities which I have described earlier. As networks of this type matured, they would significantly affect decision-making in the community. Decisions, however, would not be made on the basis of power but rather through careful dialogue between all those involved in the various questions. Communities would be ready to grasp opportunities when they were available and to manage problems before they became crises.

My work in Australia over the last couple of years has resulted in a number of dynamics which have created Conversation and Action groups across the continent. They are linked through two networks: Reworking Tomorrow and Australia Connects. Information about how to learn more about these processes is contained in the resource section at the end of the book.

These networks concentrate on creating the context where people can discover their personal passion. They are then helped to find others who share their belief in the need for fundamental change and to set up conversation and action groups to fulfil their dreams.

Chapter 10

Beyond Power, Sovereignty and Democracy

Up to this point, the approach in turning the century will have been somewhat familiar to you, assuming you have kept up with the debates raging about fundamental change over the last 30 years. For example, the need to abandon maximum economic growth policies has been relatively widely discussed, even though it has not yet been accepted nor have its specific implications been widely explored.

Similarly, the arguments for the development of a learning society are increasingly heard, although many of the implications I have raised are still relatively new. We are rapidly discovering that we cannot afford to abandon any of the people in our society without damage to everybody. We are giving more effort to improving the opportunities for people to learn and think.

This part of the book will deal with "politics" – defined in its broadest sense of collective decision making. This subject has so far received very little creative attention, and part of the difficulty is that most of us include only the process of voting and the decisions made by elected officials when talking about politics. The overall political process is, however, far wider. Politics determines whether the Chamber of Commerce or the Town Council really calls the shots in a city. Politics decides whether church leaders are significantly involved in making choices. The degree of involvement permitted the disadvantaged is also a political question.

Once we recognise the relevance of this broader picture, it is obvious that extraordinary changes are taking place in political structures and the use of power throughout the world. The failure of the coup in the Soviet Union in the summer of 1991 was a direct result of the refusal of crack KGB units to obey orders when confronted with civilian opposition – a dynamic so wild it's unlikely any fiction writer would have considered using it as a plot. The incomplete movements towards peace in the Middle East, South Africa and Ireland are tributes to the willingness of people to pursue politics in dramatically new ways. On the other hand, the progressive disintegration of current decision-making structures in the democracies results in large part from the increasing unwillingness of citizens to be forced to act in ways which seem inappropriate, or destructive, to them.

Shifting reactions to the use of power are a critical element in more personal areas also. For example, the public increasingly recognises that sexual harassment, intimidation and rape have little to do with sex, but result from the desire to dominate. These attitudinal shifts have created minefields through which we all have to tread very carefully. Dangers lurk everywhere: many North American universities have "no touching" codes between faculty and students. The fear of sexual harassment charges has been used to deny our need to touch and comfort each other.

An historical overview

The right to be involved in decision making has been increasingly widely shared over the last millennium. The power to make arbitrary choices has been significantly curbed over the same period. Democracy is now the dominant system throughout the world. Many people have come to believe it is the best possible system of government and that it will not change at any time in the future.

Winston Churchill was more realistic: "Democracy," he said, "is the worst form of government except all the others." While it does support the process of collective decision making better than any other currently available system, it is certainly not adequate to deal with the complexities of the twenty-first century.

Our current political systems are an uncomfortable, and incongruous, mix of power and consultation. To understand why politics is conducted as it is, we must look back at how current dynamics developed in the Western world. In the early part of the second millennium, the church held the dominant power. Religious and superstitious people paid a large part of their resources to the priestly hierarchy to assure their own salvation, and the Pope was the ultimate arbiter of important decisions. Even kings felt unable to ignore or overrule him because of the sanctions he could wield – for example, through an interdiction that cut a country off from the rest of the Christian world.

We can get a feel for the Middle Ages by looking at the current situation in the Muslim world. Clerics hold great power. Pilgrimages provide grace in heaven and require respect on earth. People believe that God determines their future and do not expect to make decisions that significantly alter their place in the society or their destiny. The current Muslim world-view would seem natural to those who lived as Christians in the first half of the second millennium. The Western world has since made growth its god, rather than the church, and only the very rash see this is pure gain.

Today most Christians in Western churches consider that absolute authority survives only in the claimed right of the Pope to be infallible when he speaks *ex cathedra*. In these circumstances, he claims to transmit God's views and questioning is not "acceptable", but many Catholics deny even this limited right to enforce obedience and choose to follow their own consciences and beliefs, defying church doctrine if necessary.

Kings, under the Pope's guidance, held the secular power in the Middle Ages. The dominant political philosophy was that rulers could do no wrong: they made the law, and people depended for justice largely on the character and integrity of the individual who held the position. The great kings and queens, such as Elizabeth I, commanded obedience because they incarnated the values and beliefs of their subjects. In addition they were able to restrain the greed of those who officially wielded power in their name, a skill often lacking in other rulers of the time.

While kings and queens no longer have significant power, we have not recognised the full implications of the shift that took place as royalty lost the ability to enforce its will. Power moved from the "sovereign" to the "sovereign state", and the slogan was no longer that the King could do no wrong, but rather: "My country, right or wrong." People were expected to give their loyalty to their nation regardless of its behaviour. It was this slogan which led an exasperated Samuel Johnson to say: "Patriotism is the last refuge of a scoundrel."

What powers of the monarch have passed to the sovereign state? It has inherited an absolute right to make war; it also has the right, and the duty, to make economic policy to improve the conditions of its citizens. It can determine which activities are illegal. Less obviously, the sovereign state has often demanded the right to monopolise information.

Nations have claimed that they cannot be sued. In the United States, for example, government employees cannot be forced to pay their debts. Successful challenges to many of these sovereign claims in recent years include the Freedom of Information Act, which gives people the right to discover much of what is in government records. People in Great Britain are still battling to receive this same right.

The dying sovereign state

The nation-state, in its modern form, was a European invention designed to deal with the realities of that area at a particular point in time. It was exported as Europeans dominated the rest of the world but it never proved as suitable for other places. Today countries can no longer defend their boundaries because of the dangers of mutual destruction. They are losing control of their economies, because of the extent of financial interrelationships, and as a result, the real power of the nation-state is rapidly declining. The attack on Yugoslavia continued this trend and breached an absolute prohibition in the United Nations Charter.

Humanity has always divided itself into "insiders" and "outsiders" – the difference is the steady movement to larger and larger scales of government. Decision-making was first carried out by tribes, then by cities and city-states, and finally at the national level. Until the coming of modern weaponry and particularly the nuclear arsenal, the ultimate controller of international affairs was the threat of war, and eventually war itself (Clemenceau argued that "War is the continuation of diplomacy by other means"). Military adventures cleared the air and produced a new order that held for a time until somebody else tried to change the pattern by force.

This mindset lay behind the Cold War. It dominated world thinking from the middle of the nineteen-forties to the end of the eighties. Two heavily armed blocs confronted each other. The resulting stalemate, based on the fear of nuclear weapons, kept the world relatively unchanged for this same period. Both sides were unwilling to provoke the other in a way which might cause nuclear war. A new term – "the balance of terror" – was coined to describe this reality.

At the end of the eighties, the cost of the military stalemate became excessive for both Russia and America. This led to new patterns of thinking with both nations being willing to sign treaties reducing levels of conventional and nuclear armaments. Later the Russian economy collapsed, apparently leaving the US as the remaining "superpower". The complexity of the new challenges has emerged because there has been no effective challenge to the triumphalism of the United States over the last decade.

Despite America's status, however, it is being forced to make its decisions as part of an interconnected global network. In a major summary article by Doyle McManus and Robin Wright of the Los Angeles Times Service, former Secretary of State George P Shultz is quoted as saying that the combined effects

of economic globalism on even the strongest nation's freedom
of action amount to "the decline of sovereignty". He also says:
"The concept of absolute sovereignty is long gone. As national
boundaries blur, sovereign power is dispersed and more players
vie for international influence."

The same article also quotes Francisco Sagasti of the World
Bank.

> Nation-states have become less important as political
> units in the sense of being able to control whatever
> phenomena – economic, social, environmental or
> technological – take place in the world. This is hard to
> get accustomed to, for all our political systems are
> geared to focus on the nation-state as the locus of
> power, decision-making and as the main unit of
> political, social and economic analysis. We have not yet
> learned to live with the fact that these phenomena
> transcend national boundaries.

Getting beyond the nation-state model requires a shift at a
deeper level of understanding. The real challenge of the
immediate future is to break out of the insider/outsider model
and to discover that we live on a small planet where we must all
cooperate. There are no short-cuts. This is why it is appropriate
to talk about the need for the human race to grow out of its
adolescence and into maturity. Either we learn to cooperate with
each other or conditions on earth become unmanageable.

The nation state is currently the protector of the weak and the
needy. If it can no longer play these roles effectively, there is a
need for a far greater shift in our patterns of thinking and action
than we have yet realised.

Moving beyond the dream of a planetary government

The decline of the sovereign state is now inevitable. But this
change could theoretically lead humanity in two very different
directions. One route would maintain coercive power but move
it to the global level by developing "world government".
Alternatively we can develop totally new political models

which challenge human beings to far higher levels of responsibility within their geographical, work and professional communities.

Many of those who believe that world government is the next appropriate response, look to the United Nations as the great leader of the future, pointing to its role in the Iraq invasion of Kuwait as evidence of its potential. Unfortunately, the UN cannot lead us beyond the nation-state model. There are two reasons for this conclusion.

First, the level of competence of those who work for the United Nations is not, in general, equal to the magnitude of the task which must be accomplished. While there are notable exceptions, many of the people in the UN system are unable to secure as lucrative a job anywhere else. They are attracted by what amounts in many cases to a life-long guarantee of employment. It is conceivable that this problem could be overcome but it would be a tremendous hurdle to leap.

The second, and far more serious problem, emerges because many of the issues that must be faced in the twenty-first century require the abandonment of the nation-state model. Delegates who are appointed by nation-states cannot be expected to think clearly about issues that require reducing national power.

National governments are not the most appropriate groupings to make decisions about the future. The discussions in the European Economic Community continue to be confused by this issue. Great Britain, in particular, hopes to maintain its national sovereignty and denies the fact that it is inevitably vanishing because of trends which have nothing to do with the EEC negotiations.

The future requires fundamental change in political styles. The needed shifts cannot be forced by planetary or regional governments which rely primarily on regulation, law and force. Rather, they will emerge as individuals, communities, firms, churches, organisations and businesses agree on a new story and decide on different priorities as a result. The answer is not to develop global regulation and law but to challenge people to exercise responsible freedom.

The possibility of moving in this direction will become real as we commit to developing learning institutions and societies. People do adopt new priorities if they understand changing realities. Behaviour changes are much more likely to be permanent if they are based on perceived self-interest rather than being coerced by regulation.

Setting up learning societies which rely on responsible freedom is often rejected as impossible. We forget that the movement that has already taken place towards democracy was also seen as "impossible" in earlier times. This is not the time to lose our nerve, denying the potential for human growth that has served humanity so well in the past.

Dictatorships

I am aware that many people find my proposals utopian, believing that efficient power structures are necessary and inevitable. Taken to its logical extreme, this viewpoint results in proposals that we should find a wise and benevolent dictator. Given all the problems of today, such a paragon sounds attractive – indeed, if I could believe in the effectiveness of such a person, and that of her/his successors, I'd vote that person into office tomorrow, even at the cost of my losing the franchise forever!

This approach will not work, however. The reason is simple, and was suggested by Lord Acton: "Power tends to corrupt and absolute power corrupts absolutely." I have struggled with the implications of this statement for a long time, and have always had problems accepting it as it stands because I have met people with power who have not seemed corrupted. Many of them do the best they can, although the results of their actions are often the opposite of what they hoped.

Adding one word to the Lord Acton statement changes its meaning significantly and it becomes a tautology. "Power tends to corrupt information and absolute power corrupts information absolutely." Subordinates have a natural tendency to tell superiors what they want to hear. The more power they use, the less likely it is that you'll take the risk of raising tough issues. In such a situation, a dictator would be deprived of the information needed to make good decisions.

Power, like almost every word in the English language, has a multitude of meanings. It is a word which some people use in a positive sense and others use negatively. I am using the word to cover those instances when people have the ability to control behaviour and force obedience. I include, in this definition, people who use language, style, coercion and force in ways which require people to do things they would not otherwise choose.

Power, in the definition I have used above, will therefore always tend to distort information and knowledge-flows. Lord Acton is generally assumed to have been thinking about the results of power in governmental circles, but exactly the same problems occur in all other systems. Any person who makes decisions, without hearing challenges from others, makes the same type of errors whether he or she is the head of a business firm, a school or college, a non-profit organisation, a church or any other institution.

In a recent paper, Herman Bryant Maynard Jr and Susan E Mehrtens discuss the problems which prevent most corporations from being effective.

> Much of our employees' energy goes into repression, hiding the truth, concealing problems, and refusing to face reality. We in business often fall into the Holocaust syndrome, in which people have neither the space nor the awareness of access points to get out of the box in which they find themselves... Inside most corporations there is little tolerance for insubordination or public criticism.

Power always tends to limit honesty and deter effective communication of information. Many people in our culture have the right to use power to force decisions on others: policemen, judges, schoolteachers, bureaucrats, bosses etc. are able to coerce. Power is sometimes personal, given by position or wealth. More often, in today's world, the ability to use power is primarily controlled by an intricate web of law and regulation, which provides the right to require certain behaviours and avoid others.

An anonymous fable – which made the point beautifully – came across my desk just as I was revising this chapter.

> In the beginning was the plan, and then came the assumptions, and the assumptions were without form, and darkness was upon the face of the workers, and they spake among themselves saying: "It is a bucket of bull-do and it stinketh".
>
> And the workers went to their Supervisors and sayeth: "It is a pail of dung and none may abide the odour thereof."
>
> And the Supervisors went unto their Managers and sayeth unto them: "It is a container of excrement and it is very strong and none can abide by it."
>
> Then the Managers went unto their Vice-Presidents and sayeth: "It is a vessel of fertiliser and none may abide by its strength."
>
> And the Vice-Presidents spake among themselves, saying one to another: "It contains that which aids plant growth and it is very strong."
>
> And the Vice-Presidents went unto the President and sayeth unto him: "The plan promotes growth and is very powerful."
>
> And the President went to the Board and proclaimed: "This new plan will actively promote the growth and efficiency of the company."
>
> And the Board looked upon the plan, saw that it was good and were pleased to adopt it.

Gervase R Bushe, a management consultant, makes the same point in more formal language.

> Usually, it is the people at the very bottom of the organisation, those least empowered in control-based systems, who are the closest to the key sources of information. Due to the tendency of information to distort on the way up in hierarchies, very little of this information gets to those who take the authority to make all the decisions. Eventually, decisions drift further and further away from reality and the organisation fails or becomes ripe for a takeover.

One of the core discussions during the long-running debate over Y2K, or the millennium bug, was the degree to which information was being distorted on the way to the top of systems. Some felt that the reports which the public were receiving were essentially accurate. Others believed that power was eliminating accuracy.

According to Tom Englehardt, a former senior editor at Pantheon books, a similar pattern caused the collapse of successive Chinese dynasties.

> In traditional China, it was believed that dynasties fell, in part, because of the disastrous disparities between names and the things named. The last dynastic ruler, mistaking the reassuring descriptions his courtiers offered him for the actual state of affairs in the imperial domains, found himself, in effect, blinded by names. Sooner or later, the abyss between the named and the real simply swallowed him up.

The gap between real-world activities and the arguments of elites today is dangerously wide. The plague of "political correctness" makes it difficult to challenge dangerously obsolete myths. Much of the discussion we hear has degenerated into mealy-mouthed politeness at one extreme or, at the other, into loud debates which increase heat rather than light.

Hierarchical systems always tend to block negative feedback, which is critically important to long-run success. Negative feedback tells people the things they have forgotten or missed. It provides the opportunity to do better next time and may prevent catastrophic errors. One of the greatest skills in life is making it clear to your friends and colleagues that you will not be angry, let alone damage them, if they tell you things that it may be difficult for you to hear and accept.

Similarly, an unwillingness in potential colleagues or friends to accept negative feedback should be a strong warning signal in setting up your relationships. One of the most hopeful projects with which I was ever associated failed because one of the principals had her staff screen all criticism. As a result, she continued to act in ways which made collaboration impossible.

At the nation-state level, many people believe that the fear that accompanies fascism was one of the basic reasons for Germany's defeat in World War II. From the middle of 1940, the allies read a large proportion of Germany's most confidential messages by breaking her key secret code, which was called Enigma. Although great care was taken in how intercepted messages were used, it seems impossible that nobody ever realised what was happening. Bringing bad news was, however, highly dangerous in the Nazi hierarchy. If somebody had tried to raise the issue, it would almost certainly have been blocked higher up in the system and the messenger killed.

All of us who have dealt with power systems in our theoretical democracy will have had more than a taste of this same problem. There are, however, more ways of dealing with arrogance and stupidity within a democracy than in a dictatorship. You can move out of channels with some hope that you will find somebody prepared to take risks for the sake of justice or effectiveness. But the risks nevertheless remain high and those who are willing to blow the whistle all too often suffer unreasonably. In recent years, some governments have realised that the benefits to be gained from the activities of whistle blowers are so large that their activities warrant legal protection.

Challenging inappropriate decisions is made more difficult because all too many human beings and institutions have come to believe that morality and values are not their concern. Many business philosophers have argued that the task of business is profit maximisation and that other institutions should look after societal concerns. Similarly, professional groups have often only looked at their own narrow self-interest and been unwilling to censure or control their members. It is therefore not surprising that some people and institutions cut corners and that those who challenge destructive behaviour are treated badly.

For example, the medical profession all too often permits irresponsible and incompetent people to continue to practice. The ever-spiralling costs of malpractice insurance are directly related to this failure to punish those who make the most

241

mistakes. Many doctors, particularly those in obstetrics and gynaecology, are giving up their practices because insurance costs are rising rapidly; this is depriving mothers of vitally needed services in many countries.

Rebuilding an effective value-based culture will depend on all of us doing what we know we ought to, even when it is inconvenient or embarrassing. Each of us may be more prepared to take a stand if we realise that it is the small steps which make a long-run difference. One of the lessons I have learned throughout my life is that one can never know which actions change the lives of others. Very often, it is the seemingly trivial which has the greatest impact.

New decision-making patterns

Who should be involved in decision-making and how should it be structured? Given that governments continue to make decisions, who has the right to determine how the powers of the state should be used? This question has bedevilled democracy since its beginning, and one of the most vexed questions has been the extension of the franchise.

Every shift towards a broader group of electors has been bitterly fought. It was originally argued that if people without property were able to vote, they would inevitably deprive the rich of their resources. Later, it was argued that women would "vote their emotions". Still later, the right to vote at age 18 was challenged on the grounds that people would be too immature to understand the issues. The panic-stricken opposition to more people being involved in government has always been proved wrong; voters have always done better than pessimists feared.

There is a more complex question which cannot be so easily resolved. How should the decision-making process be structured? Should there be one governing body or two? (Nebraska is the only state in the United States with a unicameral legislature.) Can decisions be reviewed for their constitutionality, or not? The United States goes to the Supreme Court to resolve questions of this nature, but Britain has no written constitution and parliament is therefore the ultimate decision-maker. How much power should be held at national, regional and local levels? Much experimentation is going on at this time. Indeed, this question is being further complicated by the growth of global organisations, such as the United Nations, and regional groupings, in Europe, Latin America, Asia and Australasia.

Many citizens and organisations are now working to reverse the trend towards centralisation which developed during the twentieth century. This trend emerged because all too many communities refused in the past to take the tough decisions which would support equity and social justice. The failure to act responsibly at local levels drove decision-making upwards; it often seemed as though forward movement would only be secured at the federal level. In addition, many state and federal bureaucrats have often believed that they are wiser than the public and should therefore determine the directions of the culture. In addition, most politicians want to point to the legislation they initiated when they stand for re-election.

These pressures for legislation are reinforced by the composition of most legislative bodies which have a high proportion of lawyers. Their mindset is based on a belief in the ability of the courts to determine right and wrong. Laws therefore seem to be the best way to achieve justice and change. This bias is enhanced by the fact that the self-interest of lawyers is in complicated legislation that has to be adjudicated.

These factors have prevented any significant movement away from federal control. Indeed, so long as communities, businesses and professional groups are unwilling to take responsibility for their own affairs, and bureaucrats and politicians see power as the way to make their mark, law and regulation will continue to be dominant. In the current climate of opinion, legislation is sought as soon as a majority can be found. It is considered appropriate to force people to obey the will of the majority – or even a vocal minority, if it has the clout to get laws passed.

Where should authority lie in today's complex world? And how is legitimacy assured for this authority? This is always the ultimate question. The key (and highly surprising) lesson we must learn is that the nation-state cannot be the dominant decision-making organisation as we move into the compassionate era. We need to return to the community level.

The nineties have seen this trend grow rapidly. Those who are concerned about the commercial globalisation of the world see community decision-making as the counter-point. More and more analysts talk about city-states.

Four horsemen of the apocalypse

The dynamics of the world were dominated by East-West issues from the forties to the eighties. The next decades will be controlled by the ways we manage the relationships between the rich and the poor nations. Unfortunately, the problems of the developing world are still low on the global agenda. We shall only change perceptions if we recognise both the real potentials and dangers in the current situation. The potentials arise from our ability to increase the standards of those who are most dispossessed among us, so they can achieve adequate levels of food, clothing and shelter. The amount of money required to achieve this goal is relatively small, certainly when compared to the amount wasted on weaponry.

One primary danger is that there may not be enough time left to prevent massive breakdowns in civil order in more and more countries of the world. Only a massive commitment to new ideas will provide the human race with the potential to resolve the immediate crises it faces. We must introduce new directions now if progressive breakdown is to be avoided. There is a point of no-return and it can be reached.

The overall picture in the suffering countries of the world worsened dramatically in the last decade. There was the mass migration of the Kurds following Iraqi barbarism after the Gulf War and the unwillingness of the West to address their plight. Famine in sub-Saharan Africa continues to kill hundreds of thousands. Cyclones in Bangladesh devastate much of the country and make millions homeless, adding natural disaster to the suffering imposed by overcrowding and inefficient government. Climatic instability caused more suffering in 1998 than ever before. The AIDS epidemic throughout the world, and particularly in Africa, is causing an ever-rising number of deaths. The number of refugees grows with wars and ethnic cleansings taking place in many parts of the world.

A 1999 report from the International Federation of Red Cross and Red Crescent Societies supports this view.

> In 1998, natural disasters created more refugees than wars and conflicts. Declining soil fertility, drought, flooding and deforestation drove 25 million environmental refugees from their land and into the already vulnerable squatter communities of fast-growing cities. They represented 58 per cent of total refugee population worldwide.

The report argues that this trend will inevitably continue and intensify as the environmental problems of global warming and deforestation on the one hand, and the social problems of increasing poverty and growing shanty towns, on the other, collide.

This list of tragedies is daunting. Confronted with the number and scope of the problems, "donor fatigue" is developing. People are ceasing to give because they feel that they cannot make a difference. It is all too possible that the rich nations, and indeed the primary international organisations, will come to believe that there is nothing to be done for the very poor. The percentage of national income given by the wealthier countries to their poorer neighbours continues to decline.

The disadvantaged countries of the world will become desperate if they do not receive fairer treatment. There is, however, a major paradox here: the need is not to intensify current activities – most existing aid policies are damaging nations rather than helping them. Totally new directions must be created which face the reality that there is no chance of the developing countries ever reaching the standards of living of those nations that are already wealthy. This reality can only be taught, and accepted, if the people of the developed world show a commitment to reducing their unfair draw on global resources.

In addition, vigorous and appropriate efforts must be made to support the poorer countries in the patterns of human and community development which are actually feasible and desirable for them. The initial requirement here is to face the highly distressing fact that most of the lending and aid to the disadvantaged countries has not only been wasted but has even acted against their best interests. A large amount of the money was never even used within these countries; wealthy individuals within poorer countries got hold of the foreign aid and immediately invested it abroad. Most of the developing nations now have such large scale debts that money is flowing away from them to the wealthier countries. Forgiveness of debt is essential – the question is how it can be achieved in the most acceptable, and least disruptive, way.

The millennium has been used as a rationale to forgive some of the debts of the very poorest nations. This could be a major step forward if it were accompanied by a change in basic thinking about development. Future assistance must operate in a very different style, and on a smaller scale, than in the past. It must aim to increase human and socioeconomic viability rather than be targeted narrowly on increasing the standard of living. For example, micro-loans direct to farmers and small entrepreneurs have been dramatically successful. If the major shifts are to be achieved, relations between donors and recipients will have to be totally different from those that have existed in the past.

The current fall into deeper poverty and degradation which is occurring in many parts of the world is unacceptable and dangerous. I have often heard people from the wealthier countries argue that the poor cannot harm them; they do not recognise that the rich will suffer from the consequences of the self-interested actions of the poor, which are designed to ensure they do as well as they can in intolerable conditions. There is no possibility that hungry people will preserve the forests needed to let the whole world breathe if they lack fuel to cook their minimal meals. There is no chance that people will refuse to use toxins and poisons which will destroy the quality of the air, land

and water on a global scale if they cannot feed themselves without them.

There is one additional way in which the breakdown of the social order in the poorer countries will inevitably affect the rich. The potential for the creation of new disease strains from slums in the poorer countries is obvious, particularly when these conditions are combined with the careless use of antibiotics and other medicines which tend to cause mutations in germs and diseases. The continued spread of AIDS shows that even if the course of a disease may be controllable in the developed world using expensive drugs, it can remain a death sentence in poorer countries. The chances of further illnesses developing which cannot be cured using existing medical knowledge is all too probable; a mutated strain of tuberculosis has recently developed which is so far immune to drugs. Cholera and malaria are also making a comeback.

People who see no danger if the poorer countries revolt against the wealthy fail to recognise just how fragile is the current world order. We do not live in robust systems where we can each look after ourselves. We cannot live in our cities without electricity and oil and transportation and water. These are all threatened by terrorism – an ever-present possibility if enough poor countries become sufficiently angry about the actions of the more powerful. The wealthier countries cannot protect themselves from terrorism without destroying the freedoms that are necessary for the development of responsible freedom and long-run survival.

One of the arguments against the intervention in Kosovo is that it increased the number of people who would wish to take revenge on the United States and Britain, the strongest supporters of the bombing. It is not recognised that any dramatic increase in terrorism would almost certainly be accompanied by a breakdown of the civil order in the wealthier countries. If the world polarises into predominantly white and non-white nations – a result that is certainly feasible – there would be both violence generated from outside the developed world and in the poorer sections of cities.

Terrorism is the "power" tool which can be used by those who feel themselves marginalised and dispossessed. It is understandable that the wealthier countries see this technique of violence as intolerable. Little useful dialogue will develop, however, until there is an honest recognition of the real role terrorism plays. One can see this pattern most clearly in the evolution of thinking in Israel. When Israel was aiming for statehood in the 1940s, terrorism against Britain, which controlled the "promised land", was the only available weapon. It was widely and effectively used. Now that Israel is herself a state, she has joined most other nations in condemning terrorism. While terrorism is all too often dispicable in tactics, this does not mean that it makes sense to deny the link between terrorism and the unwillingness of those with power to listen to the beliefs and concerns of those without it. Wilful blindness to reality is no solution to problems. The use of power by the rich inevitably leads to terrorism by the powerless: the link is obvious and unbreakable.

Terrorism has been primarily state-sponsored up to the current time. The leaders of certain nation-states have believed that this was the only way to damage the wealthier countries, which they saw as unwilling to meet the reasonable aspirations of people in various parts of the world. If the world continues to divide between the rich and the poor countries as seems all too possible, then terrorism could eventually become the technique of choice of a very large number of people and groups. The Gulf War significantly increased these dangers as did the break-up of the Soviet Union – there is today a significant prospect of nuclear scientists selling themselves to the highest bidder. Osama Bin Ladin has recently emerged as the first terrorist who has the financial resources to fund his anger. Unless we can make the twenty-first century into the healing century, he will not be the last.

A new sense of global solidarity is the only hope to deal with the growing gap between the rich and the poor and to avoid an unsustainable move towards authoritarian government. Tensions between the rich and the poor, both internally and internationally, are always high. The middle-class and the wealthy have an interest in stability. Poorer people and poorer nations, if driven far enough, can become desperate and tear down their structures even if this causes severe damage to their own situation.

The standard of living in many of the poorer countries has declined significantly in the eighties and nineties. People who have never encountered the poverty of the Third and Fourth World can hardly imagine it. What is called poverty in the United States is unbelievable wealth to many who live in the slums of the poorer countries. These people are always hungry, and usually desperate. People live from the garbage of the rich, they squat on land in hovels built from scraps. Many of them are permanently sick. Will we be bright enough, and sufficiently compassionate, to grasp this reality before it destroys us?

Will we also recognise that many of the poor have maintained a greater sense of social solidarity than those of us who are wealthier. The developed world has paid a substantial price for our ability to consume. We need to learn from each other if we are to avoid disaster in the twenty-first century.

Money is not the problem: the sums involved are manageable. Intelligence, creativity and compassion are the critical missing elements.

Chapter 11

Creating the Compassionate Era

The adversarial structures currently dominating our culture were appropriate as long as we believed that we could find truth through debate and argument. Now we know that truth is perceptual, the challenge is to find open processes that gently encourage each of us to rethink our existing understandings.

The Kosovo crisis shows the danger of closed systems. President Clinton has admitted that he expected the Serbs to give up after a couple of days of bombing. Everybody who knew anything about Yugoslav tradition, and World War II, could have told him that this judgment was almost certainly wrong. Unfortunately, it is now clear that only certain views were acceptable within the planning process. As a result of this failure in judgment, huge destruction took place in the area and included civilian targets.

Open systems will always be more effective and less dangerous in times of rapid change and crisis than closed groups. Dealing with a wide range of views, however, requires high levels of commitment. It is easier to narrow one's sources of information than to keep checking on what is really necessary and desirable. The possibility of missing critically important information is particularly high at the current time because, despite the extraordinarily large number of channels for moving information, a very narrow interpretation exists defining what ideas are "acceptable" and "publishable" in most of the media.

Creating open systems for the twenty-first century

The challenge of the nineties and the twenty-first century has been and will be to complete the movement towards responsible freedom which started with the Greeks. While the movement has often been halting and has sometimes been reversed, the overall direction has been unmistakable. Now we must move further.

The Civil War, a remarkable television mini-series broadcast on the public broadcasting stations in the US, gathered very large audiences because it showed the positive directions that emerged in the middle of the nineteenth century but also reminded viewers of the incompleteness of the American Revolution. The current challenge is to make the same quantum leap in commitments to freedom as those that developed during the 1860s. This time however we must carry through the necessary mindquakes without frustrating people to the point where violence seems the only possible response.

We need to develop "responsible freedom": a term that covers the concept I wish to express as well as any phrase I have been able to devise. The difficulty with the word "freedom", of course, is that it covers a broad range of meanings. At one extreme, it implies "licence", which is defined by Webster as "liberty that consists in breaking laws or rules either as an abuse or an exercise of special privilege".

At the other end of its spectrum of meanings, "freedom" already contains the idea of responsibility. Used in this way, it provides the right to do what one wishes without outside constraint, while remaining aware of the consequences of one's actions. If freedom is used in this latter sense, the addition of the word "responsible" is unnecessary. But in current conditions, where freedom if often the rationale for irresponsible or anti-social behaviour, joining the two words "responsible freedom" seems essential if the essence of my thought is to be communicated.

251

Responsible freedom is not possible without reducing the degree of control in today's Western cultures. The appropriate balance between personal choice and coercion through law and regulation, depends on the maturity of each culture and the people in it. Legislation can be reduced as people begin to develop a deeper and more spiritual sense of their real self-interest. Edmund Burke, a British political philosopher, caught this tension beautifully in the following statement: "Men are qualified for civil liberty in exact proportion to their disposition to put moral chains upon their appetites. Society cannot exist unless a controlling power upon will and appetite is placed somewhere, and the less there is within, the more there must be without."

What can be done to reverse the trend to overcontrol people and systems, which is currently so pervasive? It persists despite the move of recent years towards conservatism in many countries which has aimed to reduce the number of laws and regulations. One of the primary issues which arises when answering this question is the degree to which society can and should protect people from their own irresponsibility. For example, the dangers of riding a motorcycle without a helmet are very great; head injuries occur all too frequently. Legislators have therefore required use of a helmet in many parts of the world for dangerous activities such as motorcycle and horse riding. Another step along the same lines has been to require seat belts in automobiles, for they too can be shown to reduce death and injuries.

The people who make individual liberty their primary concern have fought these steps, claiming that coercion is inappropriate in cases where people are only damaging themselves. The problem, of course, is that when people are not wearing seat-belts, human bodies can become projectiles and damage others. Those who favour legislation also argue that because the costs of accidents are borne eventually by the whole society, the society has the right to impose regulations.

The problem is that this approach places humanity on a very slippery slope. A great many behaviours can be shown, statistically, to increase the costs to the total society. Does society have the right, and the ability, to control all of them? For example, the health problems of the obese are certainly far more severe than those of people of average weight. Would society be justified in aiming to control weight – and how would it do so? Should a weighing machine be placed at the entry to restaurants and those who were above their normal weight be required to eat salads?

When I wrote the paragraph above, I saw my idea as a science-fiction nightmare. I did not recognise that there was already a mechanism in place to create this sort of pattern. To my surprise, it was being created by private institutions that want to improve the health of their employees in order to reduce insurance costs. Businesses and non-profit corporations are demanding unparalleled control over human behaviour.

Corporations are traumatised by the increase in their medical costs and are looking for ways to limit them by controlling costly behaviour patterns. This was exemplified in article by Alan Spires in the *Juneau Empire*.

> Some (companies), such as Cable News Network, won't even hire someone who smokes an occasional cigarette at home. Others such as U-Haul, have begun fining their employees for off-hours smoking and being overweight.
> And a few companies have begun to regulate the amount of cholesterol, saturated fats, coffee and even fast food their workers eat.

The company town with its paternalistic policies was largely banished at the beginning of the twentieth-century. Should we permit a new form of company strategy to grow up which controls the behaviour of employees not only on the job, but also at home? What should be the limits of the contract between the employer and the employee? The answers we develop to these questions will have implications far beyond those which are obvious.

Health insurance debates are normally concentrated on controlling costs. But the real question we must answer is who has the right to make decisions? Some of the most critical problems cluster around the issue of pregnancy. For example, drug abuse of all kinds – smoking, alcohol, legal and illegal drugs – can result in problems for the foetus. There have been efforts to charge mothers who damage their unborn children with various legal offences – a trend that seems likely to grow but is unlikely to be effective. Those who abuse their unborn children normally suffer from a basic lack of self-respect. The only way this form of destructive behaviour is going to be limited is by bringing up human beings so they know how to love and be loved. We need to find ways to break through the negative dynamics that perpetuate anger and hostility in the culture.

Moving towards responsible freedom and an open society will demand that people have the following opportunities.

- The chance to learn the values of honesty, responsibility, humility and love.
- The ability to live with uncertainty.
- Equality of opportunity so that those who have been disadvantaged in the past have a chance to reach an equal starting point.
- Systems which are diverse enough for each person to develop himself or herself to the fullest extent possible.
- Majority rule and minority rights.
- Socioeconomic equity and social justice.
- Methods to ensure environmental balance for as far into the future as we can see.
- A commitment to reduce violence at all levels from the individual to the global.

One of the commitments that could have the largest impact would be to concentrate attention on the period from conception to entering school. Patterns of life are set during this period. A growing number of organisations are committing to this type of effort around the world.

Reducing legislation

My theme throughout this book has been the need to bring about change through learning rather than power. I have so far discussed how we can develop the learning side of the equation.

I now propose that it should be made more difficult to pass laws and introduce regulations. Instead of a simple majority being enough to force others to behave in a particular way, we should move forward to a point where legislation which restricts freedom requires a two-thirds majority.

A two-thirds majority seems realistic as the percentage required to pass legislation which restricts freedom. On the other hand, repealing legislation of this type should require only a 40 per cent vote. The bias should always be towards freeing people, communities and groups from control. The laws which do exist should be supported by such a strong consensus that people are unwilling to break the law because they will incur the displeasure of their peers, rather than because the police will penalise them if they disobey. People do have a right to make their own choices unless a strong case can be made for a particular law or regulation.

I am aware that my proposal for changing the percentage of votes to pass and repeal legislation would probably require a constitutional amendment in the United States and the chance of getting it passed would currently be low. In other countries, it would be equally difficult because it would change power patterns dramatically. Thinking about this issue would, however, force each of us to consider the key issues of the twenty-first century. What sort of society do we want to live in? Do we want to drift towards ever-greater controls? Or are we prepared to commit to more responsible decision-making for ourselves and our society? How much internal control will be developed and how much external control must be imposed?

Such regulations and laws as are essential should be passed in a form that emphasises the result and not the means, so as to leave as much space for creativity as possible. Suppose, for example, that there is an agreed need to increase the energy efficiency of buildings. The regulations should state the degree to which heat loss and gain should be restricted and not the building processes that must be used. If this approach is not employed, appropriate technologies will often be unintentionally excluded. For example, passive solar has often been prohibited, and still is in some jurisdictions, although it might well use less energy than other approaches.

Limiting the amount of government control seems frightening to many people. Some of those who have heard my arguments believe I am eliminating the only efficient approach to bring about rapid changes. Those who challenge my views ignore the clear-cut evidence that shows that legislation, ahead of agreement, often leads to a backlash. Indeed, there is an inherent flaw in the logic of bringing about major positive change through legislation. Legislators tend to lag public opinion rather than move ahead of it. It will therefore be quicker to encourage change using citizen energy than to push for government decision-making.

Moral judgments that restrict the behaviour of others should only be made when the case is overwhelming. Our attempts to legislate morality emerged at the time when we thought absolute answers existed. Today we know that we must live in the questions and apply the values of honesty, responsibility, humility and love to each situation. This requires that we leave people freer to make their own choices. Take, for example, the issue of life and death. "Murder" – or the taking of another's life without their consent – will still be outlawed, but each of us must learn to face up to the dilemmas which exist around life and death issues, given today's technologies.

Greater self-responsibility will require that each of us be more supportive of the laws enacted for our protection. For example, modern traffic patterns depend entirely on the willingness of people to obey the traffic code. Most people do so most of the time and the roads are therefore relatively safe, but a breakdown in traffic discipline would make life far more stressful. "Road rage" is an increasingly recognised danger.

We must also recognise that the legal system breaks down if too many activities are defined as crimes. As the burden of law and regulation increases, it is widely agreed that many people obey the law only when they are afraid they may be caught and penalised. We have long since passed this danger point; obedience to society's norms is now all too often based on fear of being caught rather than on social consensus.

There is a lesson to be learned from the different patterns in many Western nations and Japan. A foreigner was observing how the Japanese police force operated. An individual began to jaywalk, the police cruiser turned on its siren and the individual scuttled back to the sidewalk. The obvious question was then asked: "What are the penalties for jaywalking?" The response was: "There are no penalties for jaywalking. It is enough for us to remind people of their civic duty."

Finding a way back to knowing our duty is the primary challenge that confronts us all. The required shift towards responsible behaviour must affect individuals, work and professional groups, communities and those who make large-scale decisions. Fortunately giving people greater freedom does result in more effective decision-making. The feedback loop creating this result is self-evident once one looks for it.

Ed Lindaman, a futurist whose early death deprived us of his wisdom, told a story demonstrating this point. He worked at one of the large aircraft companies and was involved when an office of quality control was set up with two people. A year later, 200 people were in the office but everybody agreed that standards had declined. Personal and group responsibility had been replaced by an intrusive bureaucracy.

It must also be remembered that breaking the law is sometimes seen as a challenge, particularly by young people. On a visit to Oklahoma, I was discussing the level of losses from community college libraries. At that time, the loss from an open stack system was lower than from one with higher levels of security. People saw no challenge in taking books from the open stacks but were delighted to show that they were smarter than the systems set up to prevent theft.

Margaret Mead once questioned how society could reverse the downward slide which starts when people steal milk-bottles off doorsteps. Today cities throughout the world are asking the same question with far more urgency. The only possibility is for citizens, communities, work and professional groups to reestablish standards and norms which are accepted and enforced by their members, individually and collectively.

This is the point where responsible freedom and duty converge. There is a highly relevant biblical text: "In the service of God is perfect freedom". If one thinks clearly and widely, what one needs to do and what one wants to do and what one can do all come together in a single clear-cut direction. Only saints reach this level. The rest of us must do the best we can!

Developing leaders

Consumption has taken the place of citizenship. The psychic link between communities and their representatives is broken. People feel that most politicians are on the take, while politicians believe that most of their constituents have no interest in good governance. Campaigns get dirtier and dirtier as candidates point out the flaws in the other person rather than the positive reasons why people should vote for them.

The ever-growing drive to limit terms in office results from a profound sense of alienation. But if politicians are not able to remain in office for a significant period, decision-making power will move to bureaucracies. It is far from certain that this will produce an improvement in patterns of decision-making. Today's problems will not be fixed by moving the deck-chairs around on the Titanic; the need is to change systems.

Two challenges are most critical at the current time. First, good people feel it does not make sense for them to run for office; they object to the constant suspicion surrounding them and the negative reactions to their best efforts. Citizens are also unwilling to spend time supporting their elected representatives. Most messages that reach politicians are from those people who want special treatment or favours as well as from the "antis" and the "crazies". There is little of the creative and positive interconnections between all the parts of communities. As we move in this direction, and partnerships become the dominant mode in decision-making rather than power, the roles played by elected officials will shift dramatically. They will neither expect, nor be allowed to, make arbitrary decisions which do not reflect the will of the public. They will be linked far more closely with their constituents who will support them, and also hold them liable for their actions.

What steps can be taken to move in this direction at the current time? No magic bullets exist. The breakdown in political participation has taken place over many years and any recovery cannot therefore be expected to be rapid. The first necessary step is for people to support those leaders who do choose to operate in a cooperative and compassionate style.

Such an approach is particularly important at the current time because it ensures a victory whether the candidate gets the most votes or not. If the candidate wins, he or she reaches office with a committed citizenry who will be supportive of the changes that are necessary in the immediate future. If the candidate loses, then a process of education has been started which will make it easier for the next person to do well, and eventually win.

Choices in a pluralistic universe

Almost all adults grew up believing that the "right" answer could be known and society would then be able to force this answer on its citizens. We are now moving into a pluralistic world with very different belief patterns. People are no longer willing to be dominated by thinking that does not fit their own viewpoints. Western cultures, which have tried to control others for centuries, find it difficult to come to grips with this new reality.

How can different groups and viewpoints learn to live with each other without forcing shifts either by coercion or, more subtly, by imposing expectations that others have to accept? Many years ago I read *The Helping Hand* by Paul Anderson, which told the story of negotiations between earth and two planets that had been at war. Earth was willing to help because of the long-run benefits it would receive from the economic recovery of both systems. Each planet sent negotiators who were told to get the best terms they could, and both of them instructed their Ambassadors to do anything necessary to get help. The Ambassador of one planet did exactly what he was told and resources were promised – the negotiator from the other planet disobeyed instructions, insulted the people of earth who turned against him and refused help, and came home in disgrace, refusing to explain his actions.

The short-run results of these planetary choices were what would have been expected. The aided planet flourished and was able to restore its standard of living relatively rapidly, becoming a tourist destination. Earth people found themselves increasingly "at home" because hotels and eating places provided familiar standards and foods. Industry moved ahead because it was able to use existing earth technologies.

The planet without aid found it immensely difficult to pull itself up by its bootstraps. It was isolated and had to depend on its own resources because it had bankrupted itself during the war. Necessities were in short supply for years and many died. There was little commerce with earth because there was no real mesh between the thinking of the conquered planet and earth's ideas.

In the long-run, however, the picture was very different. The aided planet stagnated. In order to fit in with the styles of earth, it had to abandon the wellsprings of its culture and the way it had previously been organised. There had been no conscious imperialism demanding that things be done the same way as on earth, but if the conquered planet wanted to take advantage of what was being so generously offered, the only way it could do so was to manage its affairs in the same way as earth.

The planet that refused aid was forced to restudy its roots and to discover its own deepest learnings and knowledge. It examined the achievements of earth and found that their planet's traditions made it possible to surpass them. It developed methods of space flight which baffled earth scientists because they came out of a totally different cultural structure. Earth eventually became allied with the resurgent planet, while the other was essentially relegated to being a colony. Just before his death, the thinking and actions of the Ambassador who had anticipated these developments were made public and he was honoured as a hero rather than reviled as a traitor.

The Ambassador who refused aid forced his planet towards pluralism. The Ambassador who accepted aid unconsciously opted for an imposed uniformity. This is the same choice which the world, and particularly the poorer countries, face at the current time. Will there be a commitment to building out of the strengths of each of the cultures of the globe or will there be a continued effort to impose the viewpoints of the West?

Historically, each area throughout the world has believed in the superiority of its way of life. Other traditions are seen as inferior and dangerous. If you think in this way, it inevitably follows that real progress can only be achieved if your ideas continue to dominate. This attempt to maintain superiority is then buttressed and reinforced by distortions, half-truths and outright lies about the attitudes of other nations and religions.

Colonial powers have been totally convinced that their world-view was the right one – and indeed it was perceived as the only way to look at events. A slow erosion of this form of narrow-minded thinking is taking place today. Unfortunately, rhetorics such as those coined by George Bush, when he talked about "the American century", suggest that there is a possibility of slipping back into patterns of thought that are obsolete. There is little difference between current "American century" rhetoric and nineteenth century European expansionism. Indeed, the triumphalist American themes have become even more visible in the Clinton era.

An alternative way of looking at cultural norms does exist already. We can recognise the seeds of positive directions in all areas of the world. We should nurture positive processes wherever they are found. It will be easier to build from deeply-rooted indigenous beliefs than to graft ideas onto a culture from the outside. The difficulty with this approach is that the West has undercut the wellsprings of most cultures; whether the blocks are temporary or permanent is one of the most critical questions of our time.

How should poorer areas and countries, which still have significantly different cultures, think and act at this time? Instead of rushing to adopt the styles which have emerged in the relatively wealthy countries, they should dig back into their traditions. They need to ask how their religious, moral and ethical systems will help them preserve ecological systems and eliminate violence. They also need to find out how responsible freedom can be achieved by building on their own traditions.

The province of Kerala in India has been one of the success stories. Committed to social justice, it has developed hybrid forms between capitalism and socialism. These have produced significant movement towards better health, education and a high quality of life despite severe limits on the availability of goods and services. Two very different visions are advanced for the future: one sees current Western culture spreading all over the world, while the other believes that diversity will be maintained.

One of the most depressing aspects of my work is the level of negativity which exists in many geographical areas. I did a great deal of work in Nebraska in the eighties, and one of our efforts was to encourage people to become involved in two exercises. One of them asked for the list of adjectives that should be used to promote business and industry in the state – this task was found to be very difficult by many participants. The other was to develop descriptors which could be used to stereotype the region and might be used as a basis for a sitcom. Most people found it far easier to come up with a large number of negative words.

Confidence and hope are the minimal requirements for positive decision-making. There is growing evidence that the success of communities depends less on whether they have resources and more on the levels of commitment of their citizens. Communities that seem poised for great success based on objective factors can fail badly. Those with few resources and vibrant leadership can easily beat the odds.

Developing local value-based cultures will undercut the development of fundamentalism, which is a primary threat to the world's future. Fundamentalism is strengthened when people perceive that the certainties of their lives are being undermined and they feel a desperate need to find some rock to support them. The easiest place to find the certainty they want is in the sacred texts of their culture. The texts are then treated as absolutes that must be accepted exactly as they are written.

When new truths are drawn out of old cultures, on the other hand, individuals feel their past is still being honoured. The stress from change still remains, of course, but it will be far more limited because people feel they are following in the footsteps of their ancestors. They will find it easier to accept new approaches that honour old beliefs but can be adapted to modern conditions.

We must honour today's many world views. Diverse societies are the basis for a healthy world culture in just the same way as healthy ecologies require a complex balance of organisms, none of which dominates the others. Many reject the relevance of pluralism, however, arguing that other traditions are too flawed to enable positive growth. The best cure for this negative attitude is to face the extent and depth of the difficulties of using even one's own culture as the basis for moving towards more compassionate values. Others will reject pluralism because it is not efficient but rather messy and untidy. The message of chaos theory, however, is that untidiness is healthy rather than destructive.

The problem with pluralism, of course, is that it makes effective communication very difficult, and also guarantees high levels of conflict. There will be a need for very careful dialogue if conflicts are not to escalate into violence. The central requirement for the future, therefore, is not "efficiency" but "resiliency". It is critically important that a large number of approaches are tried so that humanity can discover those that work best. Adaptability is supported by a wide range of diversification – overspecialisation, on the other hand, leads to rigidity and increased vulnerability.

Ethnic pluralism

Much of the tension and violence in the world today stems from competing ethnic groups in nation states. There has been a strong tendency for the heritage of these ethnic minorities, and their rights, to be abridged by dominant majorities. Ethnic tensions have, therefore, been endemic throughout the world during the second half of the twentieth-century, with long-running civil wars. In some cases, the violence has threatened to cause the break-up of many African nations as well as resulting in large-scale loss of life in such countries as Cambodia. The same type of problems have caused civil unrest in many countries of Latin America.

This issue has become dramatically visible as Communist power has disintegrated and past hatreds have resurfaced. The civil war in the former Yugoslavia showed the dangers of massive fragmentation, as provinces declared themselves independent of the centre and their sovereignty was officially recognised. The break-up of the Soviet Union restored Estonia, Latvia and Lithuania to nationhood.

Solutions to ethnic issues require that the redefinition of sovereignty, discussed in the last chapter, be constantly kept in mind. Current definitions of "absolute" sovereignty cause two destructive patterns. One has been a largely unconscious assumption of superiority, causing the majority group to believe it has the "right" answers. The fact that others might see the world in a different way has been ignored. This was the primary pattern that controlled the thinking of the colonial powers who assumed they were bringing the gift of progress and order to the "lesser breeds".

The other process is totally conscious. It is the deliberate use of power to ensure that one ethnic group – which has an electoral majority or economic or military superiority – gets what it wants at the cost of others. This pattern has been all too common throughout the world.. Instead of recognising the need for majority rule and minority rights, the majority all too often uses its power to dominate.

The tragic, long-running Sri Lankan civil war emerged from majority pressure. In 1983, the Presidential campaign promised "Sinhalese in 24 hours" if an election was won. The language of the majority was made official, replacing English, which had been more effectively learned by the Tamils. The Tamils naturally felt that this was unfair and responded with the violence which has resulted in thousands of deaths and gravely damaged the development dynamics of a nation which were previously very promising.

The ethnic issue is often deliberately downplayed by those who believe in nation-state models because recognition of its importance challenges current structures. For decades, and indeed centuries, the goal has been to break down and eliminate ethnic differences. For almost a quarter of a century, I lived for part of the year in Scotland. When we arrived in the mid-seventies, the uniqueness of the Scottish culture was well on its way to being lost. Today, there has been a recovery – indeed, a huge experiment has been launched to enable Scotland, Ireland and Wales to make decisions within Great Britain.

Given that the nation-state is not a viable organisational form for the twenty-first century, the nature of the ethnic question shifts in critical ways. We can no longer assume that the nation-state will be strong enough to suppress ethnic vitality nor that it will be wise for it to do so. Moving from nation-state dominance to the reemergence of ethnic strengths is going to raise very difficult questions. Ethnic memories are very long. Violence tends to develop as each group tries to take revenge for past "injustices". Because all sides have their own tragedies to avenge, the potentials for escalation are enormous.

Kosovo is showing us how complex are the problems. The Serb minority felt besieged by the Albanian majority and used its power to carry out atrocities; some of these were almost certainly government ordered but others were obviously the result of passions which flared out of control during the NATO bombing. When the Kosovars returned, they took their revenge on the Serbs. All of the dynamics were complicated by long memories of the atrocities in World War II and the hundreds of years before.

Cultures all too often define their experiences in terms of their past tragedies rather than by looking at their own unique strengths. Only as each ethnic group regains pride in its own history, and moves beyond defining itself as superior to its past enemies, can societies grow beyond violence. If ethnic groups can regain their self-respect, then they will learn to collaborate. Violence is the resort of the weak, not of the strong.

Fortunately, more progress has been made towards positive images than is commonly realised. Referring again to our Scottish experience, dance, music and the Gaelic have been revived, together with a sense that Scotland can be proud of its own heritage rather than angry with the English. Other ethnic groups have moved in similar directions. They are coming to see their history as providing values to the world.

Ethnic strength could provide a reservoir of solidarity to the world if we are willing to tap into it rather than fear it. The roots of ethnic groups go deep into the soil. Each area also supports its own vision and its own humour: I remember walking to our home in Scotland carrying one of the old-fashioned vacuum-cleaners with hoses sprouting from every part of it. A passer-by saw its resemblance to the bagpipes and told me; "You'll never got a tune out of that, laddy!" He assumed that I would get the joke because the bagpipes are central to Scottish culture.

We need to move beyond the anger of the past and towards a recognition of the need for diversity. As discussed, the appropriate image for the future is that of a tapestry with a very rich pattern rather than a melting pot in which all differences are submerged. The tapestry image encourages each group to develop its own primary colours while committing to a total picture of which each person and culture can be part.

The future depends on whether we see the world as fragmented and broken or diverse and exciting. This is largely a matter of the way we choose to view reality.

Patterns of intervention

If we are to provide greater local freedom, we must also ask what happens when local dynamics go wrong. Given that more rights and responsibilities will be held close to the people, when do other groups have a right – and a responsibility – to intervene? There are several different aspects to this question. What's appropriate when a community is harming its members?

What about the region that uses so much water that its downstream neighbours are deprived? What about the nation-state which fails to live within its resource base?

It is extraordinarily difficult to get our heads around these questions. Because of our history, there is an assumption that not only does government know best but it will always be effective when it tries to control problems. The idea that "masterly inaction" may be a healthy policy is almost always a subject of ridicule – thus the first natural reaction, when things get out of line, is for an outside group to come in and straighten things out.

We forget that there is another possible model. This aims to challenge people to organise themselves to produce the direction they want. *Glory Road*, one of Robert Heinlein's stories, deals with this issue on a very different scale. The plot assumes that there is a government covering a myriad of galaxies, its leader imprinted with the wisdom of those who have held power before. The main lesson that has been learned from millennia of history is that intervention usually makes things worse. Letting things work themselves out, however messy and unsatisfactory this may be, often proves to be the best course.

The real choice which lies before us is whether to concentrate on the negative or to accentuate the positive. Western societies have spent much of their time drawing attention to the weaknesses and failures of people and institutions. Far less effort has been made to inform people about the positive and to spread information about what can be done. There is far more chance of making the necessary transformations if all of us concentrate on what is possible, rather than bemoaning the seriousness of the current crises.

Negativity and whining disempower; they make people feel that things are hopeless. Change agents need to help individuals and groups believe it is possible to deal with issues. While there will be times when intervention is required to prevent totally unacceptable dynamics, we should always remember that spending time fighting the negative takes energy away from developing the positive. Building is always tougher than tearing down and it takes great persistence to stick with it.

John McKnight, an American thinker, can take great credit for a widespread shift from deficit to asset thinking. In the past, communities were largely dominated by explorations of what was wrong with them. Today, more and more discussions start from the positive. People look for potentials and opportunities.

Obviously, there are times when situations are so serious that intervention is essential. Any decisions to use power to interrupt local evolution should be tested using several criteria. The first is to be sure that the standards being upheld are really applicable in the situation rather than resulting from one's own cultural background. Given the desirability of creative actions throughout the culture, one must be absolutely certain that those who are acting contrary to one's own instincts are not pioneering a possible new route into the future. During the industrial era, the tendency has been for those at "higher" levels to believe that they knew better – in the compassionate era, the bias must be exactly the opposite.

The second need is to apply the message of the serenity prayer, which demands that we distinguish between what can be changed and what cannot. Some interventions are possible and others will not work or may even be counterproductive. All too many people still feel it is enough to do the "right" thing; they feel justified in shrugging off any undesirable second and third level consequences resulting from their interventions. This approach is intolerable in the compassionate era.

The third need is to remember what will not be thought about or done as a result of choosing to intervene. Resources are always scarce. The decision to be active in one area implies that one will pay less attention to other issues and questions. It is relatively easy to see that it would be desirable to do something – it is far harder to weigh whether one area of activity is more helpful than another. Attention is today's scarcest commodity. If it is used for one purpose, other potentials and dangers will be treated less seriously or ignored.

Finally, one must ask whether a community is more likely to be effective in the future if an outside intervention takes place.

In the long run, the only way to develop a self-governing community is to encourage people to become committed citizens. If people come to believe that outsiders are willing to make the tough decisions for them, they will be less likely to make an effort of their own. If they find that outsiders are unwilling to let them make their own choices, on the grounds that they are inappropriate or wrong, they will simply back off and lose interest in leadership.

Good decision-making in the twenty-first century requires that we learn to think and act despite our inability to be certain. We must learn to focus our gut feelings and intuition rather than hope to find hard data. We need to rely on contexted knowledge rather than information.

Population issues

In more and more parts of the world, population is growing beyond the carrying-capacity of the land, water and air to support it. To what extent can, and should, the global community deal with the consequences of this situation. Alternatively, should problems of this type be confined within national boundaries?

In the poorer countries, the most urgent need is to provide birth control information to all those who want it. Failure to move in these directions will force compulsory efforts to limit births in wider and wider areas of the world. Even the most immediate action in this area will not prevent crises in a number of countries, the most obvious of which are Bangladesh, China and some of the Saharan nations.

Many years ago, Garrett Hardin, who has written extensively on population issues, suggested a way to deal with the issue of inadequate resources. He proposed that there should be a conscious adoption of "a lifeboat ethic". He argued that if a lifeboat was full already, those in it were justified in keeping others out even though this resulted in people drowning. His parallel was with the world that he claimed was approaching the limits of its carrying capacity. He argued that keeping people alive through aid would only worsen the problem. His thesis was very simple: if people get food, they will keep on having babies. The only way to prevent them from doing so is to permit starvation to occur when a country is unable to support its population, thus bringing the area back to an equilibrium position.

Population experts have feared overpopulation ever since the traditional high birth-rate and high death-rate pattern in the poor countries was broken at the end of World War II. Medical care led to the survival of more and more children as well as rapid lengthening of the average lifespan. Garrett Hardin was right to draw our attention to the emerging problem, however I have always felt that Hardin's model doesn't work, even at the level of the image. Suppose a lot of people are in a lifeboat and a lot are outside. Suppose further that those outside feel that those inside gained their position in the lifeboat unjustly. In this case, they are likely to try to upset the lifeboat even at the risk that nobody will be saved at all.

The fact that the image is flawed does not undermine the validity of the question. When conditions become intolerable people are likely to try to flee their situation – are other countries responsible for taking them in? There are four significantly different situations.

A conference called by the Council of Europe to look at the possibility of massive migration from Eastern to Western Europe, estimated it might reach as high as 30 million people. According to the report in the *Wall Street Journal*:

> There was unanimous agreement, according to delegates, that a strict separation must be made between genuine refugees, as defined by the 1951 Geneva Convention – those fleeing wars or religious or political persecution, and so-called economic refugees – people seeking to migrate for better economic opportunities.

The United States uses the same distinction to exclude many people from Latin America while letting in most Europeans, claiming the same status without serious challenge. Refugees, however, find such a distinction highly theoretical, because the very act of fleeing a country will often be seen as a political act which makes return highly dangerous.

Bangladesh forms a second type of case. What is the appropriate response to the ever-worsening population pressure in this area of the world? Should more and more resources be provided from outside? Should outward migration be permitted? Or should the area be warned that it cannot expect continuing aid from the rest of the world – and what would this mean?

The third type of question emerges because overcrowded, overextended cities may break down in the twenty-first Century. The most immediately challenging problem for the United States is Mexico City. There is growing evidence that the combination of environmental damage and poverty is leading to the potential for a massive collapse. Can the United States do anything significant to help prevent this possibility and, if it did occur, what would be the correct attitudes? What are the implications of the fact that the largest cities will be in the poor nations and that, unless trends change dramatically, most people will live in shanty towns.

A fourth question develops when countries, such as China, impose draconian limits on births because, in their view, their country cannot support a significantly larger population. The United States has argued against this strategy. Does it have any standing to act in this way?

Limiting violence

How are areas of the world which use very different approaches to governance going to be able to avoid wars during the next half-century, when communication failures will make conflicts difficult to resolve? This is a key question that must be faced if the number and intensity of wars are to be reduced. How are the wounds of centuries and millennia to be healed? There are several core needs to address, and these are set out below.

1. To avoid building up tyrants for reasons of Realpolitik. (Realpolitik is a word used to imply that moral values must take a back seat to pragmatic issues.)

The time has come for the world community to demand certain basic standards. Saddam Hussein and Hitler have often been compared; the real parallel with Hitler is that neither he nor Hussein would have become major threats if the world community had been willing to deal with them before they built up their power. Hitler would have been forced to withdraw his invading armies if European countries reacted strongly to his early breaches of the Versailles treaty; the failure to protest encouraged his future conduct. Similarly, the decision of the Western powers to build up Iraq in order to prevent a victory by Iran produced the invasion of Kuwait.

Future directions should be chosen in terms of whether they will lead to a world order of responsible freedom. While Realpolitik will still sometimes be more important than the long-run need to build towards a value-based culture, positive stands should only be abandoned when the case for doing so is overwhelming. In our rapidly changing, and heavily interconnected world, the consequences of Realpolitik decisions will haunt the future. The forces that support responsible freedom should be encouraged wherever they surface throughout the world.

2. To prevent tyrants from gaining possession of modern weaponry.

Unfortunately, the international sale of weapons, particularly to countries in the Third World, has been a major factor in achieving economic growth in the wealthier countries. Almost all the governments of the world support arms sales. Businesses have all too often been willing to break the few regulations that have been imposed by governments.

In the thirties, there was an outcry against "merchants of death" – ie. companies who sold weapons to any purchaser who could pay. Today, more and more countries are destroying the quality of life of their citizens by spending an increasing percentage of their budgets on arms. In their own long-run self-interest, all countries need to de-escalate tensions and reduce arms expenditures. Global public opinion must demand that countries cease using weaponry exports as a prime means of supporting economic growth and balancing foreign trade. Citizens should also support treaties which lead to disarmament rather than the constant increase in the destructive potential of regional enemies. Japan, for example, has decided that the military policies of developing countries will be a factor in deciding how much aid they receive. This is the type of government initiative which can help shift priorities.

3. To reduce the vulnerability of nations to behaviour they cannot control.

Disruptions in the Middle East are intolerable to the United States because of its excessive dependence on oil – which is, in turn, a result of past policy failures. If America had done as much as Japan and many European countries to develop energy efficiency, the importance of the Middle East to the US would not be as great. Indeed, Japan's view of the Gulf Crisis was very different, precisely because it was less vulnerable to disruptions of its oil supply. The debate over how to reduce energy demand, and the right mix of sources for the energy still required, must now take centre-stage.

The United States used massive power following the invasion of Kuwait because it feared interruptions in the supply of oil. This danger was greatly overstated. Most Middle East countries can no more afford a stoppage in their oil exports than importing countries can cope with a significant decrease in availability. The world is increasingly tied together in a web where disruptions cause damage all around. We can only flourish if others do well.

One of the elements in the Y2K debate is around the issue of our growing interconnectedness. Those who think that the issue is serious are very aware of the links between systems and our inability to determine how important they were. Just as nature forms a seamless, interconnected web, so increasingly does our technology. Interruptions – whether caused by terrorism, strikes or errors – are increasingly dangerous.

In the industrial era, humanity thought in win-lose terms: "If I do better, then you will do worse". In the new compassionate era, we are understanding that life is a seamless web. John Donne knew this centuries ago when he said: "Do not ask for whom the bell tolls, it tolls for thee".

Building a transnational web

Some of the most visible of the existing coordination groups work on international transportation (both sea and air), weather, telecommunications and mail. Nations are also just beginning to collaborate on environmental issues.

Ceding considerable decision-making authority to transnational organisations now seems essential. The Universal Postal Union facilitates the movement of the mail throughout the world. Every country has an interest in a common set of patterns to facilitate sea and air transportation. Transnational rules are seen as a way of supporting the concerns of everybody involved and relatively few tense disagreements therefore develop. There is a growing commitment to clear, understandable rules.

Weather is another area where better knowledge is recognised as critically important by all nations. This information is now perceived as so vital that reporting often continues despite wars. Weather reporting has indeed become "transnational" in nature.

Telecommunications pose far more difficult problems. The number of bands for electronic communication are fixed. While the supply is being stretched by technological innovation which permits more efficient usage, it is still finite; the question of which countries and areas of the world get what shares of the limited pie involves difficult and tough negotiations. Discussions in this area are models for the decision-making processes that will have to take place as more and more of the products and services in the world have to be fairly allocated. Southern nations believe that the north already has too large a share and will inevitably strive for reallocation.

Another area where changes have been taking place in the last decades is around the issues of the seas and oceans. Transnational agreements on limitation of whaling and fishing have been given more and more "teeth" as the seriousness of the situation has become apparent. As a result, nation-states have ceded authority not to a transnational government, but rather to ecological realities. The self-interest of everybody is today seen differently than in the past. – the international treaty on the use of the oceans has brought some sanity to many aspects of this shared international resource, despite the failure of the United States to ratify the treaty.

The agreement to phase out the use of chlorofluorocarbons and to report progress to a supranational body represents a new level of transnational cooperation. Some of the wealthier countries agreed that the need to ban CFCs was so important that they have committed to providing technological support to the poorer countries to aid the process of phasing out these products. The loss of ozone over temperate zones hastened commitments significantly.

The issue of most tension at this point is global warming. Countries agreed at a conference in Kyoto to cut emissions of greenhouse gasses substantially. Many countries have not yet ratified the agreement, and the goals that were set will require far larger shifts in behaviour than those yet contemplated. Nevertheless. we can expect transnational agreements to continue to develop as we recognise our interconnected self-interest. This is one of the routes into the compassionate era.

Once again what we choose to see is determined by the story we use to make sense of the world. The same set of trends can be seen as desirable or dangerous depending on the beliefs one holds about the future. As I have constantly stressed, I believe that survival requires the recognition of the need for a radically new story that promotes social cohesion, ecological integrity and effective decision-making.

Chapter 12

How to Sing Our Story

We have lost our sense of celebration of ourselves and the universe. Human survival does not only depend on getting our thinking right. We are all "artists" who need to create a cultural picture, or story, which will satisfy our soul. Joy is as much a part of a good life as rationality.

Each culture has a "story". This story is normally invisible because, in stable times, most people take their beliefs for granted. They act within set norms and do not even recognise that there are other options. Today all of us being forced to deal with mindquakes. We are half-way through the eye of the hurricane.

One of the primary causes of the sudden fundamental changes taking place at this time is that human relationships with the planet are coming full circle. Hunting and gathering religions had rituals that continuously reminded them of the need to be thankful for the benefits they received from earth's bounty. Populations rose and fell as a result of high fertility, on the one hand, and the toll of war, famine, pestilence and plagues, on the other. It rarely reached the level where it could significantly impact even on local environments.

Dynamics changed dramatically as animals were domesticated and crops cultivated. Significant environmental damage developed in the Middle East over two millennia ago when populations grew and human beings became more and more convinced that they could outpower nature. Damage began to affect planetary systems in the twentieth-century as industrial production increased to the point that it interfered with global balancing systems.

What approaches should we now develop to reintegrate human beings into natural systems? One step has been stressed again and again in this book: the need to move beyond the current commitment to maximum economic growth. However, this change will not be sufficient unless there is also a sharp shift in the way that human beings and organisations think and relate to the world around us.

Garrett Hardin wrote a classic article around this theme many years ago with the title 'The Tragedy of the Commons'. He explored the reason why European common land, where everybody could graze animals, was often destroyed by overgrazing. He pointed out that each person would place additional animals on the land, in the knowledge that the impact of their flock was not large enough, by itself, to do damage. The overall impact, however, was disastrous. Similar problems have emerged in Africa as tribes, which count their welfare in cattle, have destroyed the habitats on which they count for survival.

Hardin argued convincingly that this same phenomenon was developing on a very broad scale throughout the world. The "commons" of the air, water and land were being despoiled because they were "nobody's business" and everybody saw their own contribution to the damage as marginal. Having posed the dilemma, he provided no answer, but as people have struggled with this issue in the years since he wrote, two answers have emerged at different ends of the spectrum.

One group believes that the only hope is to increase the amount of power that nation-states have over individuals and institutions. For example, Donella Meadows, who has been one of the most creative people in the movement towards a sustainable society, has proposed limiting the amount of CO_2 in the atmosphere in order to reduce the "greenhouse" effect. She then makes the following suggestion.

> The amount of human-generated carbon emission the planet can take without being clinically deranged is perhaps one billion tons per year. That requires an eighty per cent cut from present emissions – to about zero point two tons per person on earth. Now suppose that we allocate to every nation the right to emit zero

point two tons per person of that nation's 1990 population.

Any nation that wants to burn more fuel or cut more forest than that would have to buy emission rights from a nation that won't or can't use up its allowance. The price per ton of emission would be set in an open market. It would undoubtedly be high enough to eliminate any need for foreign aid, to pay off Third World debts, and to settle the problem of economic inequity forever. It would also be a powerful incentive to practice energy efficiency, to develop solar energy, and to preserve and replant forests.

Here's an important kicker. Since total emission rights would be set at what the planet can ever tolerate, each nation's allocation would be fixed forever. If the population of that nation grows, that's too bad – its emissions per person would have to shrink. If the population slowly decreases, as some European populations are now doing, then each person's share would increase.

Stop and think for a moment about this proposal. According to Meadows, the first reaction of those at a meeting in Denmark where this idea surfaced was rejection – and, after a while, a belief that it would be fair. I understand the temptation to adopt a model of this type but I would suggest to you that, hidden within its logic, is the inevitability of a terrifying police state.

It all sounds so easy. But who is going to collect the statistics, and how are people going to be compelled to do what they must to reduce the amount of CO_2? In addition, once this type of regulatory principle has been agreed for CO_2 emissions, there are inevitably going to be quotas set for other noxious products. We would therefore move further and further into a controlled society with "thought police" everywhere – and because there would be increasing law and regulation, people would try to cheat.

This approach represents the exact opposite of the directions I have been proposing throughout this book. The conclusion from all my arguments is that people must learn the need to preserve natural systems. Many different patterns can be combined to create this result. Support can emerge from an instinctive negative reaction to the smell of chemicals and the sight of garbage.

It can also result from a highly sophisticated understanding of the dangers that arise if natural cycles are interrupted to the point that the long-run climate on earth is drastically changed. As this value-shift occurs, each one of us will need to reexamine our lifestyles and life-choices so that preventing damage to nature and ecological systems is higher on our personal priorities, and on our institutional, economic and societal agendas. The more open the political system, the more rapidly these new choices will impact upon current structures.

Free markets can be successful in determining how pollution is reduced. But they will only do so if we first decide, as a society, that this goal is high on our priority list. (Let us remember again that free markets are effective when they determine our "hows", but that they should never be permitted to become the arbiter of what societies want to support.)

This approach also throws new light on the issue of private property. An enormous amount of damage has been done in the past as people have claimed that ownership of land and resources has given them the right to destroy the land and use resources carelessly. As the human race moves towards an understanding of ecological necessities, the rights inherent in private property can make it possible to ensure that the land, water and air is once again seen as a sacred trust.

The costs of destructive use of private property by a few can again be exceeded by the benefits of responsible decisions by the many. We can redevelop a belief in "usufruct", where people had the right to benefit from the fruitfulness of the land but were required by tribal ethics to pass it on undamaged and, indeed, improved. This approach requires that not only private individuals but also corporations and governments recognise that they have responsibilities to the land.

The central challenge our societies face is to rethink our fundamental attitudes. Traditional Christianity believed that human beings had a right to subdue nature; there are a growing number of biblical scholars who believe, on the contrary, that

Genesis has been misunderstood and that human beings are meant to be stewards of nature rather than controllers of it. Lynn White sums up the challenge.

> Since the roots of our trouble are so largely religious, the remedy must also be religious, whether we call it that or not. We must think and re-feel our nature and destiny. The profoundly religious, but heretical, sense of the primitive Fransiscans for the spiritual autonomy of all parts of nature may point a direction. I propose Francis as a patron saint for ecologists.

In the last decade, we have seen the issue of spirituality move to the centre of the dialogue about the future. People are realising that rationality is not enough either for our personal lives nor for our social interaction. The old dogma of original sin that saw us in thrall to our worst natures is dying. We are recognising the potential of Matthew Fox's concept of original blessing.

This does not mean however that we can believe in Utopia – a world without problems. Some people, some of the time, will still want to cheat, steal and lie. Some people will seek power and misuse it. The price of freedom is still eternal vigilance, but we can afford to believe that most people, most of the time, want to make things better rather than worse.

We need to fully confront the question posed by Bacon. Is the control on our appetites to be placed within us or outside of us? I believe that the human adventure can only continue if we commit ourselves to a process of education which will help us all make responsible choices about our own lives and the planet.

Seeing everything as politics

The essential revolution that has to take place if we are to resolve the crisis of governance now afflicting us is to broaden our definition of politics. Politics should not be thought of only as the thoughts and actions of our elected officials. Rather we must understand that it is the sum total of our actions as they affect our collective decision-making. Our purchases are political. Our commitment to our church, and feelings about its involvement in the world, are political. Our activities to support, or ignore, education are political. Our attitudes towards the disadvantaged and the dispossessed are political, and our choices about our entertainment dollars are political.

Citizens, moving together, make the waves that define political options. Politicians merely ride them, often changing their opinions to make sure they are re-elected. The critical part of the political process is not the decisions on issues that have already surfaced – rather, it is the effort given to surfacing new questions. The movement to ban smoking has been a highly significant political effort. So has the movement against drink-driving and the decision to bring AIDS out of the shadows.

For too long, we have been concentrating on what happens in national, state and provincial capitals. Our challenge today is to learn how to help people change their ideas of appropriate directions and their self-interest. All of us who are interested in developing a better world need to discover how to help people move beyond their current definitions of self-interest.

The division between "learning" and "politics" will vanish over time; if I were writing about these topics in the middle of the twenty-first century, there would be no difference between them. However, as we are so accustomed to putting these two activities into separate boxes it will be easier to understand them if I continue the tradition.

There are three necessary steps as we move from industrial-era to compassionate-era institutions and communities. The first is to build trust and relationships. Industrial-era systems are meant to operate on logic, structure and hierarchy; compassionate-era systems operate on hunch, intuition, perception, and even "magic". At a recent meeting, where companies were taking the first steps towards a supplier council and talking to each other about how to cooperate, this word "magic" was frequently used to describe the effectiveness of interactions after trust had developed.

As people learn to work and play together, levels of activity and performance rise dramatically. Many people are today ready to commit to trust and relationships but there are few places in our current society where they can "try their wings".

We must recognise, however that we are all different in our thoughts and action. Even when we are aiming to support others, we shall disappoint them. It is easy for people to see these failures as deliberate, rather than the result of different perceptions and understandings.

Industrial-era systems deny the importance of trust. Today's approaches, as we have already seen, are all too often adversarial. We believe that the only way to make forward progress is to fight those with whom we disagree. The idea that we could get more done by working with people – rather than disagreeing with them – is largely foreign to dominant cultural norms. Even our forms of discussion tend to be in the "but" rather than the "and" style.

Those people who are in the minority can be permanently embittered if they are constantly put down and overruled, and the validity of their ideas continually denied. We shall only build trust if we can convince people that they have been listened to and heard – then they may be willing to listen to others. This approach is critically important both when setting up small groups and in working with continuing political processes.

Meetings in Renton, a small town outside Seattle, made the need to think seriously about these dynamics very clear. Both the Council and the Planning Board were basically destroying themselves because there was no trust within the groups. In a long discussion, a few of us agreed that the key task was to help people understand that they would be listened to even if all of their ideas would not necessarily be adopted. It is amazing how much wisdom can be garnered once one admits that it can come from a large variety of sources rather than only one's friends.

I recently read about a psychiatrist who learned the same message on a one-on-one level. He tried a large variety of techniques to help people to see into their own lives, and eventually recognised that there was a common denominator behind all of these methods: the existence of careful and respectful listening.

The second step is to create new ideas and structures for the future. When people trust each other, they are willing to say what they really think and believe. This is the raw material for new ways of seeing the world. Creativity provides the potential for totally novel understandings of how we can create equity in the world. It permits us to break out of the obsolete ideologies that are still controlling our world and preventing us from seeing the new opportunities and dangers which surround us.

In recent years we have tended to assume that "brainstorming" and creativity are the same thing; when we need to come up with new ideas we bring out flip charts and let people state their ideas. After this process has taken place, we classify all that has been said and assume that this represents the best thinking of those in the group.

We often fail to remember that most people, for obvious reasons, tend to raise the issues they think are acceptable – this is particularly true when the results of an activity will affect the credibility and power of those involved. If one wants individuals to talk about their real ideas, this can only take place after trust has been built. The specific requirement is that those involved in a creativity process know that the results of their thinking will not be held against them.

People must not lose brownie points because they say things that are not "politically correct". The purpose of a creativity session is to find new ways of dealing with tough questions – the only way this can be done is by raising all the critical issues. Wild ideas must also be encouraged. Some of the thoughts will be "stupid", but they may trigger better ideas down the road. Individuals need to be clear about the expectations for this type of activity, otherwise they will be excessively careful.

In today's world when people are so fearful for their future, the problems in ensuring creativity are even more difficult. All too often it is the person who goes along who gets promoted rather than the person who takes risks. We need to learn to support those who challenge the status quo rather than those who support the inertia of current systems.

The third step is to create effective action. "Partnerships" – where the various "players" in a situation get together and decide to come up with action steps they can all accept – are a good way to support new directions. These partnership models are only effective if people have already been through the stages of trust-building and creativity within their own systems. Partnerships require that people are honest with each other in terms of what they want and what the politics of their systems are. In addition, partnerships demand that people know how to look for novel solutions rather than be blocked by their current ideological thinking.

A growing number of partnerships involve public, private and non-profit groups. They would spread more rapidly if the law could be redesigned to make cooperation between these groups easier. All too often, collaboration is restricted by fears of liability and legal suits. We need a new hybrid legal form permitting public, private and governmental cooperation. We also need to recognise that the ideal of a "riskless" and "perfect" society currently underlying so much of our legislation is totally unrealistic.

Despite all the problems of our times, a very large number of new models are developing around the United States, and across the world. We need to ask why it is so difficult to learn about the many exciting ways in which people are seizing opportunities and dealing with problems. There are two primary reasons. The first is that the media still define news as "bad news" – there are few slots for positive events.

In addition, many of the groups that have been creative feel no responsibility to spread the word about their efforts. There seem to a number of motivations for this failure. Some people do not want to take time away from their local work, while some don't want to be seen as blowing their own horn too loudly. Some don't want to give away the results of their work for free.

I suspect that there may also be one overarching block to communication: many of the most exciting programs and processes cut across the current success criteria of our industrial-era culture. People are therefore not sure that what they are doing is important, and even if they are personally convinced that their activities are valuable, they may fear they will be attacked by those who still want to preserve the old-style culture. This is particularly true in the field of education. There are a lot of people who don't want significant educational change – they are often extraordinarily vocal and even violent. People may not want to expose themselves to the dangers that come with going "public".

One of the most critical needs of our time is to make it clear within each system, and the culture as a whole, that innovators and leaders will be respected and honoured. This change of emphasis would be of great value to those who have devoted their lives to bringing about fundamental change. Perhaps one can look forward to the day when those who have struggled to build a just society will get as much attention as athletes!

New measures of success

One way to improve communication among those who are creating positive changes is to encourage people to feel that their efforts are in the mainstream, rather than isolated on the frontier or even running against the dynamic of the culture. Healthy human beings and societies want to succeed, and if we can show individuals and groups that what they are doing is valued, they are more likely to be open about their activities.

A book written by Marilyn Ferguson in the seventies discussed the problem of the isolated few – the fact that there were people who were aware of the need for change but they did not know how to contact each other. Bob Stilger, my closest colleague, has enlarged this statement and talks about the "isolated many". He says that there are now a large number of people who are ready for change but we still have not found the linking mechanisms to bring us together.

The success criteria that dominate behaviour vary from era to era. The primary success criterion for the industrial era was maximum economic growth. One purpose of this book has been to propose new images of success, while the next challenge is to find ways to measure how successful we have been.

It is a basic truth that what cultures measure, they will also value. Once a measurement has been established, and is seen as having consequences, efforts will be made to move it in positive directions. For example, schools have recently been fixated on improving performance scores. Doctors try to reduce death rates. Capitalist firms focus on increasing profits. Government organisations aim to meet targets, and countries want to increase Gross Domestic Product (GDP).

Some goals are valuable, some are neutral, while some are positively damaging. Many of the measures we have inherited from the industrial era fall into this last category. The GDP is one of the most seriously flawed. GDP figures were created to measure industrial productivity. They are totally unsuitable for determining whether the social welfare of a culture is improving or worsening. In particular, they do not take into account the implications of extreme poverty.

In looking at the flaws of the current approaches and examining future potentials, I cannot do better than state the measurements proposed at a meeting on 'Redefining Wealth and Progress' held in Caracas in 1989. It started from the approaches that could be used to measure success in countries where the level of poverty is so desperate today that calculations must be simple. The primary suggested measures were the:

- percentage of the population below the poverty level
- success rate of completing first grade at school in the allotted time
- levels of pollution and the degree of destruction of natural resources
- mortality index of children under five
- number of children with low birth weights
- weight and height measurements in relation to age.

The report then proposed that countries with larger data bases study public safety, nutrition, health, education, basic services, shelter, child development, employment and the status of women.

As we move away from money measures to broader social indices, we need to decide whether we should aim to ensure comparability between areas and nations or whether we create measures particularly suitable for each geographical area. In the industrial era, the emphasis was always placed on comparability. In the compassionate era, the need will be to concentrate on the specifics of a local situation. Thus an arid area needs to pay particular attention to its success in water conservation while one with lots of water will see measures in this area as less important. Similarly, an area with a mild and equable climate will have very different views about housing than one with temperature extremes.

Planetary networking

New images of success change our self-perceptions. In the fifties, for example, many companies throughout the world had murals featuring clouds of black smoke because this was seen as a symbol of prosperity. As people became more aware of the environmental issues, smoke became a negative. Murals were then repainted to show a clean, pastoral scene with cows and factories coexisting. Some people deny the importance of this change in images, dismissing it as mere public relations and image-making; they fail to understand that when images change, they create a different set of priorities. The environment is now a potent force in transnational decision-making.

The really critical struggle is always for the hearts and minds of people. The fundamental, although largely unnoticed, debate in the second half of the twentieth-century has been around the "success criteria" each person should adopt for themselves and their societies. Major changes in thought patterns have taken place since World War II and action priorities today differ significantly from those of the fifties. People are demanding more of themselves and of their cultures.

As people become more comfortable with their potentials, they link with others who are also working towards new and positive directions on a world-wide basis. As discussed earlier, Teilhard de Chardin grasped the importance of this process at the beginning of the twentieth-century and developed the concept of the "noosphere", which would tie together all those who were being creative about the direction of the world. He saw it as a set of invisible threads connecting thinking people everywhere. Today his concept is being created as millions of people throughout the world are interconnected through thousands of networks.

The operation of networks is based on very different approaches from those that control bureaucratic systems. Networks are held together by the common interests of those involved rather than by the power over resources which is available to the people at the top of bureaucratic systems. Networks last as long as common interests can be clearly enough articulated to attract time and resources from their members.

In the fifties, Charles Merrifield, who was one of my mentors, encouraged an awareness of the ever-growing number of networking nongovernmental organisations (NGOs) that were key elements in the development of the noosphere. These organisations, which cover every conceivable field, pull together the creative energy of people throughout the world and develop bonds which are often stronger than those which link people to their nation-state. Non-governmental organisations have little power but they do have great influence and authority.

They have already served to reduce some of the worst abuses against human dignity in the world. For example, Amnesty International, through its reputation and the energy of its members, has ended many political imprisonments and curbed torture in a wide range of countries. Their concentration on individual cases has led to releases of prisoners, even in countries that pay least attention to world public opinion. Increasingly, the reports of this organisation affect the standing of a country in global opinion.

NGOs have been highly effective because they help to change the views and behaviour of people. Unfortunately, however, they often limit their own potential by seeing their work as preparatory to the passage of legislation. Many of them believe that only shifts in legal structures will make them successful, when in reality, the noosphere will only become truly effective when those within it devote their efforts to providing citizens with the skills to make decisions for themselves rather than working primarily with governments to coerce behaviour.

Why is this issue critical? One way to understand it is by considering the questions which underscored the UN Conference on the Environment and Development in Brazil in June 1992. There were two ways to structure the debate – one was to concentrate on governmental agreements which would force changes in behaviour, while the other was to educate people to understand the critical importance of preserving environmental balance for their own lives and succeeding generations. The argument of this book leads inescapably to the conclusion that the largest part of the effort should have been educational and the smaller part regulatory – unfortunately the process had the opposite priorities.

The rhetorics of democracy no longer suffice. We must move towards the reality of responsible freedom. It will be extraordinarily difficult to make this shift because most existing socioeconomic systems function using coercive power. If we really believed in our democratic rhetoric, the freeing implications of the noosphere would be easy to grasp. Because our pragmatic commitment is to the power of large institutions, networking seems naive and unbelievable to most people.

The old stories by which people live and the new one which is now emerging are in conflict. The old story assumes that order must be imposed by power; the new story is based on "chaos theory" which argues that well-balanced and strong systems will show a surface disorder that conceals a deeper order. A great deal of the needed change can be expected to emerge as people and systems self-organise.

One of the most interesting ways of understanding this reality is to recognise the principles that underlie the operation of the body. Given the implications of chaos theory, doctors are taking more notice of the very wide range of hourly and daily fluctuations in such indicators as pulse and blood pressure. They are discovering that balance is preserved as movement around an "ideal" state takes place. They are also discovering that when the body does not show fluctuations, for example in pulse rates, this may be a predictor of heart attacks.

The fact that our bodies maintain stability at all is, in a very real sense, a "miracle". One task of humanity today is to discover how to design cultures to mimic the complex feedback loops in the body – or more broadly in environmental systems. Fluctuations always need to exist in healthy societies; it's commonly known that military units are in trouble when the griping stops.

Confusion and argument in democracies is a sign of health as long as everybody respects the position of others and is honest, rather than manipulative, when stating their positions. Automatic feedback loops based on broadly conceived self-interest and positive self-image will then lead in creative directions.

Moving up the involvement ladder

How does one choose where to put one's effort? What patterns of action, creation and communication are most valuable? The answer to this question will be unique to the person, group or institution which is considering what it should be doing. There is no single key to the puzzle. We need many initiatives which all lead towards a more value-based society.

Your challenge is to find activities that inspire you and give you energy. When you connect with your personal concerns, and the needs of the world, you are noticed and your opportunities develop. There are always further levels of opportunity and these will emerge to the degree that you are successful in discovering your own skills and energies and how they link to the challenges of our time.

This is a progressive process. As Robert Burns, the great Scottish poet, wrote:

Oh wad some Pow'r the giftie gie us
To see ourselves as others see us.
It would from many a blunder free us
And foolish notion.

The challenge we face is to become aware of how our actions and activities are perceived by others. As we do this, we are able to be more effective. The fundamental challenge of the twenty-first century is to live the "examined" life. Each of us needs to learn about ourselves and the world around us. I hope I have helped to move you in this direction.

This is the first step. The second is to learn how to work with others with whom we disagree. Collaboration is the core challenge of the future. Once we recognise that others see their passions to be critical, just as we commit to our own, then we can search for the common ground between us.

I have been working at fundamental change issues for almost 50 years. I am able to keep going because I am convinced that our opportunities exceed our problems. If all of us who believe in a better future were to act effectively, the dangers which are now so pressing would be overcome.

The challenge can be met. I invite you to be a part of the process. The resource guide which closes this book suggests useful reading material, videos, and websites. Welcome to an already developing positive future.

Resources

It seems to me, these days, that the goal must be to provide a very limited number of starting points to people rather than extensive lists that people will drown in. The material listed below will provide a variety of further leads.

BOOKS.

Bateson, Gregory (1975) *Steps Toward an Ecology of Mind* New York: Ballantine,
Campbell, Joseph & Moyers, Bill (1988) *The Power of Myth* New York: Doubleday
Gleick, James (1987) *Chaos* New York: Viking
Greenleaf, Robert K. (1977) *Servant Leadership* New York: Paulist Press
Hubbard, Barbara Marx (1998) *Conscious Evolution* New World Library
Johnston, Charles M. (1984) *The Creative Imperative* Berkeley: Celestial Arts
Land, George & Jarman, Beth (1992) *Breakpoint and Beyond* New York: Harper Collins
Robertson, James (1985) *Future Work* New York: Universe Books
Russell, Peter (1998) *Waking Up in Time* Origin Press
Spretnak, Charlene(1999) *The Resurgence of the Real* Routledge,
Theobald, Robert (1999) *Visions and Pathways to the 21st Century* Lismore: Southern Cross University Press
Wheatley, Margaret (1994) *Leadership and the New Science* Berett Koehler
Woodslane in Australia and a new edition available in September 99
Whitworth, Laura, et al (1999) *Co-active Coaching* ACER: Davies-Black Press

292

WEB-SITES

Context Institute www.context.org
Local Self Reliance www.ilsr.org
Permaculture www.nor.com.au/environment/perma
Resilient Communities www.resilientcommunities.org
Simple Living www.simpleliving.net
Australia Connects www.australiaconnects.net
Reworking Tomorrow www.beciwtd.org.au/reworking/

INDEX

realising that it is not the technique which is important but the ability to make people feel heard and empowered.

- People must be encouraged to participate in dialogue with one another, without taboos about stating personal perceptions. They must learn to listen to views which they do not like. One of the hardest tasks is getting people to talk about their own views rather than stereotypes. They need to move beyond such statements as: "Managers feel..." or "Teachers believe..." to "I" statements where they state their personal feelings. Generalisations can follow after people are in touch with their own patterns of thought and belief.

- Information about the rapidly changing world must be introduced. Some new ideas will develop as people talk more honestly about their perceptions, and the wide range of understandings that exist in all groups thus become visible. Typically, however, outside influences (such as speakers, reading materials and videotapes) should be introduced to make people aware of how different the future is going to be from the past. The need to bring people up to date with emerging realities grows more urgent with every year as the certainties of the post-war world are swept away and new possibilities and dangers develop.

- It is essential that the people in the organisation align themselves with one another. This is the precondition for giving people more freedom to make decisions for themselves. Until alignment occurs, top-down decision making remains inevitable and cannot be avoided. The first step in achieving alignment is the development of trust and a sense of interdependence. The second step is encouraging a process of creativity where people become aware of the options and alternatives. The third step is providing guidelines that permit people to make decisions for themselves within broad limits.

- Finally, the involvement of outsiders is usually necessary. The outsider is purposefully neutral rather than supporting any individual or group in the change process.

The outsider is committed to the program. When things go wrong, the blame can be placed on the outsider so that the internal process can go forward with as little disruption as possible. Those who want to be a consultant to change processes should not need to be "loved": rather they should be willing to carry the burden of doing the best they can without worrying about whether this will lead to recognition or permanent activity. (Nobody can think only at this level, but being primarily concerned with one's own personal success and rewards almost guarantees the failure of renewal efforts.)

Institutional renewal should not be started unless the key players are willing to carry it through. Once people gain a sense that they may have more control over their lives and organisational decision making, you cannot remove this empowerment without the high probability that the last state of the organisation will be worse than the first.

Change processes can be sabotaged in two primary ways. One danger is that existing leaders often authorise, and seem excited about, fundamental reorganisations but do not recognise that they have strong personal needs to control others. Because they state their goal as "more responsive organisations", they often fail to perceive that the directions and solutions others will propose as they gain influence, will not be the same as those they would have chosen themselves. The consequent clash of priorities then becomes unacceptable to them. Programs are therefore often killed just when they are becoming effective. People who step out of line become pariahs, deprived of influence.

The other difficulty is that movements towards greater initiative may threaten other related systems or those "higher" in the organisation. The president of an organisation might be comfortable moving towards flatter management but the board might not. A unit of an organisation might want to change towards more freedom and autonomy but the head office might not be willing to have its control lessened in this way. My work in the Dallas Community College District fell apart for this reason. We showed that one of the community colleges within the district could be more creative and responsive, which threatened the control of the District Office. The key staff person was hired away, and control was restabilised.

The guidelines I have suggested above are, of course, counsels of perfection. Very often, efforts will have to go ahead with less than fully satisfactory situations. Keeping these optimum conditions in mind, however, will help minimise the problems that inevitably arise in any change process.

Linking decision-making and action through commitment-based systems

The computer is increasingly taking the place of middle management. People at the top of systems can often discover the detailed results of different possible approaches through using simulations. In order to evaluate potentials, however, they need to be in close touch with those who are the actors. This allows them to get an accurate picture of real conditions inside and outside the organisation.

The need for closer contact between the top and the bottom of institutions results from the fact that accurate movement of information within organisations is essential. SAS, the Scandinavian airline system, has pioneered efforts in this direction. Recognising that flight attendants largely determine the image of the company, SAS has developed direct links between top management and those who work with customers, providing the latter group with a great deal more authority to make decisions. Similarly, some American hotel chains have given their managers far greater latitude to make cash payments to customers who have been badly treated.

This type of approach can also transform internal attitudes. If workers feel that management cares about them and their ideas, they will almost certainly be more productive. In addition, the chance of thefts and sabotage decreases dramatically because workers have a feeling of "belonging" to the organisation. Profit-sharing can reinforce these desirable directions.

Two major trends are therefore developing. First, closer coordination is developing between those at the top and those who know what is actually going on. Second, the ranks of middle management are decreasing rapidly. Gervase Bushe, one of the most exciting of management thinkers, suggests that top management, the shapers of the overall effort, should be in close contact with those who are doing the work. He also cites the need for people he calls "integrators" – those who ensure that work can be effectively carried out. These integrators play a very different role from existing middle managers.

There is a fourth group who are the leaders. They will often be invisible. Lao Tzu stated many centuries ago that "when the leader leads well, the people will say they did it themselves". The purpose of the leader is to create situations where visionaries, actors and integrators can get on with their tasks in ways that combine to create an effective whole.

I believe that this fourfold split is going to be critical to effective organisations in the future. One group will be the visionaries who enjoy thinking about a future which they want to realise. A second group will be the actors who like to "get on with it" but also know how to tell the visionaries when their ideas don't work or how they can be improved. The third "integrating" group will consist of those who keep the system moving forward smoothly – these are the people who support both visionaries and actors. This group includes personnel staff and accountants, for these people make the operation of the company possible. The fourth group will be the leaders who understand when to concentrate on action, vision and integration.

Such a model implies considerable changes in our thinking about institutional change. At the current time, much effort is concentrated on changing legal structures so that work places are controlled by workers or are structured as cooperatives. The implication of the argument I have made above is that it is far more important to ensure that people are placed in positions that suit their preferred style. The next challenge is to rethink remuneration structures so that the contribution of all four groups is equitably recognised. Today, leaders are seen as the